1887
The Legend Lives On!

The 1887 lever-action shotgun is considered to be the first successful repeating shotgun. The Chiappa Firearms 1887 is a faithful reproduction of this classic firearm. The 1887 utilizes the design of the original solid lever that includes an innovative internal safety. Featuring a European walnut stock and forearm and color case finished receivers, the 1887 is as beautiful as it is functional.

CHIAPPAFIREARMS.COM

The Single Action Shooting Society®

SINCE 1987

SASS®

★ ★

Cowboy Action Shooting™

Mention this Ad and Save $10 on your Membership

Join SASS® ~ Where the West Can Still be Won!

The Single Action Shooting Society® is an International membership organization created to preserve and promote the sport of Cowboy Action Shooting™. Join SASS® today and take advantage of all the great benefits of being part of the greatest shooting and membership organization in the world.

★ *Competitive shooting that is safe, fun, and welcoming for the whole family!* ★

★ *Shooting categories for all skill levels* ★

★ *Over 500 affiliated clubs worldwide* ★

SINGLE ACTION SHOOTING SOCIETY

SASS

(877) 411-SASS • (574) 598-2987 • SASSNET.COM

SHORT AND SWEET
WITH FLAIR TO SPARE

★ ★ ★ ★ ★

BARKEEP™

The single-action Barkeep™ comes chambered with the 22 LR cylinder and is also compatible with an interchangeable 22 WMR cylinder. Built for optimal concealability in a light and portable package, the Barkeep™ boasts fixed open sights for fast action and a clean sight picture.

Check with your local dealer or visit HERITAGEMFG.COM

66

38

78

FEATURES

8

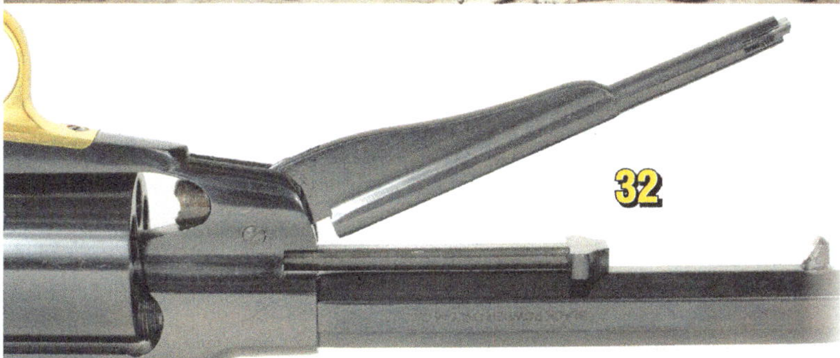

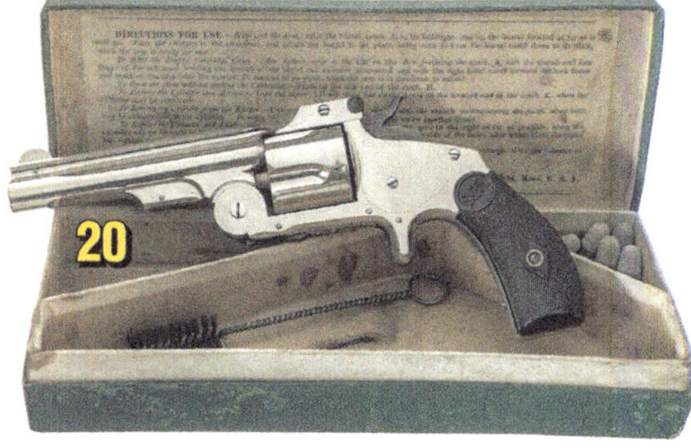

GUNS MAGAZINE SPECIAL EDITION Old West (ISSN 1044-6257) is published annually by Publishers' Development Corporation and is available on newsstands nationwide. CONTRIBUTORS submitting manuscripts, photographs or drawings do so at their own risk. Materials cannot be returned unless accompanied by sufficient postage. PAYMENT is for all world rights and will be made at rates current at time of publication and will cover reproduction in any or all GUNS Magazine editions or promotions. The act of mailing a manuscript constitutes the author's certification of originality of material. ADVERTISING RATES furnished on request. REPRODUCTION or use of any portion of this magazine in any manner, without written permission is prohibited. The opinions and recommendations expressed by individual authors within this magazine are not necessarily those of Publishers' Development Corporation. Copyright© 2022 by Publishers' Development Corporation, 225 W Valley Parkway, Suite 100, Escondido, CA, 92025. All rights reserved. QUESTIONS: call (760) 975-3880, email help@gunsmagazine.com or write GUNS Magazine, P.O. Box 460130, Escondido, CA 92025.

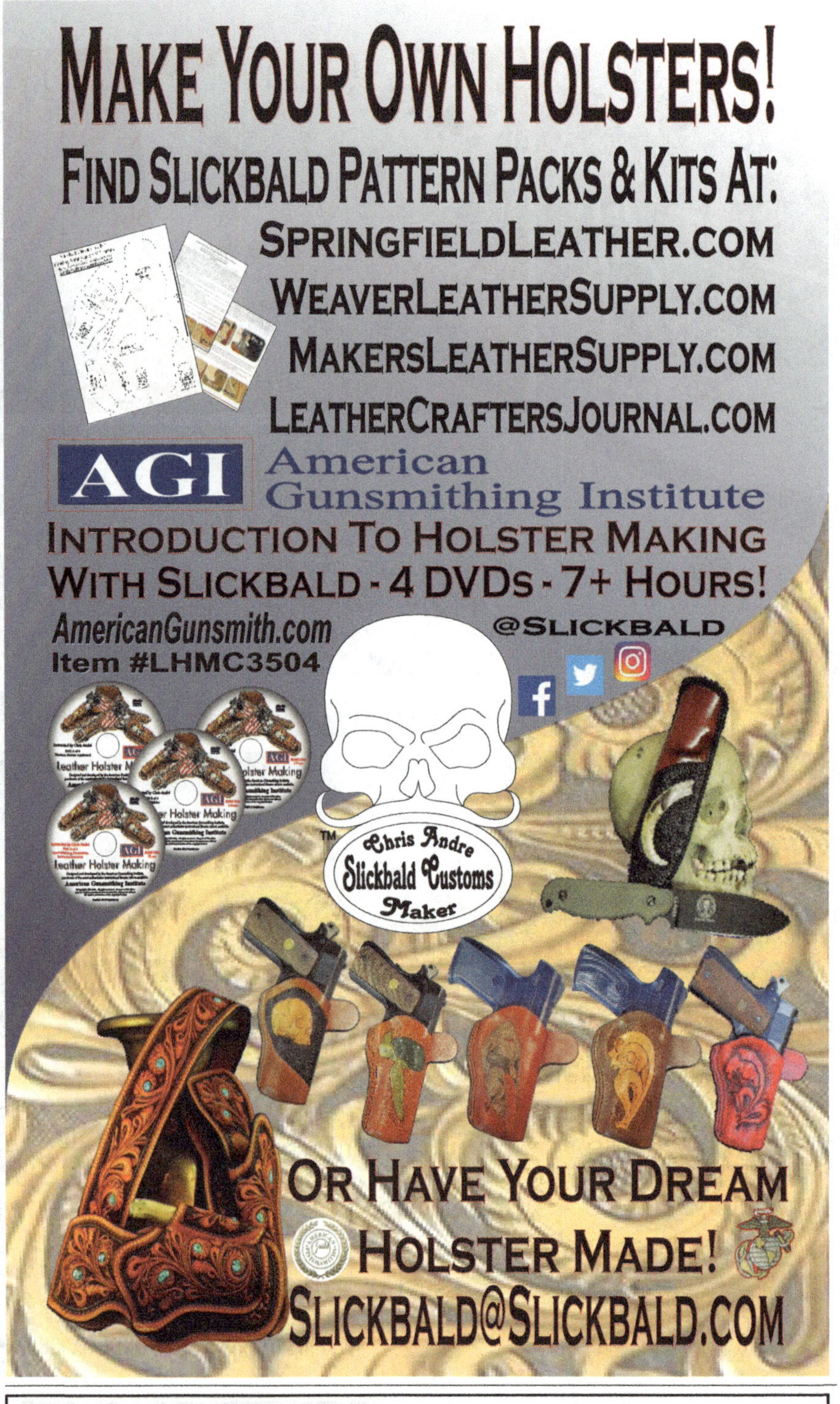

MAKE YOUR OWN HOLSTERS!

FIND SLICKBALD PATTERN PACKS & KITS AT:

SPRINGFIELDLEATHER.COM
WEAVERLEATHERSUPPLY.COM
MAKERSLEATHERSUPPLY.COM
LEATHERCRAFTERSJOURNAL.COM

AGI American Gunsmithing Institute

INTRODUCTION TO HOLSTER MAKING WITH SLICKBALD - 4 DVDs - 7+ HOURS!

AmericanGunsmith.com
Item #LHMC3504

@SLICKBALD

M1A / M14 Top Extended Rail

Made in the USA

LOW-PRO

Also Available:
Vertical Grips / Handstops / QD Mounts
Flashlight Mounts / Rails / MRD Mounts

Light Mounts

MRD Mounts

www.amsmachine.com
(910) 215-5980

OLD WEST
HISTORY, GUNS & GEAR

CORPORATE OFFICERS
Randy Moldé, Marjorie Young, Amy Von Rosen

Editor Tom McHale

Associate Editors Jenna Buckley, Jazz Jimenez

Art Director Jennifer Lewis

Circulation/Production Director Heather Arnold

Production Manager Jim Kirschbaum

Digital Content Editor Ashley McGee

Website Manager Lorinda Massey

Staff Photographer Joseph Novelozo

Editorial Review Consol Torres

CONTRIBUTING EDITORS

Will Dabbs, MD • Tom Laemlein

Frank Jardim • Alan Garbers

Jeremy D. Clough • Roy Huntington

Mike "Duke" Venturino • Roger Smith

 **FMG PUBLICATIONS**

SPECIAL EDITIONS fmgpublications.com
Editor: Tom McHale

HANDGUNNER americanhandgunner.com
Editor: Tom McHale

GUNS gunsmagazine.com
Editor: Brent Wheat

SHOOTING INDUSTRY shootingindustry.com
Editor: Jade Moldae

COP americancop.com
Editor: Erick Gelhaus

NATIONAL AD SALES advertising@fmghq.com
WEST Delano Amaguin • delano.amaguin@fmghq.com
NORTH EAST Amy Tanguay • amy.tanguay@fmghq.com
SOUTH EAST Tom Vorel • tom.vorel@fmghq.com

Online Traffic Manager: Lori Robbins • lori.robbins@fmghq.com

CUSTOMER SERVICE

gunsmagazine.com

SUBSCRIPTION 866.820.4045
EDITORIAL . . . . editor@gunsmagazine.com
PRODUCTION . . . . annuals@fmghq.com

NSSF
The Firearm Industry Trade Association

PRODUCED IN THE U.S.A.

From The Desk Of
Tom McHale
Editor

The less-tamed Wild West attracted the bold, the desperate and the occasional Renaissance man.

George Goodfellow, MD, stood apart from the typical Tombstone, Ariz., physician, as 75% of his competition never felt compelled to actually attend medical school. Growing up in the gold mining rush, Goodfellow **studied engineering** before heading off to the U.S. Naval Academy where **he was** expelled after becoming the school's boxing champ. The logical next step? Medical school. Practicing in Tombstone soon gave him the perspective and experience to become the leading authority on treating gunshot wounds. Some of his innovations are standard practice today — barring the shot of whiskey anesthetic and biting on a bullet for pain management. Oh, and if that isn't enough, he arguably launched the idea of bullet-resistant vests.

When Alan Pinkerton offers a eulogy at your funeral, you know you've earned respect as a lawman. Delos "Yankee" Bligh served as chief of detectives in Louisville, Ky., during the late 19th century. Things were a bit different then, as detectives routinely chased down villains wherever they pleased. Bligh was known to take cases hundreds of miles outside his jurisdiction chasing the James-Younger Gang. He even solved a $3 million forgery case for Scotland Yard. Warrants? Who needs warrants when you carry a lock pick set along with an S&W Baby Russian revolver? Frank Jardim explores "Yankee" Bligh's history and gear.

George Goodfellow's medical practice was located above this saloon. It's handy to have a ready supply of pain medication just downstairs.

We tackle the myth (or is it?) of quick-draw gunslingers fanning their single-action revolver hammers to fill the air with lead. Is "fanning" a made-for-movies fabrication, or was it a legitimate gunfighting skill? You may be surprised by the facts.

Speaking of quick shooting in the single-action world, in this issue, you learn the ins and outs and overall appeal of Cowboy Action Shooting. The sport combines camaraderie, costumes and skill with weapons of the West, including side-by-side and traditional pump shotguns, lever-action rifles and the classic sixgun. And don't forget the cowgirls. The Single Action Shooting Society attracts plenty of women to the sport, as outlined in "The Women of SASS."

Even into the cartridge ammunition era, many clung to the proven cap & ball revolver design. This issue takes an in-depth look at the famous Colt 1851 revolver. If you want to spare the powder and ball loading approach, we'll show you some nifty Kirst Konverters allowing the use of modern ammunition in cap & ball reproductions.

Or, you can explore new guns, like Taylor's .357 lever-action rifles and "Smoke Wagon" revolvers, a Chiappa 1887 shotgun, the all-fun Ruger Wrangler Birdshead rimfire and Marlin 1895 Trapper.

I hope you enjoy this Special Edition issue of *Old West: History, Guns & Gear.* Sit back, read a story or three and appreciate the Old West mystique.

☙ Will Dabbs, MD ❧

DR. GEORGE GOODFELLOW, MD

George Goodfellow was born two days before Christmas 1855. His father was a gold miner in California, so young George came of age in the rough mining camps that so characterized the California Gold Rush. After a year of civil engineering at the University of California at Berkeley, Goodfellow was accepted into the U.S. Naval Academy. He became the school boxing champion in short order, but was ultimately dismissed for hazing after his first semester.

Goodfellow had always held a fascination with medicine, so he subsequently attended the Wooster University Medical School. In 1876 he married Katherine "Kate" Colt. Ironically, Kate was a cousin of the legendary Samuel Colt. Dr. Goodfellow was soon to become intimately familiar with Colonel Colt's eponymous hogleg.

Dr. Goodfellow ultimately settled in Tombstone, in the Arizona Territories, as one of 12 practicing physicians. Of the 12, only Goodfellow and two others had bothered to attend medical school. Given the rampant unfettered violence endemic to the area, Dr. Goodfellow soon became the world's recognized authority on the medical management of gunshot wounds.

The Shooting

On February 26, 1882, Dr. George Goodfellow sat in the Oriental Saloon in Tombstone, nursing his favorite adult beverage. Dr. Goodfellow was by then a fixture thereabouts, and he maintained his medical clinic in a room above the Oriental. Living as he did among the trappings of the hard men of Tombstone, Dr. Goodfellow was a trusted asset to all.

Goodfellow was known to travel long distances on horseback to treat both outlaws and lawmen alike. However, it's tough to live in a sewer without getting dirty. Dr. Goodfellow was himself an inveterate womanizer and a heavy drinker.

Fly's Gallery   Tombstone, A.Z.

Luke Short was a professional faro dealer and part owner of the Oriental. At 32 years old, Short had already survived multiple gunfights. On February 26, he was dealing cards at the Oriental opposite a local troublemaker named Charlie Storms.

Storms was just born bad. Now in his 60s, Charlie Storms was likewise an experienced shootist with several dead men to his credit. Storms had been present when Wild Bill Hickok was killed six years prior and purportedly stole his pistol. Charlie was a mean drunk and had been up all night playing cards and arguing.

Bat Masterson was a well-known law officer who maintained friendships with both men. When the friction between Storms and Short began to build, he attempted an intervention. Masterson meant well but was ultimately unsuccessful.

The Killing

With the benefit of hindsight, Storms was drunk and likely just fatally misjudged Short. Masterson later opined that Storms felt he could bully Short into getting what he wanted. Storms was sadly mistaken.

Storms eventually accused Short of cheating. Masterson intervened and escorted Storms into the street before things could get out of hand. Dr. Goodfellow quietly studied the proceedings from a nearby table.

The drunken Charlie Storms then staggered back through the door, pushed past his friend Bat Masterson and grabbed

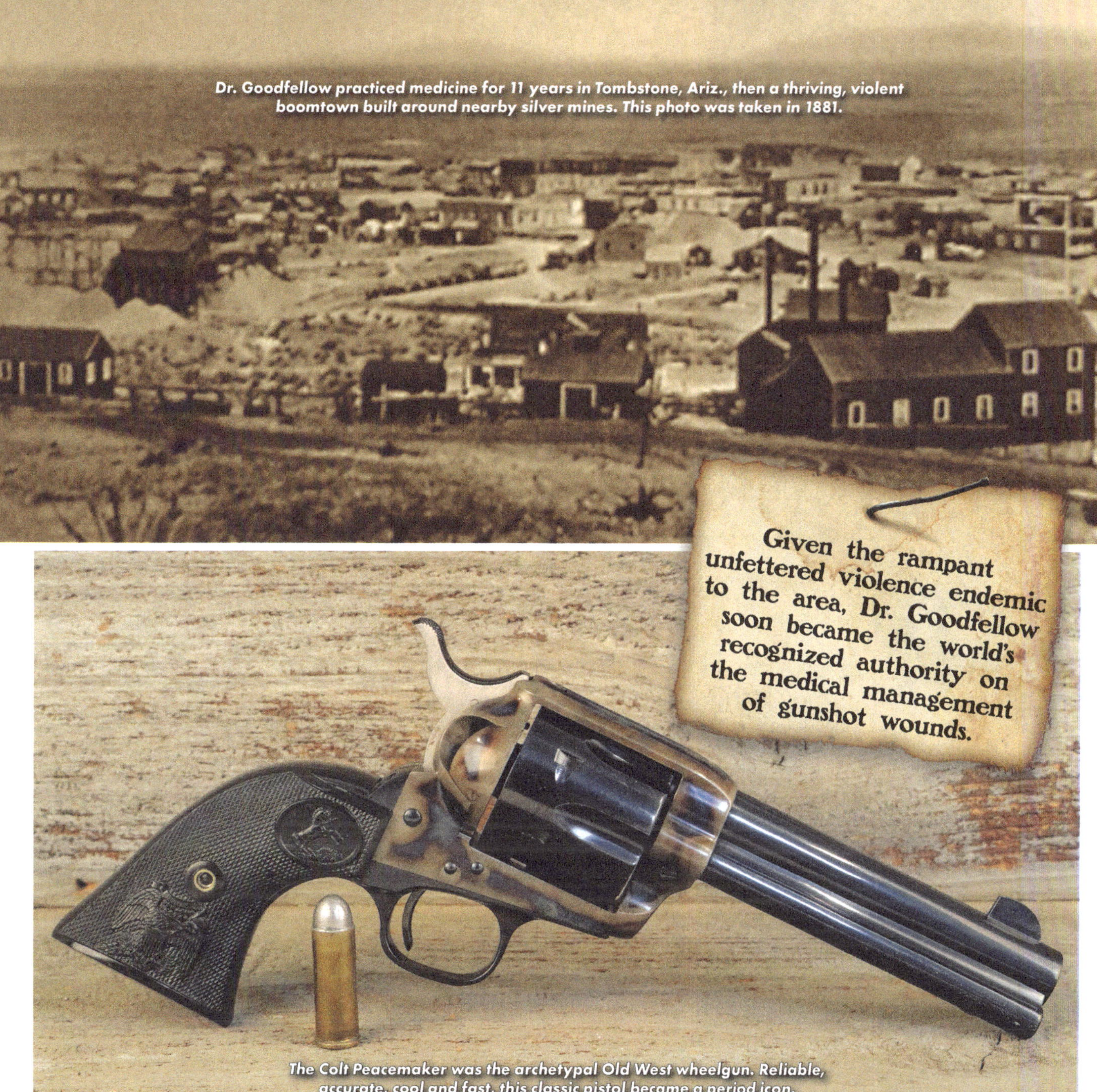

The Colt Peacemaker was the archetypal Old West wheelgun. Reliable, accurate, cool and fast, this classic pistol became a period icon.

Short's right ear with his left hand. He then reached for his gun, a stubby .45-cal. Colt Peacemaker Sheriff's Model.

Luke Short was faster on the draw. He pressed the muzzle of his own Peacemaker against Storm's left chest and unceremoniously shot the man through the heart. He then drilled the drunken miscreant a second time as he fell backward. The first round's discharge at contact range set poor Charlie's shirt alight.

Storms staggered backward about 12' and fell onto his back. He got off two shots of his own from his stubby single-action pistol, both of which ended up in the ceiling. Charlie Storms was dead where he fell.

By the time Goodfellow got to him, Charlie Storms had already shuffled off this mortal coil. The heavy 255-grain bullet from Short's Colt tore through the man's heart and flattened against his vertebral column. Dr. Goodfellow was amazed at the lack of bleeding from the wound. Goodfellow had Storms' cooling corpse moved to the local undertaker's and performed a quick dissection.

The previous morning Storms had tucked a folded silk handkerchief into his left breast pocket. By random chance, Short's big lead bullet had center-punched this expensive piece of cloth. However, instead of burrowing through, as would have been the case with cotton or wool, the silk wrapped around the bullet and followed it into the wound. The handkerchief remained otherwise intact.

Dr. Goodfellow was intrigued. He attended another unfortunate cowboy who had caught a load of 00 buckshot to the head. Several of these .33-cal. pellets punched through his face and flattened on the backside of his skull, killing him most expeditiously. However, one ball struck the man's expensive silk hatband and failed to penetrate. This got Dr. Goodfellow's intellectual juices flowing.

The Aftermath

Marshal Ben Sippy arrested Luke Short on the charge of murder. Though, by the standards of the place and the day, this was clearly self-defense, so Short was released *tout de suite*. Regardless, men like Luke Short seldom lived long. He ultimately suc-

This is Dr. Goodfellow mounted atop his favorite horse, El Rosillo. El Rosillo was a personal gift from Mexican President Porfirio Díaz for Goodfellow's disaster relief work after the Bavispe earthquake.

The Gila monster is the only venomous lizard indigenous to the United States. Dr. Goodfellow collected these things, paying locals $5 apiece for prime examples.

cumbed at age 39 to Bright's disease, a kidney malady essentially untreatable with the technology of the day.

In 1887, Dr. Goodfellow published "The Impenetrability of Silk to Bullets" for the medical journal *Southern California Practitioner.* Goodfellow's research led to the earliest examples of soft body armor. These early vests were made from multiple layers of natural silk and were subsequently lyrically expensive. A decent vest ran about $800 at the time, which is about $50,000 today. Archduke Ferdinand actually owned one of these silk vests, but was not wearing it the day Gavril Princip assassinated him and precipitated World War I.

Nowadays, nobody heads into harm's way without some kind of body armor. Today's Kevlar and Spectra obviously supplanted silk, but the theory remains the same. The number of lives saved is beyond counting, and it all began with a shootout in the Oriental Saloon in Tombstone, Ariz., in 1882.

Goodfellow's Gunshot Wounds

Dr. Goodfellow's impact on the modern science of trauma surgery cannot be overstated. Goodfellow was the first surgeon to document the need for an exploratory laparotomy in the case of gunshot wounds to the abdomen. An ex-lap is an operation wherein the abdomen is surgically opened so the viscera can be examined and repaired.

Prior to his era, the standard of care involved probing a wound with unsterilized fingers in an attempt to retrieve errant projectiles. This practice ultimately killed President James Garfield after he was shot by a homicidal schizophrenic named Charles Guiteau in 1881. As an aside, Guiteau had chosen the .442 Webley Bulldog revolver he used for the shooting because he thought it would look good in a museum afterward. Though it was indeed on display in the Smithsonian for a time, the murder weapon was later stolen. Its whereabouts are unknown today.

By contrast, Dr. Goodfellow had studied the cutting-edge research on antiseptic operative techniques and would sterilize his hands and instruments with whiskey and lye soap prior to his operations. He subsequently had a much lower incidence of post-operative infections than did his counterparts not so enlightened. Goodfellow treated Virgil and Morgan Earp as well as Doc Holliday after the famed gunfight at the O.K. Corral. At his behest, Dr. Goodfellow removed the mortally wounded Billy Clanton's boots immediately before he died. Goodfellow's professional testimony helped to exonerate the Earp party in the subsequent judicial inquest.

Luke Short was a professional gambler and an accomplished gunslinger.

Goodfellow was known to have a refined sense of humor. This wry wit often made its way into his medical logs. He once opined, "The .44 and .45 caliber Colt revolver, .45-60 and .44-40 Winchester rifles and carbines were the toys with which our festive or obstreperous citizens delight themselves."

The Rest of the Story

In addition to his seminal work on gunshot wounds, Dr. Goodfellow also conducted the world's first perineal prostatectomy to treat an enlarged prostate. In the days before CT scans and reliable anesthesia, this must have been a wild ride for the surgeon and the patient. Goodfellow also pioneered the use of spinal anesthesia. In this case, he drew off a fixed volume of the patient's spinal fluid, dissolved in crystals of cocaine, and re-injected it into the spinal canal.

Dr. Goodfellow was widely published on a variety of disparate topics. He conducted extensive research on the venom of Gila monsters and rattlesnakes. Goodfellow even once intentionally allowed a Gila monster to bite him just to determine if such an attack was survivable. He later wrote of these bizarre creatures, "The breath is very fetid, and its odor can be detected at some little distance from the lizard. It is supposed that this is one way in which the monster catches the insects and small animals which form a part of its food supply — the foul gas overcoming them."

Goodfellow also taught himself seismology. He produced an accurate map of the fault lines of the Bavispe earthquake that struck the Mexican state of Sonora in 1887 … after driving a horse-drawn wagon loaded with medical supplies some 90 miles to assist survivors. Mexican President Porfirio Díaz later awarded him a silver medal and a prize horse named El Rosillo in recognition of his life-saving work.

In 1898 Dr. Goodfellow was assigned as an Army surgeon alongside his friend General William "Pecos Bill" Shafter fighting in Cuba during the Spanish-American War. In addition to his other remarkable gifts, Goodfellow spoke fluent Spanish. Following the Battle for San Juan Hill, he broke out a bottle of "Ol' Barleycorn" whiskey, which he shared with both the victorious Americans and the Spanish General José Toral. Goodfellow's efforts helped ensure a smooth surrender of Spanish forces.

In the summer of 1910, Dr. Goodfellow fell ill. The rumor was his malady was a flare of some exotic disease he had contracted during the Spanish-American War. However, those close to him suspected his illness was simply the manifestation of end-stage alcoholism. Six months later, he died at the early age of 54. His mandatory laparotomy remains the standard of care for patients with penetrating trauma to the abdomen today. Dr. George Goodfellow is recognized as America's first civilian trauma surgeon. His was a rich life richly lived.

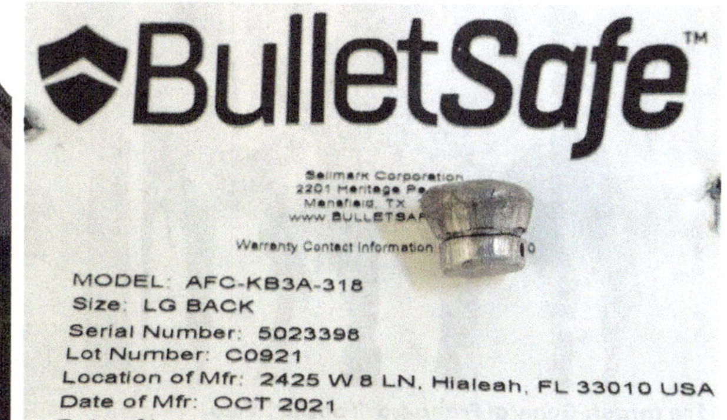

This .45 Long Colt bullet was recovered after having been fired into a BulletSafe armored vest. You can only imagine the mischief such a thing might foment inside some poor sot's chest cavity.

Tom Laemlein

THE PUNITIVE EXPEDITION

Chasing Villa

In pursuit: General John J. "Black Jack" Pershing leads the U.S. Punitive Expedition 350 miles into Mexico. Photo: NARA

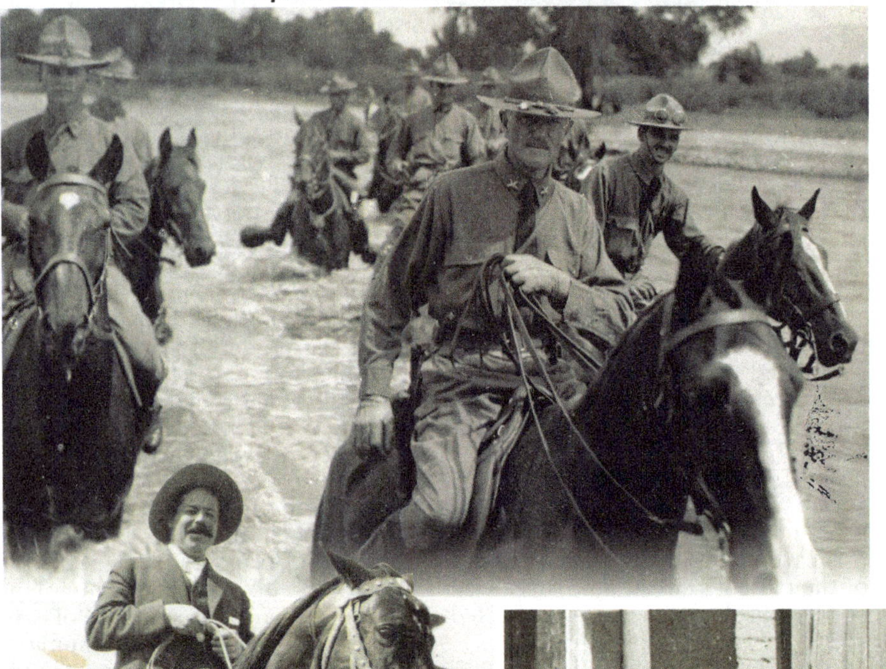

The target: General Francisco "Pancho" Villa. After Villa ordered the attack on Columbus, N.M., on March 9, 1916, President Wilson ordered the expedition that would chase Villa in Mexico until February 1917. Photo: Library of Congress

The last of the Old West: A U.S. cavalryman on duty in Columbus, N.M., during March 1916. Note the early-style magazine pouches for his M1911 pistol. Photo: NARA

After Pancho Villa's men raided Columbus, N.M., on the night of March 9, 1916, the United States and Mexico were precariously close to war. Of course, this is what Villa wanted all along, but he did not get his wish. Instead, he received the violent attention of General John Pershing and the Mexican Punitive Expedition. U.S. Secretary of War Newton Baker wrote that Pershing's mission was to "catch Villa if possible," but Pershing's War Department orders were to "pursue and disperse" the band of raiders who had conducted the attack on U.S. soil. Capturing or killing Villa was not part of Pershing's official directive.

The streets of Columbus, N.M., in early 1916. U.S. troops gather by the post office while an iron horse waits for its rider. In the background, a sign promotes WP Stevenson's "Folly Girl Company." Photo: NARA

Unfortunately, U.S. media built up the Punitive Expedition as more of an Old West bounty hunter mission conducted by the new U.S. Army. In this light, the expedition has often been portrayed as a failure. However, research shows that of the 485 known Villistas who attacked Columbus, Pershing's troops killed 248 and took 19 of them prisoner by the end of July 1916. Add to it another 69 of Villa's *desperadoes* killed or captured during the fighting at Columbus.

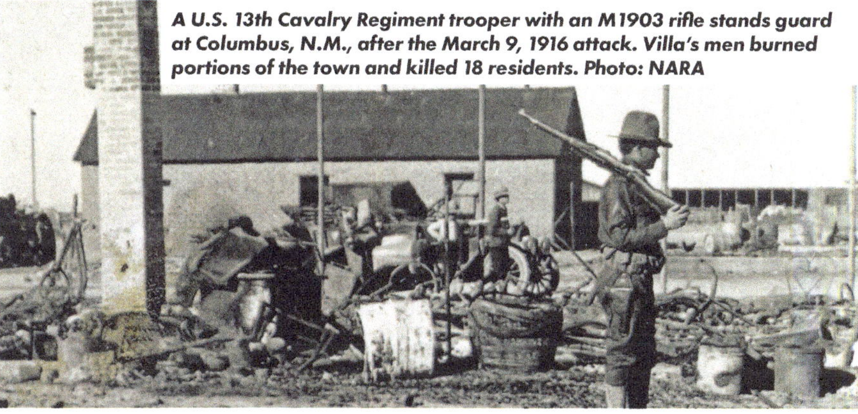

A U.S. 13th Cavalry Regiment trooper with an M1903 rifle stands guard at Columbus, N.M., after the March 9, 1916 attack. Villa's men burned portions of the town and killed 18 residents. Photo: NARA

The Citizens Home Guard of Columbus, N.M. The local residents fought back against Villa's men during the raid. This group carries a wide range of firearms — from Colt pistols and Winchester rifles to M1910 Mexican Mauser carbines (7x57mm) to the U.S. M1903 Springfield rifle (lower right). Photo: NARA

The aftermath of the Columbus, N.M. raid. Troopers of the 13th Cavalry Regiment look over the body of one of Villa's men killed the night before. Approximately 80 Villistas were killed in the raid. Photo: NARA

The townspeople of Columbus fought for their homes. Here two locals look over a Villista killed during the raid. Photo: NARA

The cost: Remains of the U.S. cavalrymen lost in action at Columbus are sent home. Photo: NARA

Gathering to pursue Villa's men after the Columbus, N.M. raid. Troopers of the 13th Cavalry Regiment assemble the morning after. Note their M1903 rifles and the Model 1913 Cavalry Saber. Photo: NARA

Securing the border: U.S. cavalrymen check border crossers for contraband and weapons in 1916. Photo: Library of Congress

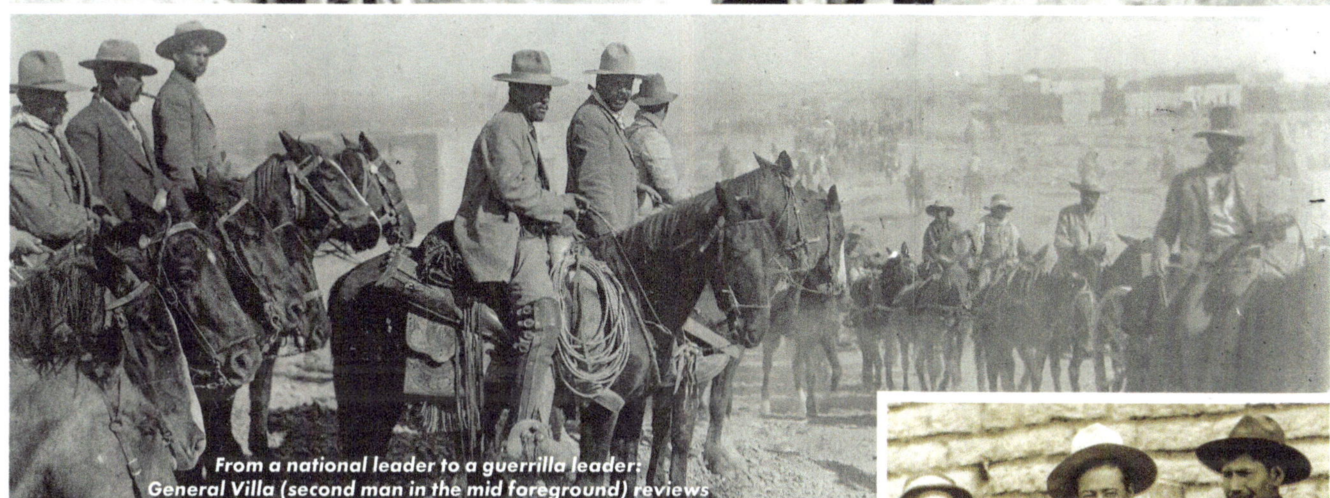

From a national leader to a guerrilla leader: General Villa (second man in the mid foreground) reviews his dwindling forces. Photo: Library of Congress

Villa poses with some of his staff; most of the men carry the Mauser Model 1910 carbine or the full Model 1910 rifle (7x57mm). Photo: Library of Congress

Villa's men came from a wide variety of backgrounds and had an even greater number of agendas. The man in the center carries a Savage Model 99. Photo: Library of Congress

Machine guns on the border: Villa's troops had a small number of machine guns, including this French Hotchkiss Model 1914 (provided to Mexico in 7mm). The Hotchkiss was a strip-fed weapon, using 24- or 30-round metal feed strips. Photo: Library of Congress

Villistas carried a range of weapons, but the Mauser M1910 rifles and carbines, along with any of the modern Winchester rifles, were the prevailing favorites. Photo: Library of Congress

The battle at Columbus and the subsequent Mexican Expedition saw the use of the Benét–Mercié Machine Rifle, Caliber .30 U.S. Model of 1909. Early use of the Benét–Mercié saw frequent jams with its 30-round feed strip loading. Field training cleared up the problems, and the 27-lb. Benét–Mercié (600 rpm cyclic rate) performed well in Mexico. Photo: Library of Congress

America's first rifle-caliber machine gun, the Maxim Machine Gun, Caliber .30, Model of 1904. A handful of the American Maxim MGs saw combat during the Mexican Expedition. Photo: Library of Congress

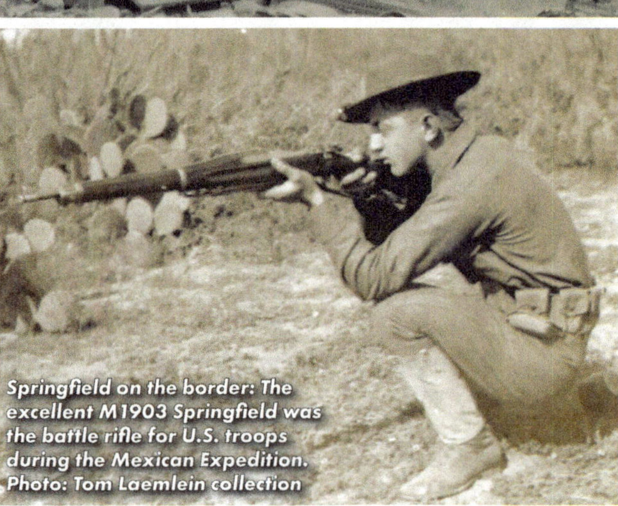

Springfield on the border: The excellent M1903 Springfield was the battle rifle for U.S. troops during the Mexican Expedition. Photo: Tom Laemlein collection

A postcard for the folks back home: Springfield rifles on the border. Photo: Tom Laemlein collection

Trench line at Las Cruces. Men of the 6th Infantry Regiment dug in. Photo: NARA

A small number of .30-caliber Lewis Guns made the trip to Mexico. Photo: NARA

U.S. troops guarding captured Villistas in the dust. Photo: NARA

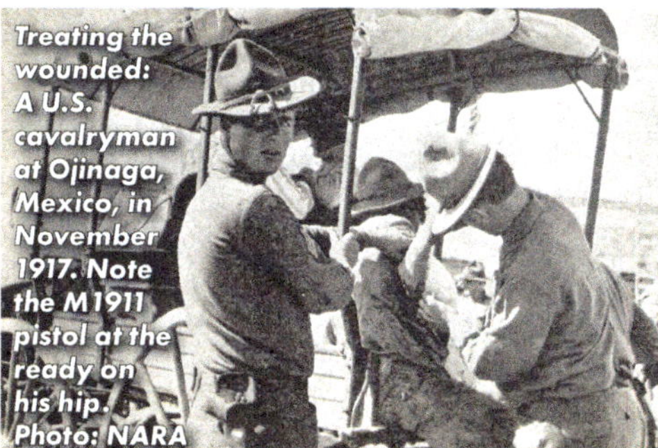

Treating the wounded: A U.S. cavalryman at Ojinaga, Mexico, in November 1917. Note the M1911 pistol at the ready on his hip. Photo: NARA

U.S. cavalry mounted on Harley-Davidson J-Series motorcycles during the Mexican Expedition. Photo: NARA

The Jeffery Quad 1.5 ton, four-wheel-drive truck bogged in Mexico. Note the M1903 Springfield rifle in the scabbard mount. Photo: NARA

American motorization: The Mexican Punitive Expedition saw the introduction of many new forms of motor transport into the U.S. Army, including Curtiss reconnaissance aircraft. Photo: NARA

Horseless: U.S. troops armed with M1903 Springfield rifles dismount from a new motor transport during the Mexican Expedition. Photo: NARA

The Jeffrey Armored Car No. 1 was present at the border during the Punitive Expedition, but there are no records of it being used in combat. The turrets were armed with one Benét-Mercié M1909 machine rifle. Photo: NARA

The Holt 75 tractor at work in Mexico during 1916. The Holt tractor was powered by a gasoline engine and could travel up to 15 mph. Photo: NARA

A Curtiss JN-3 of the 1st Aero Squadron. Eight of these aircraft deployed to Mexico during the Punitive Expedition. The expedition was the U.S. Army's first use of aviation during field operations. Photo: NARA

Mexico was highly unstable then, in the throes of a civil war, and without any semblance of legitimate governmental control. Secretary Baker later admitted the U.S. government needed to demonstrate power and eliminate raids into U.S. territory. The Punitive Expedition was successful in many ways, even if the big prize of capturing and hanging Villa was outside its grasp. Many lessons learned in chasing Villa would serve the U.S. Army well when America joined the Allies in World War I.

Trouble along the Mexican border would continue until the early 1920s. Villa would regain strength and raise a small army again, but fail to take Ciudad Juarez in June 1919; his career as a guerrilla leader was mostly over. He managed to secure a pardon from Mexico's President Carranza and retired to his hacienda near Parral, Chihuahua.

Villa was assassinated July 16, 1923, while visiting Parral — struck nine times by rifle bullets fired by a group of seven gunmen.

The Curtiss JN-3s did not fly combat missions, per se, but their use in the burgeoning role of aerial reconnaissance drew praise from Pershing's staff. Roger G. Miller referenced this quote from General Pershing's final assessment report to the government following the expedition in the U.S. Air Force History and Museums program, A Preliminary To War: The 1st Aero Squadron and the Mexican Punitive Expedition of 1916: "Under the difficulties of aviation experienced, the service rendered must be considered as most exceptional. The personnel have displayed the most commendable spirit, and personal efficiency is of the highest order. Officers have literally taken their lives in their hands without hesitation, although several aviators have had narrow escapes. Unstinting praise for the aviators who have served with this Expedition is universal throughout the Command." Photo: NARA

Curtiss depicted in "Down Mexico Way" by Colin Campbell. Photo: USAF Art Collection via NARA

Despite the new technology, horses remained the U.S. Army's best means of pursuing Villa in the rugged Mexican terrain. Photo: NARA

Miles of Sand: American troops chased Pancho Villa for hundreds of miles into Mexico, winning several battles and killing many of his men — but Villa escaped capture and extradition to the U.S. to face American justice. Photo: NARA

On the trail: General Pershing at Casa Grandes, Mexico. Photo: Library of Congress

Frank Jardim

A BABY RUSSIAN FOR SERIOUS POLICE WORK

Detective Delos 'Yankee' Bligh, Louisville, Ky.

The badge he used from 1870 to 1890.

Historical objects with bona fide provenance (that's museum talk for a true story) have the ability to engage the mind and carry you back to their time and place in history. I had a great experience years ago when a museum curator friend shared with me a small collection donated by the descendants of one of America's most memorable lawmen. It wasn't much, but what there was had obviously been thoughtfully looked after in the century before it was donated to the museum. The collection included a Mexican War Veteran's medal, Louisville police badge #1, a pocket watch, calling card, lock pick set and an S&W Baby Russian revolver. They all belonged to Delos "Yankee" Bligh.

Top Detective

Yankee Bligh was one of America's greatest 19th-century detectives, but is almost unknown today. He cracked a $3 million forgery case for Scotland Yard, received a reward from Queen Victoria, invented the first mugshot books and chased Jesse James. He was probably every bit as good a detective as his famed colleague Alan Pinkerton, but without his commercial ambition or talent for self-promotion. Though Bligh's investigations of the James Gang took him out of state, nothing could draw him away from his beloved Louisville for long. He turned down job offers from the Secret Service and Pinkerton. At Bligh's funeral, Alan Pinkerton was a eulogist and pallbearer.

Delos "Yankee" Bligh: Louisville Chief of Detectives, 1870–1890

Louisville Calls

Bligh was born in New York in 1823 and headed West at age 19 for a life of adventure as a fur trapper on the frontier, but his tenderfoot timing was poor. High water on the Ohio River in Louisville, Ky., prevented his further migration and he took what work he could find to support himself. Fortunately, there was much work to be had. Louisville had been an important trading and distribution center since the 18th century. By 1840, it was the 16th largest city in the country, with the census recording a population of 21,210 whites, free colored and slaves.

Bligh was a big fellow and he got a job as a bricklayer in the fast-growing city. At least one of the buildings he worked on still stands today — the four-story Landmark Building at the corner of Third and Liberty Streets.

Without intending to, young Bligh found a home in the city he helped make. He married, had children (ultimately 10 kids by two wives) and showed a dedication to Louisville throughout his life. The tug of Western adventure got a solid grip on him one final time during the Mexican War in 1847. Bligh volunteered for the Louisville Legion and sailed off down the river to war on the southern border.

After the fighting was done, he returned to his city, the memories of soldiering apparently adequate to sate his youthful frontier urges for the rest of his life. His veteran's campaign medal was still in his possession, beautifully cared for, at the time of his death.

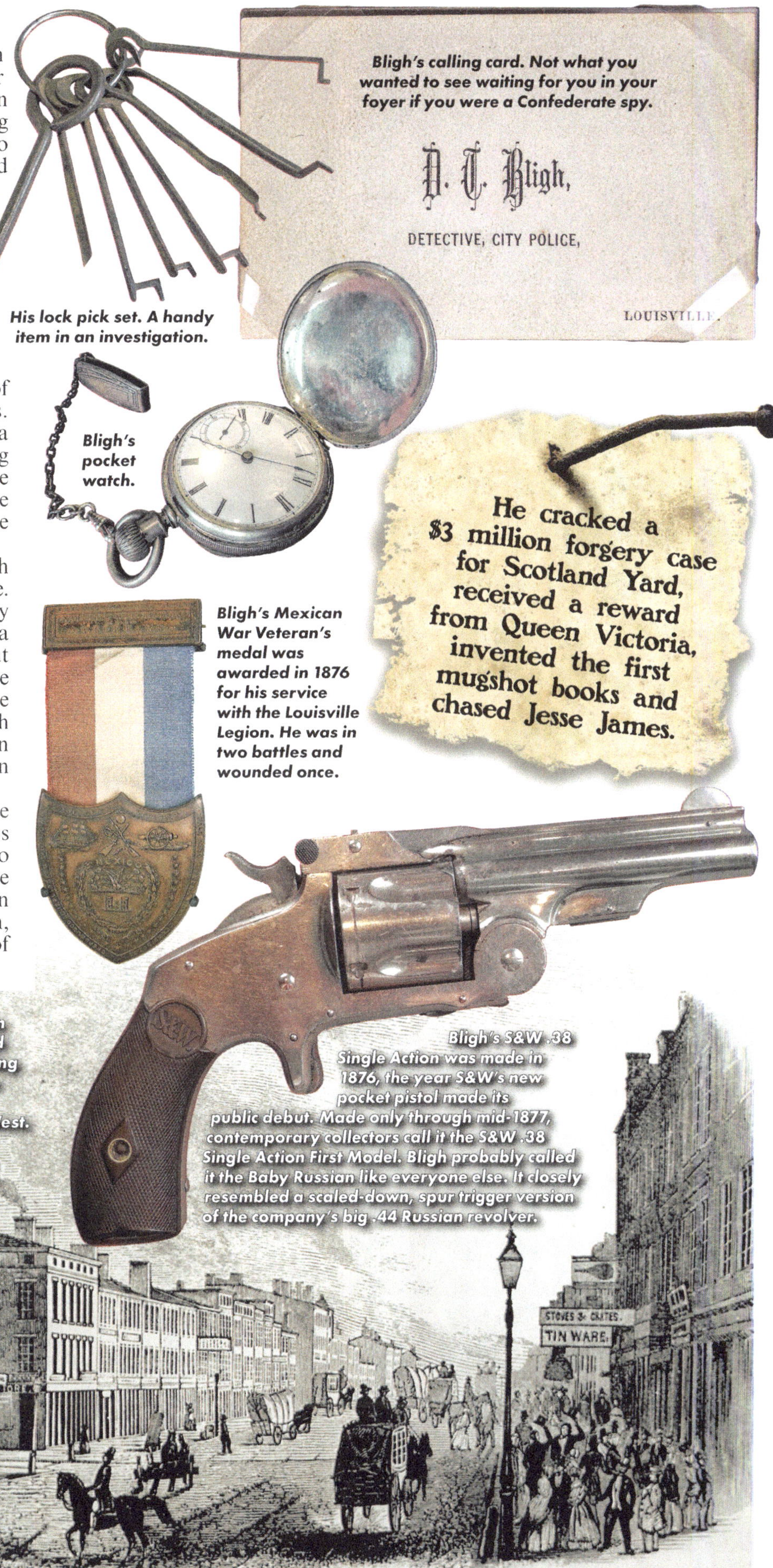

Bligh's calling card. Not what you wanted to see waiting for you in your foyer if you were a Confederate spy.

His lock pick set. A handy item in an investigation.

Bligh's pocket watch.

Bligh's Mexican War Veteran's medal was awarded in 1876 for his service with the Louisville Legion. He was in two battles and wounded once.

He cracked a $3 million forgery case for Scotland Yard, received a reward from Queen Victoria, invented the first mugshot books and chased Jesse James.

Main Street in Louisville as it looked in 1846, four years after the 19-year-old Bligh arrived, appears in this engraving to be populated by people in top hats and tailcoats. It wasn't quite that civilized, but it was hardly the Wild West.

Bligh's S&W .38 Single Action was made in 1876, the year S&W's new pocket pistol made its public debut. Made only through mid-1877, contemporary collectors call it the S&W .38 Single Action First Model. Bligh probably called it the Baby Russian like everyone else. It closely resembled a scaled-down, spur trigger version of the company's big .44 Russian revolver.

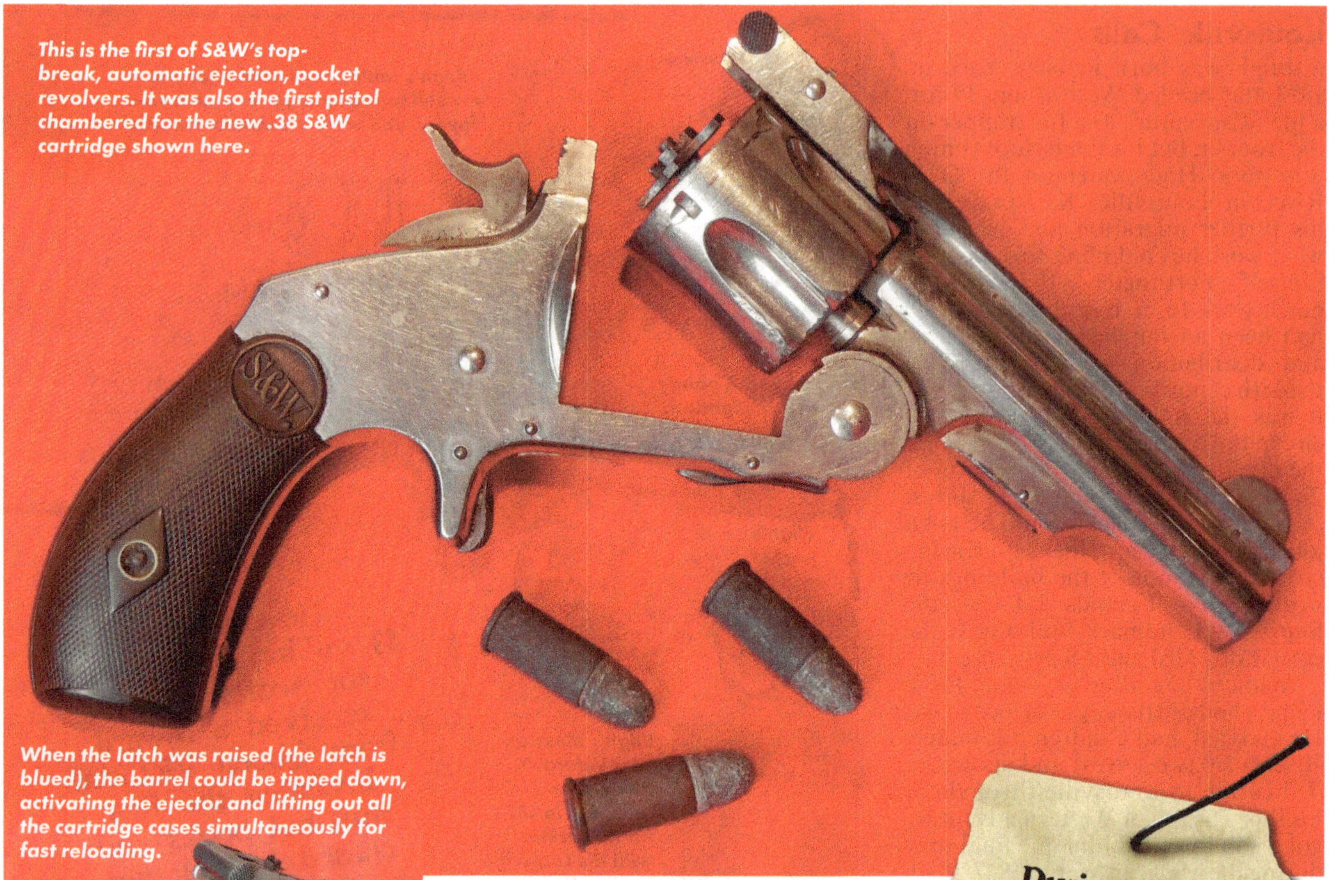

This is the first of S&W's top-break, automatic ejection, pocket revolvers. It was also the first pistol chambered for the new .38 S&W cartridge shown here.

When the latch was raised (the latch is blued), the barrel could be tipped down, activating the ejector and lifting out all the cartridge cases simultaneously for fast reloading.

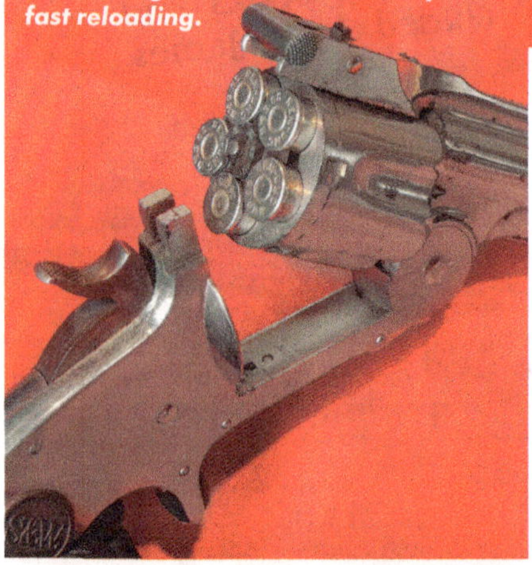

Very early box of Winchester black powder .38 S&W cartridges showing the new Baby Russian revolver on the label.

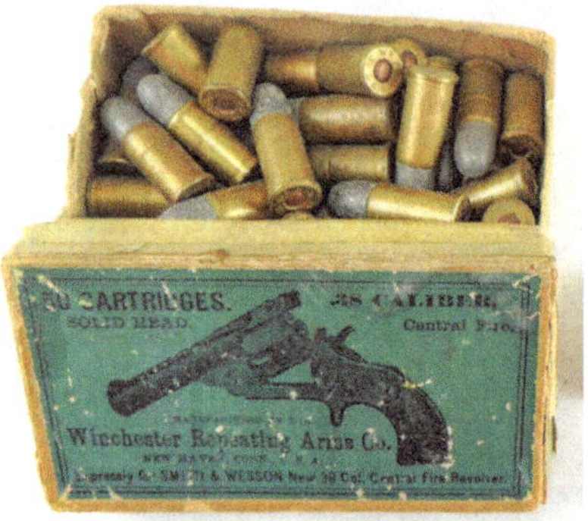

During the war, from 1861 to 1865, he was a full-time lawman and vigorously rooted out Confederate spies and sympathizers in the city, earning himself a promotion to detective by the war's end.

All of the .38 S&W pocket revolvers had five-shot cylinders. Note how tiny the rear sight is.

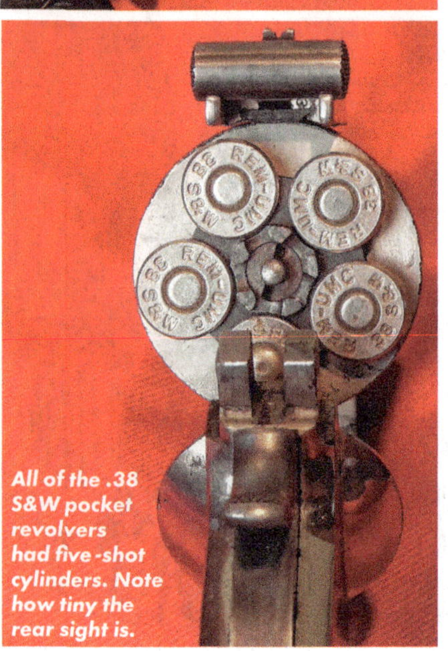

Law Enforcement Roots

As a mature 33 year old, Bligh was a powerful man and big for his time. He stood six feet tall and weighed 250 lbs. He must have seemed pretty formidable to the locals because in 1856, he was asked to join the city's nascent police force and became one of their five "supernumerary day watchmen." He was the bane of the city's criminal element and waterfront ruffians. He remained an unofficial member of the Louisville Police until the start of the Civil War. During the war, from 1861 to 1865, he was a full-time lawman and vigorously rooted out Confederate spies and sympathizers in the city, earning himself a promotion to detective by the war's end. This may have been the time he got the nickname "Yankee."

By 1870, Louisville's population had grown to 100,783 and Bligh was made chief of detectives. He held this position until his death from heart failure in 1890. It was in this period Bligh had many of his greatest cases. In his lifetime, he saw Louisville's population increase over seven-and-a-half fold and grow from a frontier river city to an urban metropolis of 161,129 people.

Louisville wasn't the exception in this respect. America was going through a growth spurt, and with more people came more crime. Just like today, the criminals vastly outnumbered the lawmen. But, unlike today, it wasn't uncommon to find lawmen working on cases outside their legal jurisdiction. The best lawmen of the day felt they had a professional

Barrel patent dates on a First Model.

responsibility to investigate crimes, pursue the perpetrators and bring them to justice to set an example that lawlessness would not go unchallenged. Bligh was that kind of lawman.

James Gang

In 1868, the Jesse James and Cole Younger gang committed a robbery in Russellville, Ky., that drew Bligh's attention though it was 140 miles south of Louisville. Bligh tracked down and captured one gang member and shot another. In 1872, Bligh investigated a bank robbery in Columbia, Ky. (100 miles from Louisville) and in 1875 another bank robbery in Huntington, WV (240 miles from Louisville). In both cases, he identified the James Gang as the culprits. Bligh's dogged pursuit of the gang made the newspapers and it appears James took the threat seriously, even publicly denouncing the detective in newspapers himself in Louisville, Ky., St. Louis, Mo. and Nashville, Tenn. and (unconvincingly) claiming innocence.

Bligh and James would finally meet without confrontation in a train station. A responsible lawman, Bligh had no intention of endangering civilians by instigating a dangerous apprehension on a crowded train platform. Had he done so, we can reasonably speculate James would have shot it out to save his skin with no concern for the bystanders. He'd done so before.

Urban Carry

Bligh's nickel-plated S&W .38 Single-Action revolver I examined probably wasn't the only firearm he owned. One does not go after the James-Younger gang with a pocket .38 after all. However, for a city detective, it makes perfect sense. Fairly potent with good shot placement, accurate and easily concealed, the little pistol was ideal for plainclothes work in urban areas. Louisville was not the Wild West. Even when Bligh first arrived, it was one of America's largest and most important cities.

Bligh is believed to have killed one man with this particular pistol in 1881. It was an unfortunate, though justifiable, shooting of a Chinese immigrant who was chasing a robber through a crowded street and excit-

Near-perfect 4" barrel nickel Baby Russian with black hard rubber grips in original box.

Exterior of original Baby Russian box.

edly swinging an ax. The Chinaman knocked Bligh down in the crowd, and not understanding Chinese, he tragically misread the situation. Believing he was under attack, Bligh shot and killed the man. It was ruled self-defense, but Bligh was said to have deeply regretted the mistake for the rest of his life.

Bligh's S&W

Bligh's S&W .38 Single Action was made in 1876, the year it was first introduced. Production of that model ended July 1877. Collectors call this pistol the S&W .38 Single Action First Model. In its day, it was nicknamed the Baby Russian. More on that later. Whether Bligh was an early adopter or bought it used, we don't know, but he clearly knew a good thing when he saw it.

S&W made 25,548 First Models before introducing a simplified design in mid-1877. Collectors call the latter gun the S&W .38 Single Action Second Model. That stayed in production until 1891, but about half of 108,225 Second Model guns made were built in the first two-and-a-half years of factory production. The S&W .38 Single Actions were hot sellers before public interest shifted toward double-action pocket revolvers in the 1880s. Had it not taken S&W six years to get the .38 Single Action in production, one could speculate they might have sold over 400,000. In their defense, they had a lot going on between 1871 and 1876.

From Russia with Love

In 1871, when S&W released the .44 Model 3 (their first big bore, single

This blued model Baby Russian came with wooden grips standard, while the nickeled guns had hard rubber grips. Nickel-plated guns vastly outnumbered blued guns. The most common barrel length for these pistols is 3 ¼" and 4".

Close-up of Baby Russian front sight and sculpted barrel rib.

Close-up of Baby Russian ejector latch mechanism. It was expensive to make and fit, so it was reengineered in 1877. Collectors call the improved design the S&W .38 Single Action Second Model. Apparently, it changed the gun's appearance enough that these later models weren't called Baby Russians.

Close-up of Baby Russian combination rear sight and barrel latch.

action, top-break, centerfire revolver), the strength of the new top-break action and advanced simultaneous ejection feature got them a big military contract with Tsarist Russia. It was a timely success for the company. Sales of the .44 S&W Russian made it possible to develop and manufacture a new generation of S&W handguns to replace the obsolete tip-up barrel rimfire .22 and .32 pocket pistols they'd been making since before the Civil War.

Graceful, delicate, well-made and beautiful to look at, the tip-up barrel gun's fragile frame hinge and weak lock were ill-suited to chambering in more powerful calibers. Reloading them required time and dexterity to unlatch the barrel, remove the cylinder and push out each empty casing on the single ejector pin mounted under the barrel. Nothing showed quite how antiquated the tip-up barrel was than a comparison to the new top-break Model 3. S&W designed and prototyped new pocket pistols but shelved the project in 1871; and shelved it stayed for years. The delay was probably due to the need to scale up their production facilities for the Russian contracts. You could argue the delay worked to their advantage regarding the engineering quality of the new pocket pistol.

The .38 S&W

The gradual refinement of the .44 S&W Russian pistol inspired a rework of their pocket pistol prototype resulting in significant improvements, including an important change in caliber. D.B. Wesson was unsatisfied with the original .38 rimfire cartridge and designed a new, reloadable, centerfire cartridge for the new pocket pistol.

The .38 S&W was the company's first small-caliber center fire metallic cased cartridge and proved immensely popular worldwide for self-defense well into the mid-20th century. The original load used a 145-grain round-nosed lead bullet propelled by 14 grains of FFFg black powder. For comparison purposes, a cap & ball 1851 Colt Navy revolver with a 7 ½" barrel will throw a 150-grain bullet around 668 FPS with 15 grains of FFFg powder. From S&W's pocket pistols, which typically had 3 ¼" or 4" barrels, I think you'd be lucky to get 550 fps. Those ballistics aren't much to brag about, but by the standards of the day, they were considered adequate. Keep in mind D.B. Wesson designed this cartridge to be accurate and manageable under recoil when shot in a self-defense revolver with really small grips and a spur trigger. There wasn't much to hold on to.

Baby Russian

When the new S&W .38 Single Action pocket pistol was finally ready for production, it looked a lot like a scaled-down S&W .44 Russian revolver with a spur trigger. That's what led to it being nicknamed the Baby Russian. Only the initial 1876-77 model bore that moniker. The later S&W .38 Single Action Second Model used a different ejector and cylinder release, giving it a slightly different appearance.

The S&W .38 Single Actions and the .32 Single Actions introduced in 1878, all shared the study S&W top-break action, simultaneous ejection of spent cases and spur trigger features. Spur trigger cries out "DANGER" to the eyes of modern shooters but consider that these guns were single action and would not have been carried around cocked and ready in the pocket. The spur trigger, out of style for more than a century now, offered some of the same advantages as the cutaway trigger guards found on custom Fitz Specials of the 1930s. There was nothing to obstruct and slow down your finger's way to the trigger when you needed to draw and shoot fast.

By the end of 1891, S&W had sold close to 134,000 of its compact .38 S&W single-action top-break revolvers. By the end of the same period, Colt had sold around 144,000 Model 1873 Single Action Army revolvers, mostly in .45 Colt and .44-40 WCF We think of the 1873 Colt as the archetype handgun of the Old West. However, production figures show that it was only one of many firearms widely used in 19th century America.

AUTOMATION

THERE ARE AMMO PLANTS CAPABLE OF PRODUCING NEARLY FOUR MILLION ROUNDS A DAY. THAT'S NOT US. WE ARE A CRAFT AMMUNITION MAKER, **AND YOU CAN'T AUTOMATE CRAFT.**

The Power of Performance
BLACK HILLS
Ammunition

TO LOCATE A DEALER NEAR YOU, PLEASE CALL 800.568.6625 | WWW.BLACK-HILLS.COM

Get our latest

FMG PUBLICATIONS

SPECIAL EDITIONS

for $14.95 each! Order online today!

www.fmgpubs.com

760-975-3880

The early .45 Colt loading was a 250-grain bullet over 30-grains of black powder ignited by an internal Benet primer (left). Cartridge advancements brought an easier-to-ignite Boxer primer (right) a few years later.

FANNING THE FLAMES

Alan Garbers
Photos: Alan and Dianna Garbers

Hollywood Lies or Old West Lore?

Many Western gunmen rejected complicated double-action revolvers like the Colt 1877 (bottom) for the reliable accuracy of the Colt 1873 single action (top).

Who doesn't enjoy a Western in which the protagonist fans his Colt and takes out the bad guys? I don't care if it's Clint Eastwood in one of the *Dollars* trilogy, Alan Ladd in *Shane* or Kevin Costner in *Open Range*, it is satisfying to watch. But, how accurate is fanning; and I mean both ways. Is Hollywood correct in its portrayal, and just how authentic was the art of fanning using period firearms?

Many preach fanning never existed and is strictly a Hollywood production. It would be more accurate to say fanning saw limited use in the Old West.

Just a quick refresher in case you're unfamiliar — fanning is holding the revolver with the strong hand and cocking the hammer with the palm or fingers of the offhand in a sweeping motion.

You may be wondering, why waste time cocking the hammer? Why not just pull the trigger? For decades, single-action revolvers dominated the market due to their simplicity and accuracy. But their one fault was the need to manually cock the hammer before each round was fired, so pulling the trigger did nothing until the user cocked the hammer fully back. By the late 1870s, double-action revolvers were available, and those models could be fired by just pulling the trigger. But designs had not been refined, so the trigger pull was comparatively long and difficult, as pulling the trigger advanced the cylinder, cocked the hammer and fired the gun. Double actions were often unreliable and broke with hard use.

Early Proof?

One of the earliest mentions of "fanning the hammer" appeared in a newspaper story circulated around the West in March 1887. The article featured Harry Whitehill, a no-nonsense gunman who served six terms as sheriff of Grant County, N.M., including the mining boomtown of Silver City.

The high hammer spur of the Colt 1873 (bottom) lent itself to fanning, while the lower profile Colt Bisley hammer (top) was for thumbing only.

Fanning is faster, but the gun movement, recoil and heavy smoke make accuracy problematic.

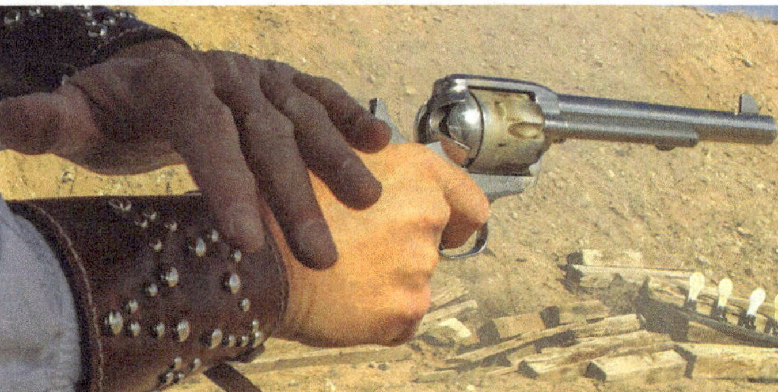

Whitehouse was a lawman criminals went out of their way to avoid. He was the first lawman to arrest Billy the Kid — and did it twice.

In the article, Whitehill joked about the notion of easterners thinking cowboys carried double-action revolvers, when in reality, the newer designs were quickly rejected in the West. The reason was due to the long trigger pull and the tendency to pull the shot off target. In many cases, the bullet would graze a rib or inner arm, leaving the opponent capable of firing back.

Whitehill's trigger was tied back, so the hammer fell and fired as soon as it was released. He gave the reporter a fanning demonstration, firing six rounds into a small tree so rapidly it sounded like a pack of firecrackers. The resulting group was 3".

Gunfight Use?

In December 1889, a newspaper story circulated about trick shooting used by gunfighters like William "Curly Bill" Brocius. The feature started with a story about U.S. Deputy Marshal David Neagle. Tombstone historians may remember Neagle as the deputy hired by Sheriff John Behan. Neagle also worked closely with the Earps when required.

Deputy Neagle had stopped an attack on a federal judge in California. The story claimed Neagle used a gun with no trigger and fanned the hammer when required. Two of his three shots struck and killed the assailant, while the third shot missed. Since the attack was indoors, his vision was likely obscured by the thick smoke from the black powder rounds.

The same article hinted the art of fanning originated in New Mexico, when cowboys entertained train passengers with trick shooting. The cowboys reportedly shot six holes in the bottom of an oyster can at 50 yards. The story became unbelievable when the can became a dime!

Fanning Hit and Miss

Another story told of an attack eight years earlier (1881). A cowboy named Bob Sinclair took exception to another named Jack Riley. Sinclair shucked his pistol and commenced fanning. None of the bullets found their mark. In response, Riley picked up a board and struck Sinclair on the side of the head.

A similar story from April 1879 came from Wyatt Earp and Bat Masterson. During their Dodge City days, a buffalo hunter turned freighter named Levi Richardson hit town. Richardson was well-known and considered a top shot with any weapon — and had killed several men in gunfights. Richardson had a strong dislike for a young gambler with the colorful name of Cockeyed Frank Loving. Richardson had been practicing fanning on targets and felt supremely confident as he stormed into the Long Branch Saloon and challenged Loving. Loving accepted the challenge with remarkable calm. Richardson pulled out his Colt and blazed away until the revolver was empty. Loving had returned fire with his Remington a little more deliberately, striking Richardson repeatedly. They were so close their barrels were almost touching. Richardson hit the floor and died soon after.

Wyatt Earp

Wyatt Earp would later tell his biographer, "In all my life as a frontier peace officer, I did not know a really proficient gunfighter who had anything but contempt for the gun fanner, or man who literally shot from the hip."

Earp may have been trying to rewrite his history.

In December 1896, Earp was asked to referee a boxing match between Bob Fitzsimmons and Tom Sharkey. He made national news by wearing his Colt .45 into the ring. During the resulting uproar, a story from Alfred Lewis ran in the *Philadelphia Times*. Lewis claimed to have known the Earps well in their Tombstone days. He maintained Wyatt had filed his front sight off to make drawing smoother and was known to fan his pistol in a fight so fast it sounded like a Gatling gun.

Fingerless Fanning

Captain J.A. Brooks joined the Texas Rangers in 1883. He was instru-

Sheriff Harvey Whitehill was a rough and tumble, no-nonsense lawman and a master of fanning. His abilities won the votes of the citizens of Silver City, N.M., for six terms.

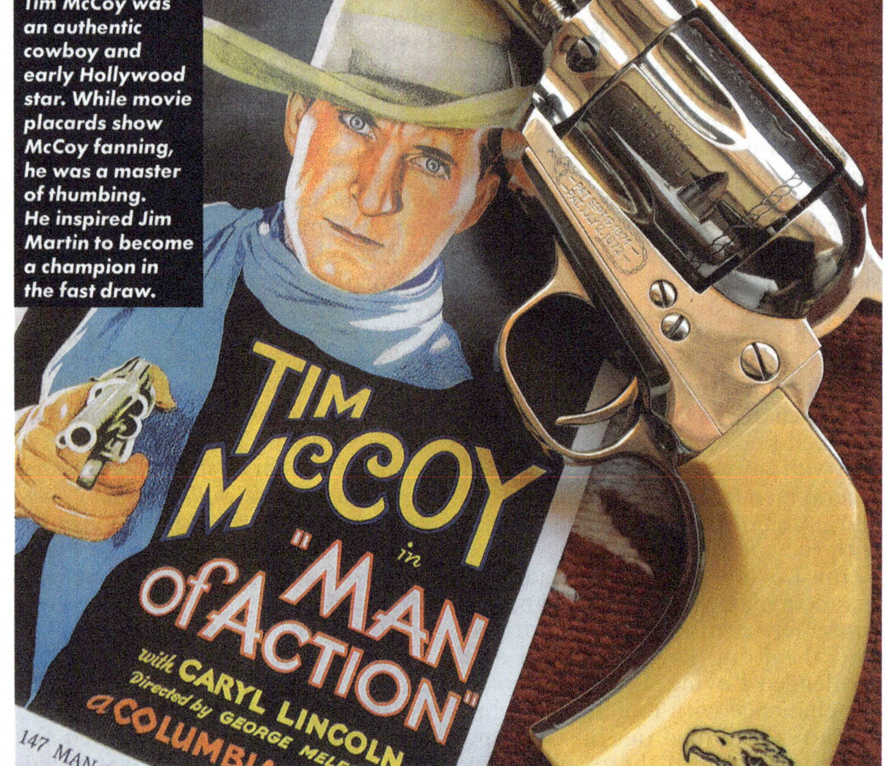

Tim McCoy was an authentic cowboy and early Hollywood star. While movie placards show McCoy fanning, he was a master of thumbing. He inspired Jim Martin to become a champion in the fast draw.

mental in eliminating the Conner Gang, but one ranger was slain and three more wounded in the process. Brooks was one of the wounded and lost three fingers on his left hand. This didn't stop him from enforcing the law for 23 years, but he did have to overcome his handicap by becoming a top gunman. After his retirement, Brooks still had the skills of his younger days.

The book, *Trails and Trials of a Texas Ranger* by William Warren Starling said this about Brooks: "Some Western historians deny that the old single-action Peacemaker was ever fired by 'fanning the hammer.' Captain Brooks used this method repeatedly, and it especially suited his lame left hand. He gave me a personal demonstration of how it was done.

"When Capt. Brooks was well past 60 years old, I saw him shoot five shots at a knot on an oak tree. He fanned the hammer of an old .45 so fast that it sounded like an automatic and hit the target four times."

A More Modern Take

The evidence shows fanning existed long before Hollywood made it what we see on the screen. But why fan when it seems more natural to thumb the hammer as intended by Colt? For that, I went to renowned fast draw, artist Jim Martin.

Jim is a legend in the world of the fast draw, and while retired, he is still amazingly fast. Jim is famous for his skill at thumbing. In his opinion, fanning is easier to master than thumbing. It makes sense. In thumbing, one hand does everything: drawing, aiming, cocking, firing and reholstering. In fanning, the tasks are divided. The strong hand draws and aims. The offhand cocks the hammer, which is the hardest task.

In the early days of cartridge guns, the hammers had extra-strong hammer springs to assure the hammer had enough energy to set off the unreliable primers. So, many users developed a throw-down style of drawing so inertia helped cock the hammer. Using the mass of the offhand to cock the hammer was easier and sped up the process.

Cons ...

So why didn't all gunmen fan?

First, the Colt was made for a deliberate, well-aimed shot with one hand. Speed came with familiarity and use. Thumbers also had the advantage of using either hand to keep fighting. If a fanner was incapacitated in either hand, they were vulnerable and likely a second-place finisher.

Second, fanning is very hard on the revolver. The energy caused by the sudden acceleration and lockup of the cylinder will quickly damage or break the internal parts, in some cases within a few-dozen shots. The inertia can also over-rotate the cylinder, causing the chamber and barrel to be out of alignment. This can result in damage or total failure of the gun when needed most.

Third, the .45 Colt cartridge was a 250-grain bullet propelled by 30 grains of black powder in most cases. It was the Magnum of its day! Rapid firing of the gun created recoil that was hard to control and voluminous clouds of dense white smoke. Those two made accuracy on a moving target almost impossible, especially in a dingy coal-oil lamp-lit saloon. In the cases documented, the fanner rarely hit their mark. And the demonstrations given for the press were done outside, in daylight, on a stationary target that wasn't shooting back!

So, was fanning a product of Hollywood? No. It did exist in the Old West, but it was enough of an oddity to make the front-page news, and those who genuinely mastered it were exceptional gunmen.

DIXIE
Gun Works, Inc.

We're living America's history. Everyday.

The blackpowder era is proudly woven into our rich American tapestry. And today, thousands of blackpowder enthusiasts—from primitive and military re-enactors to modern hunters and competitive shooters—keep the tradition alive. Everything you need to take part is right here in the **2022 DIXIE GUN WORKS'** catalog—the world's largest selection of blackpowder replica arms, accessories, antique parts, muzzleloader hunting and sport shooting equipment.

PROFESSIONAL SERVICE AND EXPERTISE GUARANTEED

ORDER TODAY!
STILL ONLY $5.00

VIEW ITEMS AND ORDER ONLINE!

www.dixiegunworks.com
Major credit cards accepted

FOR ORDERS ONLY (800) 238-6785

DIXIE GUN WORKS, INC.
1412 W. Reelfoot Avenue PO Box 130 Union City, TN 38281
INFO PHONE: (731) 885-0700   FAX: (731) 885-0440
EMAIL: info@dixiegunworks.com

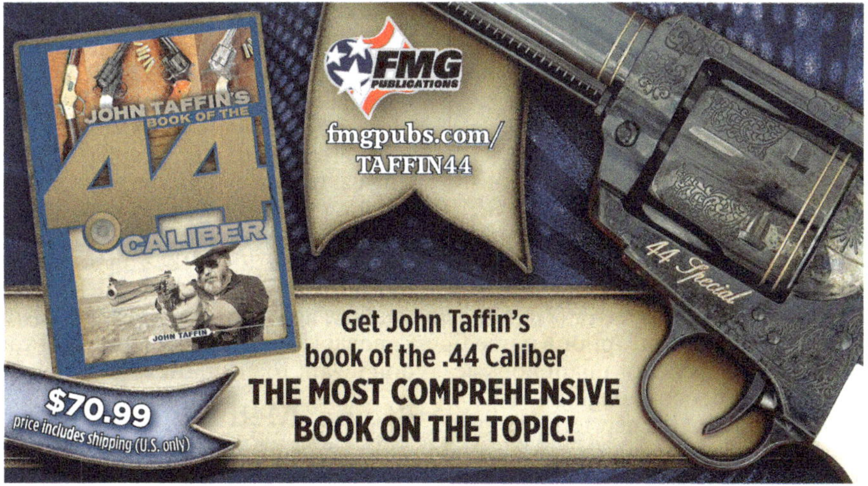

Jeremy D. Clough

LOADS A MITE SLOW …

Modern Ammo for the Cap & Ball Sixgun: Kirst Konverters

" y very first pistol was a cap & ball Colt. Shoots as fast as lightning, but she loads a mite slow."
— *Devil's Right Hand* by Steve Earle

Anyone who's loaded a black powder sixgun knows Earle was right. Loading requires four operations: measuring and pouring the powder charge, seating a ball on top of it, either using a wad or seal to avoid chain firing and then capping the nipple. That's for each chamber, so a total of 24 different tasks to get the gun full up, something I imagine would be hard to do while getting shot at.

The advent of the self-contained cartridge dramatically changed that. While loading a single action is still basically a one-at-a-time thing, dunking that big brass cartridge into its charge hole is a far more efficient way to keep a single-action revolver functioning. For those of us who enjoy shooting more than loading, it also makes for a more pleasant afternoon at the range.

Birth of the Cartridge

Cartridges were in use previously, but a Rollin White patent held by S&W kept other companies (read: Colt, for whom White had done work) from boring revolver cylinders through to take a cartridge until it expired in 1870. While the newfangled contraption's immediate reception was not unanimous acclaim, it came soon enough, and with it, a desire to adapt the new technology to the black powder revolvers in which the post-Civil War world was awash. This

was no small thing: over a quarter million Colt 1851s were made, nearly that many Remington 1858s, a couple hundred thousand Colt 1860s and many others still too good to just throw away. The same technology that kept those guns relevant then makes them more enjoyable now, thanks to Kirst Konverters.

Converting Cap & Ball

The mechanical challenge of swapping from cap & ball to cartridge consists of boring through the cylinder and adding a firing pin since the hammer shape required to pop a cap will not necessarily line up with a primer nor set it off. Early Richards conversions used a non-rotating plate containing a single firing pin. In contrast, some modern drop-in conversion cylinders use a cylinder-mounted plate with one firing pin per charge hole.

Kirst Konverters incorporate elements of the Richards design and generally use a single firing pin, with the Konverter plate indexed by its flat bottom.

There remains the problem of getting cartridges in and out: The nipple relief on the right side is nowhere near big enough for a cartridge, so you either scoop out the side of the gun or remove the cylinder to reload it, which is particularly attractive for guns with easily removable cylinders — especially if you don't want to grind on your pistol

Movie Methods

In *Pale Rider,* Clint Eastwood reloads his converted Remington 1858

by swapping loaded cylinders whenever he runs dry. It's thus no surprise Kirst, a pioneer of modern cartridge conversions, calls one of the Remington units the Pale Rider. It's a little more fiddly than in the movie, but the process is essentially as Eastwood demonstrated. With the hammer at half cock or partially withdrawn, pull down the loading lever, which frees the cylinder pin to move forward and release the cylinder, then roll a new one in. Slide the pin backward, rotate the loading lever upward, latch it in place and you're ready to go again.

Despite the famous gun shop scene of *The Good, the Bad and the Ugly* where Tuco ("the Ugly"), mixes and matches Colt parts like a 1911 aficionado with a Brownells' catalog, swapping cylinders in an open-top Colt is not so easy. It requires pressing out the captive barrel wedge and pulling the barrel forward off

Kirst Konverters, a pioneer in modern cartridge conversion cylinders, makes it simple to shoot fixed ammo from black powder revolvers like this Pietta 1858 Remington (top) and 2nd Gen Colt 1851 Navy (bottom).

Loading a black powder revolver requires four actions per charge hole: measuring and pouring in the powder, seating a ball, sealing the cylinder and capping it. Or you can just drop in a loaded round.

The .45 caliber cylinders are marked "A" (shown) and "C" for ACP and Colt, respectively. And yep, the .45 ACP one is dirty because Jeremy shot it.

For those willing to modify their cap & ball guns, Kirst offers a gated conversion as well as an ejector assembly, so no disassembly is required for loading. This one is for an 1860 Colt.

The Kirst .22 conversion for the '58 uses its customary adaptor ring with a single firing pin, with a clearance cut for loading and unloading. A .22 LR won't quite clear the frame, so you either make a clearance cut or remove the cylinder when it's empty — no great task on the '58.

The chamber area of the .22 LR cylinder has been thoughtfully machined, so it's easy to get a fingernail under the case heads to empty the cylinder. Or you can punch them out with a brass rod, as Jeremy did.

the cylinder pin, which will likely require tools.

Safety First

We'll start with the easy one, but as a safety precaution, simply changing what an old-school sixgun shoots does not eliminate the safety problems inherent in the original lockwork. Always leave the hammer down on an empty chamber and do not trust half cock. While rimfire conversions can be used on brass-framed pistols, the centerfire ones are only for steel-framed pistols, and all should use lead bullets exclusively.

Remington '58s are typically .44, but every .44 is a lie: No ".44" caliber I know of is actually that dimension. Most are smaller (0.429"), but .44 black powder barrels fire a 0.454" ball. While the loads used should either be black powder or equivalent — leave the +P stuff for something else — this means the '58 can be readily converted to fire

centerfire .45 ammo. For this article, Kirst kindly provided its Pale Rider Double Up converter, which comes with one conversion plate and two five-shot cylinders. In this case, they're .45 ACP and .45 Colt, conveniently marked .45A and .45C to tell them apart.

Some Assembly Required

As with all aftermarket parts, some fitting may be required for the cylinder and converter plate. Both cylinders were a bit long for my Pietta '58, something you figure out quickly because they won't go in. The instructions say to slowly remove material using sandpaper. I'm sure that works, but I'm more confident in the precision of my lathe than my hands, so to the South Bend we went.

I first used painter's tape to keep the jaws from marring the bluing on the cylinder. After checking the alignment with a center before firmly clamping it

Pietta 1858 with its cylinders (left to right): standard .44 cap & ball, .45 ACP with Konverter ring in place, .45 Colt (which also chambers .45 Schofield) and .22 LR. The ring on the .22 Konverter has been scooped out to allow it to be loaded/unloaded in the gun, but that requires clearing the pistol's frame.

Pietta's reasonably priced clone of an 1858 Remington in .44, like other blackpowder .44s, shoot 0.454" projectiles. With the addition of Kirst Konverters, it now shoots .45 ACP, .45 Colt, .45 Schofield and .22 LR. Black Hills provided the .45 Colt and Schofield, while Jeremy loaded the ACP with 200-grain bullets from D&L.

in place, I barely surfaced the face of the cylinder repeatedly until it would go in, checking every complete pass. Once it cleared, though, the cylinder pin would not fully seat, indicating the bottom of the converter plate needed to be relieved to align its central hole with the one in the breech.

A Hammer is Not a Precision Tool ...

Several times in the fitting process, the cylinder pin got stuck and required a whack or two with a rubber mallet to remove. Spoiler alert: Don't do this. The pin is two parts and those mallet raps weakened the joint enough that the end of the pin cheerfully departed the gun during the first range session. One trip to the Dixie Gun Works website and $15 later, I had a new one.

Unfortunately, the barrel-mounted stud to which the loading lever latches also took flight during that first session, a result of the manufacturer's choice to solder the stud in place rather

Both .45 cylinders were just a bit long; rather than using sandpaper as the directions suggested, Jeremy shortened them in the lathe, carefully making passes and checking until they fit. The blue is from painter's tape used to avoid scratching the cylinder.

than dovetail it like the originals. No doubt it's part of what contributes to the gun's super-reasonable price, but I'll be cutting a dovetail for the replacement I have on the way. This is partially because as I was preparing to solder the original back into place, the spring clamp holding

it in place shifted, launching it to parts unknown.

Konverter Success

The Konverters, on the other hand, worked flawlessly. Having rubber banded the loading lever in place, we put some 150 rounds through the '58, consisting of light .45 ACP handloads assembled using D&L Sports' 200-grain bullet and cowboy loadings of the .45 Colt and shorter .45 Schofield provided by Black Hills ammunition. ACP hit to the point of aim at 25 yards, while the two rimmed rounds hit somewhat high.

With the light loads and weight of the 8" barrel, recoil was minimal, and accuracy was good. While I struggled a little with the sights (the rounded top and V-like rear-sight groove made it hard to shoot groups), when the cylinder pin departed, we were happily banging steel at 50 yards. And while I'm not movie-quick, it was easy to swap out cylinders to reload. Empties

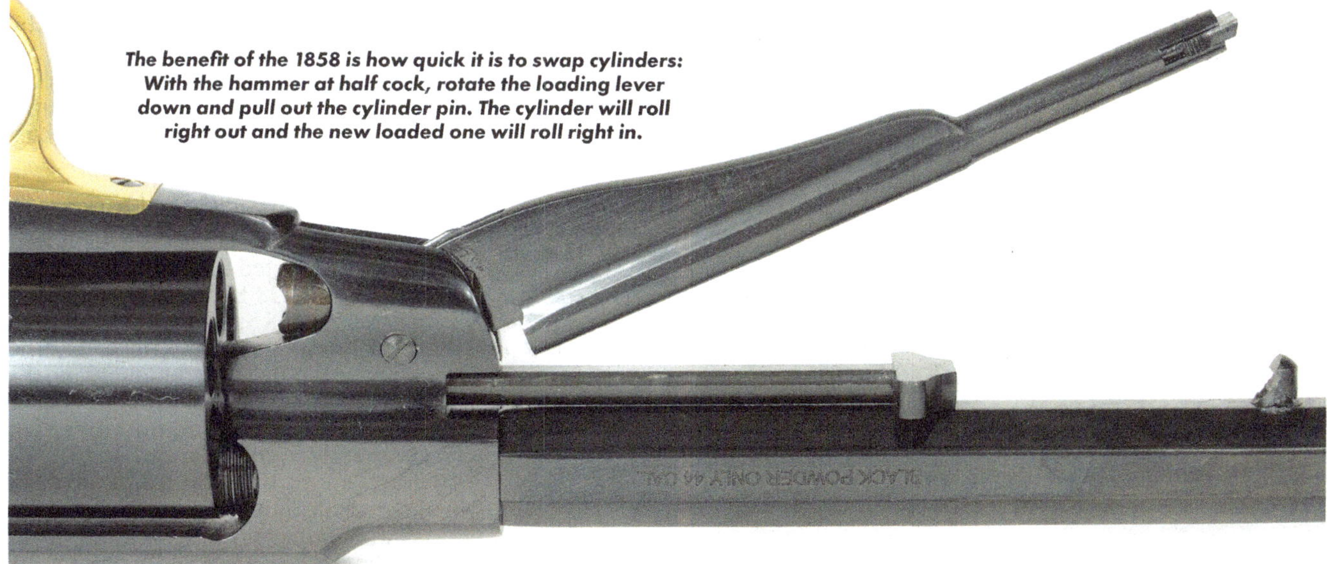

The benefit of the 1858 is how quick it is to swap cylinders: With the hammer at half cock, rotate the loading lever down and pull out the cylinder pin. The cylinder will roll right out and the new loaded one will roll right in.

The .36-caliber 2nd Generation Colt 1851 Navy. While Kirst and others make .38-caliber cartridge conversions, the Colt's significantly larger bore diameter and difficulty in removing the cylinder are obstacles. Kirst's .22 unit, however, installs with no modifications and is pure joy to shoot.

While banging steel back to 50 yards was easy, Jeremy struggled shooting the Remington on paper. Note that while he strung this .45 ACP, 25-yard group over 4 ½" horizontally — clearly shooter error — vertically, it measures just over 1".

The 1851 conversion comes with a cylinder with a six-firing-pin back plate and a barrel liner with shims and a .44-caliber adaptor. No shims were required on Jeremy's gun.

Unlike the '58 rimfire conversion where the single-firing-pin ring stays in place, the '51 uses a six-firing-pin plate keyed to the cylinder by a unique spring-loaded pin arrangement. It lets the two rotate separately for loading and unloading through a hole in the back plate.

either fell out, or I punched them out with a brass cleaning rod.

Rimfire Options

And then there was the .22 conversion. Installing with no modification, it consists of a .22 cylinder and converter plate as well as a stubby little .22 barrel insert short enough to fit into the rear of the barrel through the cylinder window. It was accompanied by shims to get the cylinder gap just right, as well as a pair of sleeves that allow it to be used in .36- or .44-caliber pistols.

The converter plate has a groove to allow the cylinder to be loaded and unloaded in the gun (Kirst also sells a no-modification ejector rod assembly that replaces the cylinder pin), but .22 LR is a bit too long to clear the gun's recoil shield without modification; I imagine .22 short would do just fine. No worries: Roll it out just like the center-fires, punch the empties out and reload. Be aware there's a small clearance cut on the flange of the barrel insert and you'll need to keep it aligned with the center of the cylinder during installation.

It is ridiculously fun, with little noise, zero recoil and none of the pungent black powder cloud of smoke. It's even more fun with Aguila's gleefully anemic Colibri ammo. While Kirst advertised its .22 conversions as accurate to 50', we stretched it to 25 yards, where the Colt Navy version did particularly well.

More Conversion Options

In addition to .22 LR, the Colt 1851 can be converted to fire centerfire cartridges like .38 Short/Long Colt and (very mild) .38 Special, but unless you want to cut the frame for a loading groove, the need to hammer out the barrel wedge every six rounds makes it less attractive. And nominal bore diameter is something like 0.375", much larger than the 0.355" or so of loaded .38 ammo. Skirted bullets such as wadcutters can help, as does lining the barrel to a tighter diameter, a fix

The window in the side of the cylinder gives the shooter access to the spring-loaded plunger that locks the cylinder and back plate together. Pull it forward with a thumbnail and the two rotate separately for loading and unloading.

that Kirst and others offer, but makes the gun unusable for black powder.

Since I want to leave my 2nd Generation Colt unmodified, it left few options — which, fortunately, included Kirst's .22 conversion. Like the '58 conversion, it includes a barrel insert with sleeve and shims and a two-piece cylinder, but unlike it, the cylinder has a unique latching arrangement where the cylinder can be rotated separately from its six-firing-pin backplate to load and unload. There's a loading hole in the backplate, and the cartridges easily clear the gun's frame, so there is no need to take the gun apart to reload; just use a brass rod or hex key to push out empties.

To install, gently tap out the barrel wedge from right to left, then line up the loading ram on a solid part of the cylinder and use it to force the barrel forward off the cylinder arbor. Remove the cylinder, grease the pin and slide the conversion cylinder on. Slide in the barrel liner, shimming if necessary (it wasn't on mine), then index the barrel on the cylinder arbor and frame and tap the barrel wedge back into place. It's now the coolest .22 I've shot in a long time. Like the '58, there's no recoil, and it is a pure joy to hear the little "snap" of the .22 and see it hit whatever you were aiming at. I managed to put five out of six rounds into about 3" at 25 yards, resting my hands, which is plenty accurate for plinking, especially considering the rear sight is, you know, a notch in the cocked hammer.

Converted guns were a critical part of the opening of the American West, making *blackpowder* revolvers easier to shoot and load. Kirst Konverters do the same thing today, so you can enjoy your classic sixgun without all the mess and time involved in shooting black powder … and in .22, they're just ridiculously fun.

For more info: Black-Hills.com, DLSports.com, DixieGunWorks.com, KirstKonverter.com

THE COWBOY WAY

Risk Everything,
Fear Nothing,
Have No Regrets.

Shoot HSM ammo to get the job done right.

.32-20 Winchester	.41 Remington Magnum	.45 Schofield	.32-40 Winchester
.38 Special	.44 Russian	.45 Colt	.38-55 Winchester
.357 Magnum	.44 S&W Special	.30-30 Winchester	.44-40
.38-40 Winchester	.44 Magnum	.30-40 Krag	.45-70 Govt.

When ya round 'em up and count 'em, who has more to offer a cowboy than HSM? More calibers. More selection. Both pistol and rifle. Each round crafted with cowboy integrity and grit.

Perfect for your personal cowboy pistols and rifles. And, HSM is always affordable.

So, get at it. The cowboy way. With complete confidence. Shoot HSM!

To learn more, please visit www.hsmammunition.com.

HSM
SINCE 1968

WANT MORE?

Click Here:
gunsmagazine.com

Bat was the real deal and we're betting he would've carried a 1907 as a handy backup if he could have.

"Bat" Masterson Says:

"A tenderfoot with a Savage Automatic and the nerve to stand his ground, could have run the worst six-shooter man, the West ever knew, right off the range."

Mr. Masterson, famous Sheriff, of Dodge City, and Government Scout in the early days, gives these two sound reasons for the above positive assertion.

First, anyone, without practice, can shoot the Savage Automatic straight. You point it naturally, off hand, just as you point your finger, yet you hit what you aim at!

10 Shots Quick

Second, the Savage Automatic is quicker and gets in the first shot every time against a revolver. You can fire 10 shots as fast as you can *press* (not pull) the trigger.

Mr. Masterson has written in a fascinating vein about the expertness of the most famous six-shooter men of the early days. We have published it in a handsome booklet. Free. Write for it. You should know about this wonderful, modern pocket-arm; not like other automatics in action. Safer and easier to carry than a revolver. Powerful, (32 cal.); light (19 oz.); short (6½ in.); fits flat in pocket. Try it at your dealers. If he hasn't it, you can buy from us.

THE FAMOUS SAVAGE RIFLES

have been used for years by sportsmen and are known to be the most skilfully built rifles in America. The sporting size, '99 Model, 303 Repeater and the '03 Model .22 cal. Repeater, are premiers in their classes. We will send you the new Savage Rifle Catalogue, handsomely illustrated, full of rifle information, for your address on a post card. Address, SAVAGE ARMS CO., 471 Savage Avenue, Utica, N. Y., U. S. A.

The New SAVAGE Automatic

"10 Shots Quick" and a bit of "magical" ergonomics kept the 1907 popular, with more than 208,000 sold.

Roy Huntington

BAT MASTERSON APPROVED

The Delightful Savage 1907

o less a gunfighter than Bat Masterson had this to say about the Savage 1907: "A tenderfoot with a Savage Automatic and the nerve to stand his ground, could have run the worst six-shooter man the West ever knew, right off the range."

Perhaps even more interesting to me is the fact in the same ad showing Bat brandishing a 1907, the "Second" reason for Bat's assertion is: "The Savage Automatic is quicker and gets in the first shot every time against a revolver. You can fire 10 shots as fast as you can *press* (not pull) the trigger." The italics and "(not pull)" are in the original ad copy. Bat knew the ropes, and it's why he eventually died of a heart attack at his desk writing sports copy for a newspaper — rather than in the dusty streets of Dodge City.

While the Colt 1903 and even the Remington 51 are the darlings of classic pocket-pistol admirers, it wasn't until I bought this Savage 1907 in .32 ACP I realized I had been missing out. I always enjoyed their ads with Bat, the distraught "housewife at home facing a burglar" ("Victory And Your Savage!") and even Buffalo Bill Cody himself touting it, but I had never actually fired one. I thought them strange-looking, and they just didn't look as if they'd feel good.

I was exactly wrong.

The Origin

Many 1911 fans don't realize Savage's original design in 1907 by Elbert Searles for an 8-round double-stack .45 ACP was a finalist in the great race for a new fighting handgun for U.S. forces. Up against the 1911, the Luger and others lost out until it came down to the Savage and the Colt. Alas, the Savage cost considerably more and had manufacturing quirks causing malfunctions and parts breakages during extensive testing by the military. It was the "big boy" Colt up against a smaller company, and Colt won handily due mostly to John Browning's genius. The 195 .45 ACP Savage test guns were returned to Savage, where they were eventually sold. Value today is in the $20,000 to $40,000 range.

But Savage realized scaling things down to a pocket pistol might work, and they did just that. The "Model 1907" was introduced in .32 ACP in 1908. First-year production was about 2,000 guns, but in 1911 alone, they sold 20,000 guns. This trend kept up, with total production figures topping out in 1920 at about 208,800, with an additional 9,845 in .380 ACP models.

Interestingly, while the U.S. military didn't buy any, the French did purchase 27,000 in .32 ACP for use in WWI.

The Design

I was amazed, frankly, at how good this gun feels in the hand. Savage made a great fuss about how it "points naturally," and I confess it points better than the Colt 1903. They talk about there being "… no need for any experience as it shoots just like the way you point your finger!" Great advertising copy, but not entirely true. I did find it very easy to shoot fast and accurately in close, though, and I do think there's a bit of magic going on.

The "hammer" isn't really a hammer, which fools most people. It's a "cocking indicator" since the 1907 is actually striker-fired. If it's back, you know the gun is cocked. However, I wouldn't ever use it to "lower" the striker, as there just isn't any way to get a good grip on it.

Like the CZ 75, the slide rides "inside" of the frame, so it's hard to grab onto. The burly serrations you see are there to lend a good gripping surface. The external safety (marked *Safe* and *Fire*) is "on" when up and can be brushed downward into the off position easily. I'm not sure I'd carry it "cocked and locked" like a 1911. Besides, you honestly shouldn't rely on an antique like this for protection unless you're really in a pinch.

The magazine holds 10 rounds and is a double stack. Most pocket guns held six to eight at best, so the Savage won the cartridge-capacity battle handily. What's funny is, at a glance, it's hard to tell the mags apart from the "new" breed of similar capacity

Top to bottom: Savage 1907, Colt Pocket Positive and the Colt 1903 were peers for personal protection in the teens of the last century.

Roy shot this offhand 5-shot group at about 12 yards with the Savage. Make fun of the tiny sights if you want, but it still shoots.

Ruger LCP Max double-stack mag on left, Savage on right. Savage beat everyone to the draw for that design in 1907!

Some old Hirtenberg .32 ACP clocked 980+ out of the Savage. Some of the old Euro stuff was hot!

That "hammer" really isn't; it's just a cocking indicator for the striker hiding inside the slide. The scalloped section rotates right as part of the takedown procedure.

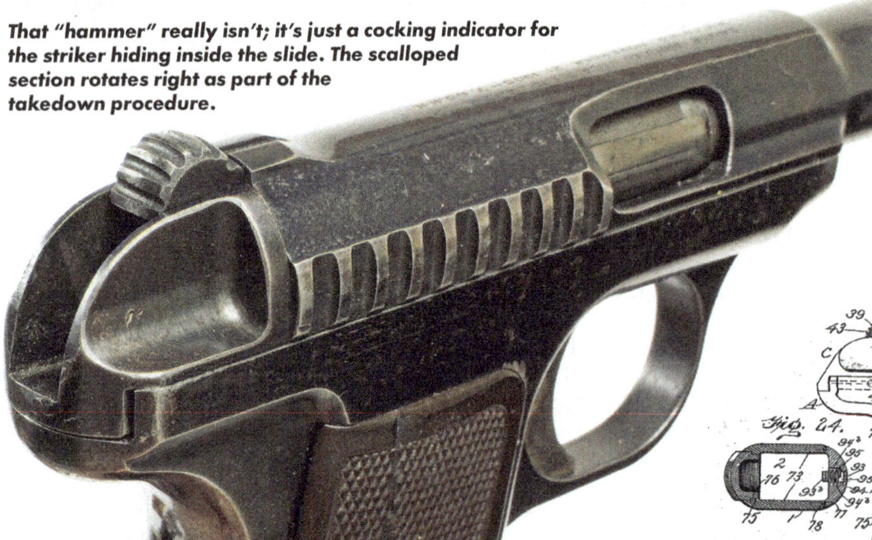

pocket- pistol magazines. Savage beat everyone to it — 110 years ago.

The mag is released with a tiny lever on the front strap. It's purported to be able to be released with your little finger, but it's pretty fumbly for a "speed" load. Still, I think it's better than the classic heel release on so many of these guns. Sights are tiny, of course, but it adds to the charm of shooting the old guns.

Takedown is clever. You move the slide to the rear, then pull the cocking piece (the hammer-looking thing) down and twist the rear of the slide to the right. This rotates the fire-control assembly, and it will eventually pull out the back. The slide then goes forward off the frame, with the barrel, etc., coming free. You'll end up with six parts, and it's very easy to clean and lube. The key is to remember to pull the cocking piece all the way down before you try to turn the assembly.

Shooting

Unfortunately, my gun has an after-market magazine, so mine is "Eight Shots Quick" rather than 10. But I put about 50 rounds through it for this little exposé, and it ran just fine. A fast mag dump at about 5 yards showed a nice tight group, without really looking at the sights, just pointing. Maybe Savage was right? I slowed down and used the tiny sights at about 12 yards and got a tidy 1.5" group. And yes, I tried my 80-yard steel torso target and, in eight rounds, hit it three times once I dialed in the elevation. Now tell me that's not great fun!

I recommend if you like this sort of thing, keep your good eye open for one. They tend to sell for modest prices, say $400 or so for a "shooter" to more than $1,000 for a really pretty one. And pretty they can be with their amazing polish and blue the old gun-smiths could manage.

But be warned, your first gun like this is only your first step on a long journey of marvelous fun. Suddenly, the used-gun section of 1903s, 1907s, Remington 51s and the like will beckon. Prepare to lose your heart!

TURNBULL
RESTORATION
SERVICES

Shown: Restored Colt SAA Revolver from 1874

Preserve

Saving cherished memories and reviving past stories while
returning heirloom firearms back to their original condition.

(585) 412-2930
quotes@turnbullrestoration.com

CONTACT US FOR YOUR NO-FEE,
NO-OBLIGATION RESTORATION QUOTE

TURNBULLRESTORATION.COM/TFW

TURNBULL
RESTORATION

WIN A STACCATO C 2011 & MORE!

CONCEALED CARRY & SELF-DEFENSE

THE SCOOP ON APPENDIX CARRY

LIFESAVING FLASHLIGHT TIPS

WILL YOUR CARRY KNIFE SAVE YOU? OR GET YOU KILLED?

HOME & SELF-DEFENSE
• Suppressors? Really?
• Pistol? Rifle? Shotgun?
• Intervention, Vel Non

DAILY CARRY ESSENTIALS
• Vehicle Carry Solutions
• Less-Lethal Tricks
• Mobilizing Mouse Guns
• Pocket Carry CQB

USING WEAPONS OF OPPORTUNITY!

VOLUME #29
AmericanHandgunner.com

ARE YOU PREPARED TO
PROTECT YOUR
FAMILY?

You are your own first responder. Investing
in knowledge, training and practice is the
most effective thing you can do to increase
the odds of successfully protecting yourself
and loved ones. This issue of
Concealed Carry & Self-Defense 2022
has more useful, and practical, educational
self-defense content than ever before.
Order now!

AVAILABLE IN
PRINT & DIGITAL FORMAT
FMGPUBS.COM

ALSO AVAILABLE ON
amazon Prime

Colt's first actual revolver meant for carrying in a holster on a person's belt was the Model 1851 Navy .36. This one is cased with all the accessories needed to fire and maintain it.

Mike "Duke" Venturino · Photos: Yvonne Venturino

BEYOND THE PEACEMAKER

The Other Old West "Belt Pistols"

Colt's main rival in the revolver market in the early 1860s was Remington. This is their .36 Belt Pistol.

Do you believe movie and TV portrayals of America's frontier firearms? I don't. But if you do, I will forgive you for thinking only the Colt Single Action Army, aka the Peacemaker, saw significant carry in every frontiersman's holster. Until recent years, rarely were other late-1800s sixshooters shown on either big or small screens.

To cover the myriad of sixguns that saw frontier use, we must go back decades earlier than the Peacemaker's introduction year of 1873. Colt didn't get practical (read: successful) cap & ball revolvers on the market

until the late 1840s. A few years later, the company named the first of their new genre the .36 Belt Pistol. Today it's Colt's Model 1851 Navy .36. There were earlier .31-caliber peashooters, but mainly they were carried in pockets. Ten years later, Colt was seeking government contracts when they scaled down their behemoth Walker and Dragoon .44s. This new and graceful revolver was commonly called the .44 Army, but today is known as the Model 1860 Army. At about the same time, Colt rounded the contours of the .36 Navy into what is known today as the Model 1861.

Colt wasn't the only brand of revolver floating about back then. Remington had both .36- and .44-caliber sixguns with some advantages over Sam Colt's designs. For instance, the Remington revolver frames had top straps with a groove down their middles for rear sights. Colt rear sights were only notches in the ham-mers. Also, Colt cap & ball revolvers had to be dismantled into three parts for thorough cleaning. Remington's cylinder could be removed in seconds without tools.

Belt Pistol Action

It seems the five years immediately post-Civil War were some of the most violent "out West," especially in terms of Indian fighting on the plains. Both Colt and Remington .44s saw considerable action. For instance, when General Sheridan enlisted 50 "frontiersmen" to serve as a "quick reaction" force in Colorado and Kansas in 1868, they were issued Spencer lever-action carbines and .44 Colt "Army" revolvers. Their only big fight was when they were besieged on a Colorado river island by Cheyenne warriors. Also, tales of the 7th Cavalry's adventures in the same area at the time make mention of their Remington .44s. In one

skirmish, six soldiers were trapped in a buffalo wallow by a war party. When help finally arrived, four were completely disabled with wounds; one soldier only had 13 Spencer cartridges remaining for his carbine and another was only able to fire a Remington revolver with his left hand because a bullet had broken his right arm.

Conversion Era

After the Civil War, S&W had .22 and .32 cartridge-firing popguns, but the first American cartridge-firing "belt revolvers" were conversions of cap & ball sixguns. Without proof, it seems most were based on Remington's cap & ball models. There was a .46 Remington and different conversions chambering .44 Henry Rimfire. However, it does seem like some famous frontiersmen, such as Wild Bill Hickok, clung to their tried-and-true cap & ball revolvers. His Colt '51 Navy .36s supposedly were in

These three Colts show the evolution of Colt cap & ball .44s. First came the Colt/Walker .44 in 1847. Over the next few years, the design was reduced to the Colt Dragoon .44, which appeared in three slightly different versions. Lastly, in 1860 Colt produced its last .44 cap & ball revolver, the Model 1860 Army .44, which many consider the most graceful revolver ever made.

After the Civil War, S&W had .22 and .32 cartridge-firing popguns, but the first American cartridge-firing "belt revolvers" were conversions of cap & ball sixguns.

his room when he was assassinated at Deadwood, S.D., in 1876.

.44 Russians

Newly manufactured cartridge-firing belt revolvers finally appeared in 1870. Smith & Wesson was first with their Model No. 3 top break. It was made as .44 Henry and .44/100 S&W (later .44 American) and .44 Russian. Speaking of Russians, they colluded to get S&W building several alterations of their Model No. 3s in the early 1870s. Of course, all were .44 Russian. These were shipped offshore to the tune of tens of thousands, but a considerable number also found favor with American gun toters.

When Jesse James' gang attempted a bank robbery at Northfield, Minn., in 1876, most of them packed one sort or another of S&W .44 Russians. Another famous western lawman who supposedly liked S&W .44 Russians was Virgil Earp. However, which revolver he fired at the O.K. Corral fight in 1881 is not known with certainty. It seems for sure he did own an S&W New Model No. 3 .44 Russian after leaving Tombstone. That particular version was introduced in 1878.

Schofield Modifications

Smith & Wesson did sell 1,000 of their Model No. 3s in .44/100 caliber to the U.S. Army in 1871. Major George Schofield appreciated their fast ejection of empty cases, but patented some designs to better S&W's No. 3s. The company didn't appreciate this, but by the mid-1870s adopted the changes at the behest of the U.S. government if the revolvers could be supplied as .45s. S&W did so, but this .45 Schofield/.45 Government/.45 Colt situation has led to considerable confusion. The Model No. 3's frame would not accommodate a cylinder long enough for the govern-

Remington again tried to rival Colt with their Model 1875, aka New Model Belt Revolver.

However, because Colt had gained the government's contract for a Single Action Army .45 in 1873, Remington's '75 failed to thrive.

Perhaps the ultimate regarding S&W's single-action No. 3 revolvers is the New Model No. 3, in which .44 Russian was the predominant chambering.

ment's standard .45 Colt with a case length of 1.285". S&W's new .45 was made with a case length of 1.10". Not only did the new round fit well in S&W's new "Schofields," but it also did in all .45 Colt revolvers. In 1882, when Bob Ford shot Jesse James in the back of the head in his own home, his revolver was supposedly an S&W Schofield .45.

Some folks mistakenly call all S&W No. 3s Schofields. They are not! Only the specific Model No. 3 .45s using the Major's patents were Schofields.

Alternate Belt-Pistol Players

When S&W and Colt were rivaling each other in the mid-1870s, a couple of other manufacturers entered the "Belt Pistol" market. Those were Remington and Merwin, Hulbert & Co. It would be fair to wonder if Remington was such a big player in the "Belt Pistol" field in the 1860s, why did they wait until 1875 to introduce the New Model Belt Revolver? We call it Model 1875 now. It's probably because they were making big money building single-shot No. 1 military-style "rolling blocks" and shipping them literally around the world. I have an original 1877 Remington catalog saying they had built over 900,000 No. 1s by that time.

Their wait perhaps caused them to miss the boat because, in 1873, the

From left to right are three versions of Schofield: Original S&W Model No. 3 .45, Uberti Model 1875 .45 and new S&W No. 3, of which a special run was produced in the year 2000.

U.S. Army adopted the venerable Colt Strap Pistol, which came to be called Single Action Army. The big Remington and Colt SAA are near identical in size and operation, but each has a few points over the other. Remington's cylinder is easily removed without tools. A screwdriver was necessary for SAA cylinder removal until its design changed in the 1890s. Remington's grip frame was forged integral with its main frame, and a trigger guard was attached with a single screw. The Colt grip frame was two pieces held together to the main frame by six screws. Colt ejector rods were protected better than Remington's, but then again, another screw was needed to hold it to the barrel. Remingtons had a large web between barrel and frame, making it a better club in hand-to-hand combat than a Colt. I have seen 7 ½" barreled Colt SAAs with the barrel canted a mite upward, obviously from smiting something hard.

Remington 1875s

The U.S. Army tested Remington Model 1875s, and both officers presiding over the testing gave the model high marks. However, the army was receiving thousands of Colt .45s by then, so no Remington orders resulted. About 25,000 to 30,000 Model 1875s were made before production ceased about 1888.

I must admit Remington's Model 1875 caused egg on my face. I'd written many times that '75s were only made as .44s — .44 Remington and .44-40s. However, a reader sent me proof that, indeed, some were made as .45s — specifically the .45 Government. With chambers bored straight through, they could chamber both .45 S&W and .45 Colt. Most Remington .45s seem to have been sent to Mexico. Remington

This Colt Model 1851 .36 with chambers still loaded was dug up near a Civil War battlefield.

The least known of Old West six-shooters was the Merwin & Hulbert. Named Pocket Army, although it was far too heavy for pocket carry. This one in Duke's collection is a .44-40.

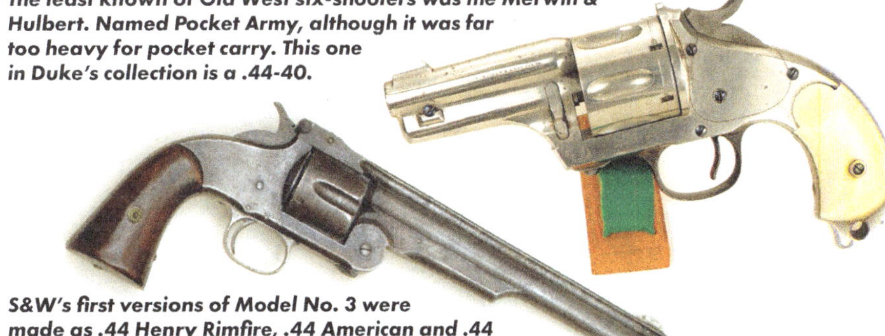

S&W's first versions of Model No. 3 were made as .44 Henry Rimfire, .44 American and .44 Russian. Most of them were sold with 8" barrels.

introduced a remodeled Model 1875 as the Model 1890, but it was dropped due to slow sales after only about 2,000 were made. When Jesse James' brother, Frank, surrendered to Missouri authorities, he turned over a brace of Remington '75 .44-40s.

Merwin Hulberts

This brings us to the most unusual frontier "Belt Pistol." The Merwin Hulberts featured frames and barrels that detached from one another and turned 90 degrees for case ejection. Some were sold in sets with 3 ½" and 7" barrels that could be interchanged in seconds. They were and are examples of the machine craftsman's art. It may be why they are the only revolvers mentioned here that have not been replicated today. The one in my collection is named their Pocket Army, although it's way too heavy to tote in a pocket. It is definitely a "Belt Revolver." The large-frame MHs were all .44s — .44 M&H and, of course, .44-40. I know of none used by any famous personage or in any famous altercation. I've tried shooting mine with black powder handloads, but it fouled up in a single cylinder full. Perhaps it's why it never hit the big time.

There were other "Belt Pistols" in the late 1800s, especially Colt and S&W double actions. They may deserve an article of their own someday.

Will Dabbs, MD

IMITATION IS THE SINCEREST FORM OF FLATTERY

The 1851 Colt Navy

Obadiah Sutcliffe had been a schoolteacher before. He and his wife, Abbie, had settled in Portland, Maine, and planned to raise a family. Then the war happened.

The 5th Maine had mustered in the summer of 1861 when spirits were high. Men flocked to the flag, ready to put down the rebels and save the Union. Sutcliffe had been one of them. In their first parlay, he had been elected company commander. Four years later, he was a different, broken man.

Across places like Bull Run, Gaines' Mill, Antietam, Spotsylvania and Cold Harbor, Sutcliffe's men had fought, bled and died. Through their many campaigns, Sutcliffe's 5th Maine had captured six enemy standards. It seemed important at the time. Now three years after its initial muster, Major Sutcliffe and his mates were finally going home. Of the 1,046 men who had begun the war, only 216 remained.

Major Sutcliffe removed his government issue Colt revolver from its holster one last time and wrapped it carefully in a cloth before pushing it to the back of his trunk. It was another month before the children came in from the fields and were ready to start school. That was time to get reacquainted with Abbie.

Abbie's presence was a soothing balm. She never asked questions when he fell into bouts of inexplicable weeping or awoke in a mighty terror. The war was a part of him now, something foreign and black irrevocably grafted into his soul. However, like so many soldiers who had come before, Obadiah Sutcliffe resolved to spend the rest of his days worthy of what he had seen and done.

Obadiah and Abbie never had children of their own, but he taught hundreds over the decades that followed. At the appointed time, Obadiah died, and his meager teacher's possessions were sold. His shopworn service pistol passed through several owners, some more responsible than others until it came to me. Now old, gnarled and pitted, like its original owner's soul, this vintage gun tells a story. It embodies something deep and wise. It is a tangible connection to something at once both profound and terrible.

History Personified

Guns are just tools. Not unlike a power drill or a claw hammer, a military firearm is designed for a certain specific task. Whether it is a

vintage British Brown Bess musket, an MP40 machine pistol built by the Nazis or a modern tricked-out M4A1 carbine, these weapons reflect the skill of their designers and the will of the nation-states that produced them. However, unlike a carpenter's tools, weapons used in combat embody something more.

A soldier's individual weapon is his most intimate possession. I have shared a sleeping bag with mine and kept it close when answering the call of nature. When that tool is what stands between life and death for some terrified young soldier, it suddenly becomes more than its component parts. To heft such a rarefied historical artifact is to connect with something deep and timeless.

In the case of the 1851 Colt Navy, these elegant old pistols armed patriots on both sides of the line. It's

the seminal problem with war. With few exceptions, all soldiers view theirs as the righteous cause. Were it not so, these same young men would still be at home occupying themselves with the business of living.

Major Sutcliffe's Pistol

Samuel Colt originally titled his remarkable contrivance the Ranger Model, but the proper appellation evolved into the Colt Revolving Belt Pistol of Naval Caliber. Most of the originals were chambered for .36-cal. balls. The Navy served throughout the American Civil War and beyond until it was supplanted in the Colt catalog by the Single Action Army in 1873. The Colt Navy was also produced in the U.K. and ultimately sold well around the world.

The Colt Navy, in its day, was the weapon to the stars. Wild Bill Hickok, Ned Kelly, Doc Holliday, Nathan Bedford Forrest and Robert E. Lee all went into harm's way bearing one. Cartridge conversions of the 1851 Navy in classic Spaghetti Westerns defined a genre.

The original 1851 Colt Navy drove a .36-cal. pure lead ball to around 925 feet per second. This put the gun on par power-wise with a modern .380 ACP. The Confederacy frequently used brass for their frames, as it was cheaper and easier to machine than steel. More than 250,000 of these iconic pistols rolled off the lines. There is an almost unnatural elegance to the gun's architecture.

Colonel Sam Colt built his guns in Hartford, Conn. A massive factory fire in 1864 was a setback, but his pistols were still everywhere during the war. Soldiers like Obadiah Sutcliffe typically carried their Navy revolvers butt-forward on the right to keep their strong hand free to wield a saber.

The Imitators

The same features that made the 1851 Colt Navy so popular back in the 19th century make it a reliable seller today. The sensual lines strike a visceral chord, and the design is relatively easy to produce on simple machines. The four distinct clicks the action makes when cocked ever so slowly are what made Clint Eastwood a household name.

The vast majority of the reproductions available on the American market today are made in Italy. I bought my first when I was 13. Italy's gun-making heritage goes back centuries. Every Italian reproduction Navy I have ever hefted was sturdy, reliable and cool.

Nowadays, you can get these guns from a variety of sources. Dixie Gun Works offers a broad selection. From pocket pistols to mountain howitzers, if they don't have it, you likely don't need it. If you're handy with tools, there are even unfinished kits that let

you imprint your unique personality onto these cool old guns. I have built two with hand tools and loved every minute of the process.

As these guns are crafted using modern steel and advanced production techniques, they are completely safe to shoot. There are several black powder substitutes available, but I prefer the smell, smoke and performance of the real deal. When it comes to black powder, GOEX is the only game in town. Black powder can be hard to source, but it is inimitably cool. I just sucked it up and bought enough to last me until I die, so I wouldn't have to search for it anymore.

Shooting these old black powder pistols is great fun. Pop a cap on each empty cylinder to ensure everything is clear before loading. Hold the gun muzzle up and charge each cylinder with powder. Once that's done, drop a ball in place and use the rammer to seat it snugly.

If you don't have much experience with these old cap & ball revolvers, greasing the end of the chambers after loading is a critical piece of the process. A couple of companies make dedicated chamber grease for this purpose, but axle grease works just fine. It's all filthy.

Reloading these old guns is undeniably laborious, but failure to grease the chambers can be terribly exciting. I once had five of six chambers spontaneously detonate when firing a reproduction 1851 Colt Navy. In case you're wondering, this chain-fire event produces enough billowy white smoke to be seen from space. Additionally, while the recoil from a single ball is delightfully mild, that of five at once is actually quite attention-getting. In this case, I had actually greased the chambers, just apparently not terribly well.

Once the chambers are loaded, put the hammer to half cock and place a

percussion cap on each nipple. Always leave an empty chamber under the hammer unless you are planning to shoot immediately. Black powder is corrosive, so set aside most of an hour and plenty of hot soapy water for cleanup afterward.

Similarities and Differences

When comparing my original with a modern Italian Pietta reproduction, a few things jump out. Colonel Colt placed a serial number on the frame, cylinder, barrel, trigger guard and grip strap. The front sight on the Civil War gun is secured via a dovetail, while the reproduction sight is a brass screw threaded into the barrel. The octagonal barrel and other sundry parts look about interchangeable otherwise.

My original gun has indeed been ridden hard and put up wet. The pistol is badly pitted in places, and it has clearly been cycled about a billion times. However, the action remains

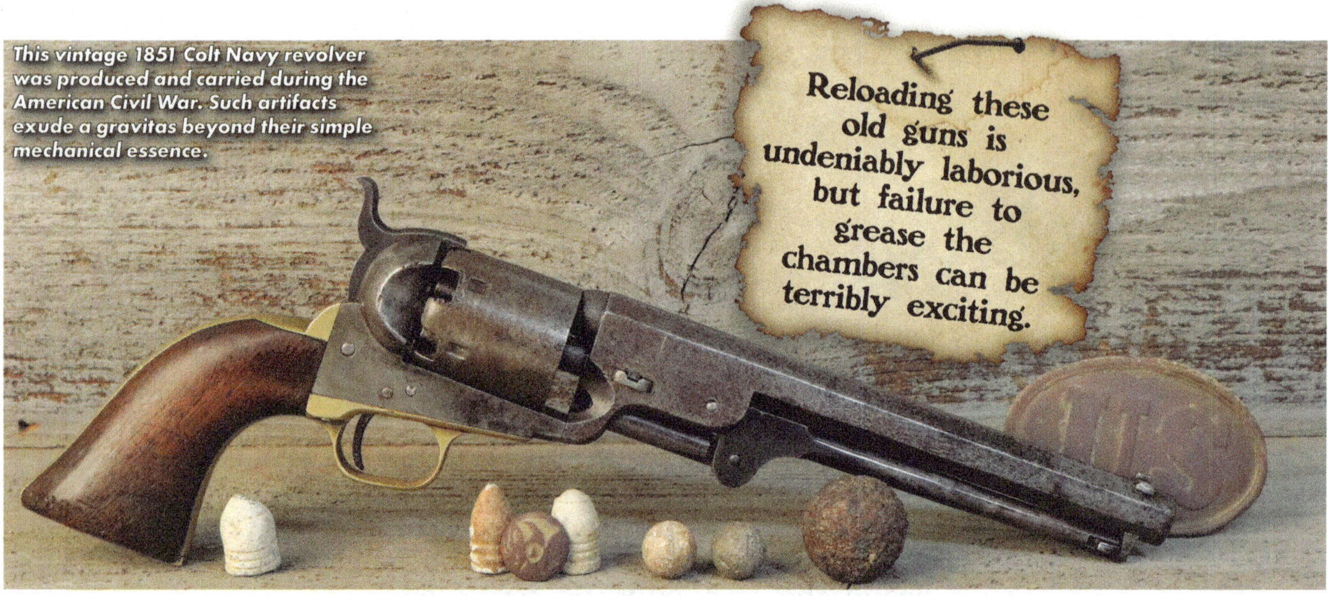

This vintage 1851 Colt Navy revolver was produced and carried during the American Civil War. Such artifacts exude a gravitas beyond their simple mechanical essence.

crisp, and the lockup reliable. All this is just a tribute to how well old Sam Colt made guns despite the pressing exigencies of total war.

My modern reproduction still sports a fair number of machining marks. I finished the brass bits myself by hand, so they're a bit austere. However, Dixie Gun Works sells these guns in kit form for as little as $245 online. For another 30 bucks, they'll professionally finish it out for you. You'd be hard-pressed to find this much cool for such little money elsewhere in the gun world.

Ruminations

I'm inexorably drawn to most anything that shoots in a fashion that can border upon unseemly. In these elegant old pistols, you can conjure some unique stories. Some Union soldier like Obadiah Sutcliffe really did carry this cool Colt Navy into battle more than a century and a half ago. Relative to other collectible firearms, these vintage Civil War-era handguns are not terribly expensive. That I get to be a custodian of such a remarkable artifact, even just for a time, is a tremendous privilege.

No matter how wizened and muscular your trigger finger might be, there remains a great deal of fun to be had by building and running one of these classic old wheelguns. The financial outlay is a mere fraction required to land more modern iron. A modest investment in components will also keep you shooting long after the guy with the fast-firing AR has run dry, packed up and gone home.

Now, after four decades, it seems I have come full circle. Along the way, I found out dual wielding a brace of classic Confederate sixguns is a reliable rush no matter your age, gender, background or comportment. Building one of these historical old revolvers is also a simply wonderful way to kill a lazy afternoon.

For more info: DixieGunWorks.com, GOEXPowder.com

AMERICAN HANDGUNNER

Plus FREE Digital Download with your paid order.

Call (866) 820-4045
www.fmgpubs.com
($54.75 outside U.S.)
P.O. Box 460100, Escondido, CA 92046

ONE-YEAR PRINT SUBSCRIPTION
ONLY $19.75!

The Bird Cage in 1937, shortly after its conversion to a coffee shop. Photo: Library of Congress

Roger Smith

AN ENTERTAINMENT VENUE OF MIXED REPUTE

The Bird Cage Theatre

The news of a rich silver find in southeastern Arizona Territory in 1877 quickly attracted the usual crowd of claims filers eager to work hard and get rich quick. And the usual tent saloons and whorehouses promptly appeared as well. The providers of other needed goods and services were not far behind, all looking for the adventure and excitement of the Old West as they plied their trades and occupations. No time was wasted in plotting and platting the town of Tombstone in the nearest relatively level area, and tents soon enough gave way to buildings.

The saloon trade was consistently profitable but also very competitive, all vying for the dollars of the miners and those who provided whatever else was needed and wanted. Coaxing, willing women displaying lots of skin were the norm, and salty free lunches were common.

Individual and traveling troupes of entertainers, mainly originating in San Francisco's notorious Barbary Coast district, were always welcome in saloons throughout the Old West and especially in the mining camps and towns.

Dedicated Entertainment

In 1871 variety performers Billy and Lottie Hutchinson decided to outdo them all with a purpose-built building designed as a theatre to draw entertainment-hungry throngs to their cathouse/saloon to be efficiently relieved of their dollars and pesos. Their Christmas gift to the men of the town opened on December 26.

Deep in relation to its width, some commented on its coffin-like dimensions. Customers were asked to leave their weapons in the lobby. The main room featured an orchestra pit and a 15'x15' elevated stage, lit by gas lights to make the performers easy to see. A long bar dominated the right side and featured a large, risqué painting of "Fatima." Customers had to get past the bar and the faro and poker tables to reach the large seating area. It held rows of backless benches, which could be quickly moved aside after the performances to create a dance floor.

More Than a Show ...

Best of all were the elevated private boxes, seven on each side, which rented for $50 per night and were accessed by narrow stairs to the rear. Expensive drinks and cigars were hustled, lifted to the serving ladies by dumbwaiter to avoid spillage. The boxes were equipped with a chair, a small table, a gas lamp and a bed for conducting business. Lush red velvet curtains were drawn for experiencing the most personal services. At the rear of the main floor beneath the boxes was a curtained area for less expensive quickies.

For the Big Spenders

In the basement were dressing rooms for the performers and a few nicely appointed small private rooms for the best-looking, most expensive ladies of the night to ply their trade. A special room hosted an exclusive high-stakes poker game that ran 24/7 from 1881–1889, the house taking 10%.

"Sophisticated" Theater?

Shakespeare (1564–1616) proved long ago that "bawdy" sells. Our modern lack of understanding of the English vernacular of his day conceals the fact his works were so raunchy his plays were actually banned in London thanks to the innuendo, double-entendre and just plain filth of all sorts. Just Google "Shakespeare bawdy." The commoners loved it and willingly paid to see and hear it back then. Two hundred eighty years later, all over the Old West, Shakespearean skits and plays were still popular among those with little formal education. A hundred and fifty years ago, they still "got it" and loved it, often shouting out The Bard's lines as the actors recited them.

Fresh Variety

Variety shows of every conceivable sort and quality made the rounds of the Western saloons every couple of years — the more vulgar, the better. Sometimes they were paid by management, sometimes they passed the hat and sometimes they had to settle for throw money. The Bird Cage was considered a better paying gig, and owner Hutchison had a lineup of entertainers that constantly changed before they got "old" and bored his clientele. New acts kept the cash flowing, while a few favored acts enjoyed very long runs.

Vaudeville acts were relatively new and welcomed in the Old West. Minstrel shows and every conceivable circus sideshow made the rounds. The design of Bird Cage was well-suited to an especially popular act — the scantily clad girl on the trapeze, flying just over the heads of the lustfully cheering audience.

The Bird Cage quickly acquired the reputation as being the hottest, wickedest night spot between the Barbary Coast and the infamous Basin Street in New Orleans. It reeked of cigar smoke, booze, cheap cologne and unwashed bodies and never closed. Most evenings saw a line of men of all occupations and stations in life eager to pay their 50 cents cover charge to squeeze in and spend far too much money to enjoy the libertine licentiousness inside. Masked costume balls were held now and then to conceal the identities of those in the community who would never want it to be known they did such things.

Infrastructure Challenges

Lack of water was a problem for Tombstone from the beginning. The Sycamore Water Company and the Huachuca Water Company were both formed in 1880. They delivered water to customers, laid water mains and began placing fire hydrants at intersections. Fire companies began forming in 1880

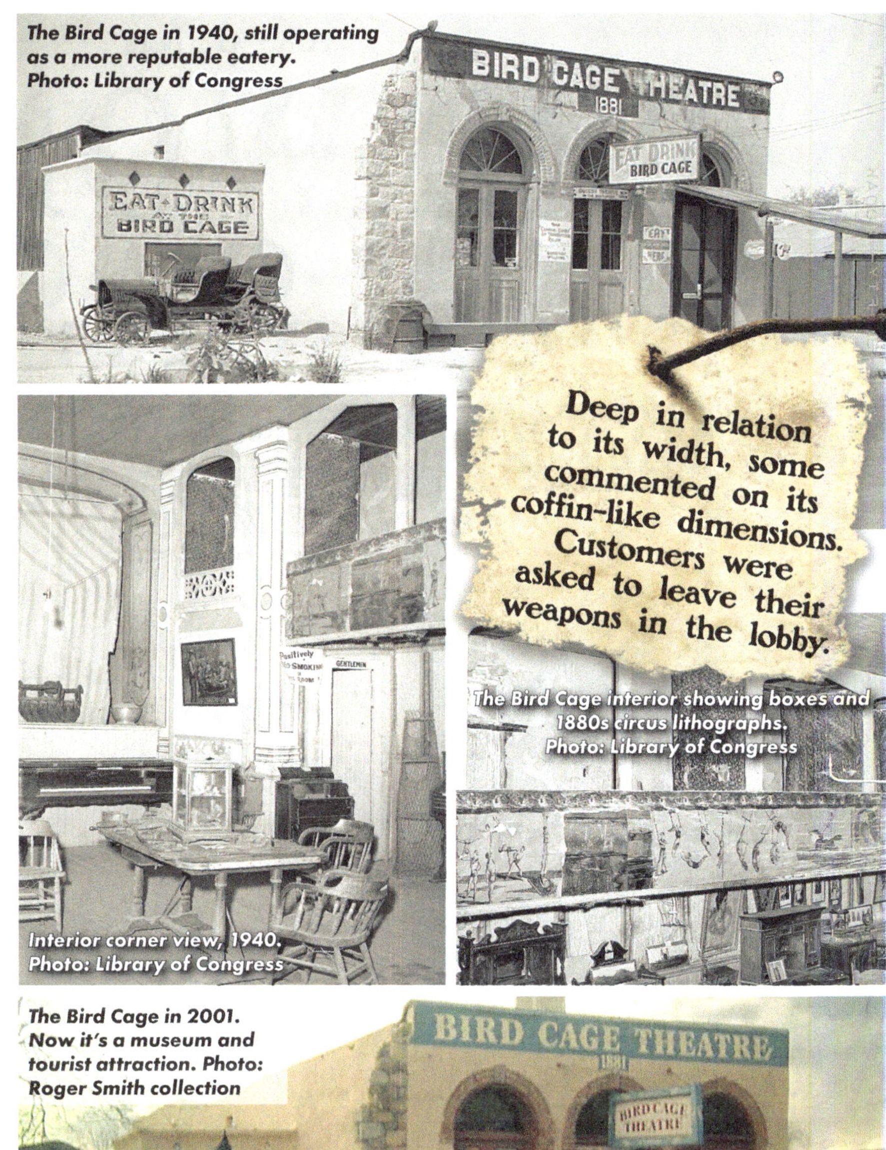

The Bird Cage in 1940, still operating as a more reputable eatery. Photo: Library of Congress

Deep in relation to its width, some commented on its coffin-like dimensions. Customers were asked to leave their weapons in the lobby.

The Bird Cage interior showing boxes and 1880s circus lithographs. Photo: Library of Congress

Interior corner view, 1940. Photo: Library of Congress

The Bird Cage in 2001. Now it's a museum and tourist attraction. Photo: Roger Smith collection

and 1881. In spite of these, a disastrous fire wiped out the wooden buildings of the business district in 1882, just before the high-pressure hydrants came on line. The adobe Bird Cage at the far end of Allen Street survived, though, and enjoyed a short monopoly while the insured haggled with the swarm of claim adjusters.

The silver mines hit water and flooded in March 1882, requiring Cornish engines, massive steam-powered pumps, to be brought in. The Grand Central Mine went out of business when its hoist and pumping plant burned in May 1886. A few months later, the money and commodities manipulators drove the price of silver down to 90 cents per ounce, the rest of the mines laid their workers off as well and the population of Tombstone quickly plummeted. The Bird Cage and the soiled doves had always depended on volume to make their businesses work. With the miners, who only averaged about $20 per week ($567 in 2022) and their dwindling support infrastructure gone, the Bird Cage changed owners a couple of times in 1885 and 1886, finally closing in 1889.

Tombstone bills itself as "the town too tough to die." As it remade itself into a tourist destination, the Bird Cage reopened briefly for Tombstone's first Helldorado Days in 1929 to celebrate the past. The sadly deteriorating building was sold again in 1934, its name briefly changing, and then operating as a coffee shop until at least 1950, before closing again. Today the Bird Cage is back open as a museum and tourist attraction.

Alan Garbers

THE WOMEN OF SASS

Making the Wild West Look Good

If you think a gun belt and holsters are naked without 5 lbs. of bling, you might be a woman of SASS.

If you get fashion tips from Dale Evans, you might be a woman of SASS.

If you struggled for three months to pick the perfect alias, you might be a woman of SASS.

If you think a matched set of Ruger Vaqueros is the perfect anniversary gift, you might be a woman of SASS.

Cowboy Action Shooting (CAS) is a sport dominated by male shooters, but female shooters make up a large portion of the winner's circle. Having shot with many female champions, I always admire the skill and dedication they possess.

While Cowboy Action Shooting is a sport played worldwide, Arizona is an epicenter. The Single Action Shooting Society (SASS) is the dominant affiliation. Matches occur every weekend around the state. Cowtown, just north of Peoria, was one of the

SASS sweethearts Cyanide Sue and Chance Derringer often dress in matching outfits.

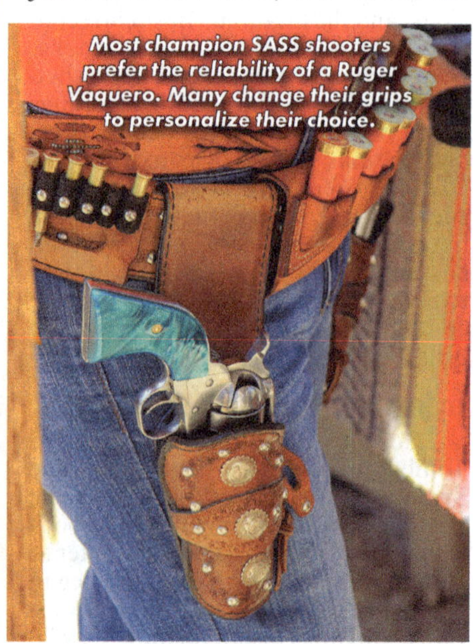

Most champion SASS shooters prefer the reliability of a Ruger Vaquero. Many change their grips to personalize their choice.

first clubs to start CAS, and it has a continuing tradition of generating champions. It is the perfect location to find the ladies of the SASS.

Women who have never participated in Cowboy Action Shooting have many questions. As a male SASS shooter, I know what advice I give, but every woman I interviewed said women should seek advice from female shooters, not men! So here goes …

Pronghorn Patty

Pronghorn Patty wasn't interested in competing when she started attending SASS matches with her husband, Tramp, but things quickly changed. She shared, "When I started seeing how many women and kids were competing and were better than the men, I thought, 'I can do this!'"

At first, Pronghorn Patty was terrified of the guns, but she swiftly overcame the apprehension with coaching and practice.

Pronghorn Patty has taken on a new challenge: stage writing. She's always thinking of how to make the stages engaging and challenging. The club often gets visitors, and Pronghorn Patty is a gracious host, answering all questions.

Her best advice is, "Find a new shooter clinic." It can be expensive to get started between buying firearms, gun leather and reloading equipment. By attending a clinic, a new shooter can try various guns and see if they enjoy competing.

Double Tap

Double Tap was the top shooter in the Ladies Senior B-Western category at the SASS End of Trail World Championships in 2022. Like most champions, she goes out of her way to help new shooters and her posse. Her

years as a USAF Colonel (retired) give her the confidence to push her limits and motivate her fellow shooters to do their best. Double Tap competes in B-Western, one of two costume categories. B-Western emulates the style of the Saturday matinee stars of the 1940s and 1950s: Big hats, embroidered smile shirts and fancy-tooled Buscadero holster rigs are standard. Bling and flash are critical fashion points. Double Tap excels at it. Double Tap is working to become the top overall female shooter. Her practice regiment involves lots of dry-fire drills.

Claudia Feather

Claudia Feather was a USPSA shooter, but gave it up to focus on CAS. In 2022, she landed in the top three in her category at End of Trail. But it wasn't always the case, and she laughed at the memories.

"In the beginning," she recalled, "more female shooters were focusing on costuming and less on speed,

joking, 'I may not have shot fast, but did I look good?'"

Claudia Feather and her husband saw a growing demand for period-style clothing and started the Wild West Mercantile in Mesa, Ariz.

Along with shooting in Cowboy events, she competes in SASS's offshoot category, Wild Bunch. Following true to the William Holden movie, Claudia shoots a Kimber 1911, a Winchester '73 lever-action rifle and a Winchester '97 shotgun.

Like many other SASS members, Claudia Feather enjoys lifelong friendships and the competition. Another aspect Claudia appreciates is the motivation to keep physically and mentally fit. Socializing, remembering the shooting sequence of a stage and planning how to shoot it keep her mind active. The physical part of moving from station to station while transitioning from gun to gun motivates her to stay fit, and her times at End of Trail show it.

Shooting in the Gunfighter category is challenging. Scarlett Darlin' works out the shooting sequence to alternate shots from her revolvers. Photo: Weinberg Studios

Ramblin' Rose and her husband love attending SASS events together.

Waiting to be called to the firing line, Miss Becky plans her strategy.

There are no cash prizes in SASS. At the End Of Trail, a cherished buckle is awarded to the winners. Double Tap wears her buckle with pride.

Cyanide Sue

Cyanide Sue is a bubbly fashion plate of the Old West. No matter what she is doing, she makes it look good. But don't let her fashion fool you. She recently decided to take on the challenge of shooting in the Frontier Cartridge Gunfighter category. The acrid sulfur from burning black powder is perfume to her. The boom of her pistols is the bass line to her theme song.

Why Cyanide Sue? "First, it sounds cool," she asserted. "Second, I love chemistry, and cyanide is the base of all poisons. Cyanide has one blue and one black element."

The color theme is common to many of her outfits. She even has a matching reticule to hold her bullets for each stage. *(I had to look it up: A reticule is a ladies' drawstring handbag.)*

If you didn't notice, Cyanide Sue is passionate about SASS. The one thing she wanted to make clear? "Just do it! Cowboy Action Shooting is so fun, and the people are so friendly, you'll get hooked," she said.

Romance? Yes, she found a sweetheart on the range, but we will save love stories for another day.

Ramblin' Rose

Ramblin' Rose was first attracted to SASS because of the Old-West fashion and social interaction. But with coaching from lady shooters, she became a serious competitor. Like many other female shooters, she chose the Ruger Vaquero, Winchester '73 and an SKB double-barrel shotgun.

Over the years, Ramblin' Rose has tried many different styles of shooting, including the Frontier Cartridge category that requires the use of black powder in all guns. Ramblin' Rose now competes in the La Patrona

Many shooters carry accessories to complement their outfits. A period-style reticule makes a great ammunition bag.

(80+) class, but since few shooters compete in her slot, she competes mentally against younger shooters and averages 30 seconds per stage. Her lifetime of experience gives her a perspective few have. Her goal is to be the oldest female shooter in SASS and still compete in her 90s!

Miss Becky

Miss Becky became a SASS shooter when ballroom dancing became more frustrating than fun. She had never fired a gun before getting into SASS. Luckily, fellow female shooter, Half-A-Hand Henri, gave Miss Becky some coaching, and her game drastically improved.

Miss Becky shoots with many championship shooters, which can be a double-edged sword. On one side, it is intimidating to compete with shooters who clear a stage in record time, yet having those same shooters provide mentoring on the physical and mental aspects of the game is priceless. Miss Becky made it into the top 10 in her category at the End of Trail 2022. Her mantra is practice, practice and the hope of breaking into the top five in 2023.

Scarlett Darlin'

If there is one shooter almost every SASS shooter knows by sight or reputation, it's Scarlett Darlin'. Along with being a well-known ambassador for the SASS, Scarlett Darlin' and her husband, Tom Eagle Talker, also offers bullets and powder through her company, Bullets By Scarlett.

Scarlett Darlin's adventure into SASS started 10 years ago when she and her husband attended a Palmetto Posse match to offer custom earplugs to shooters. The match director, alias Dun Gamblin', offered to let them shoot a stage, and the rest is history.

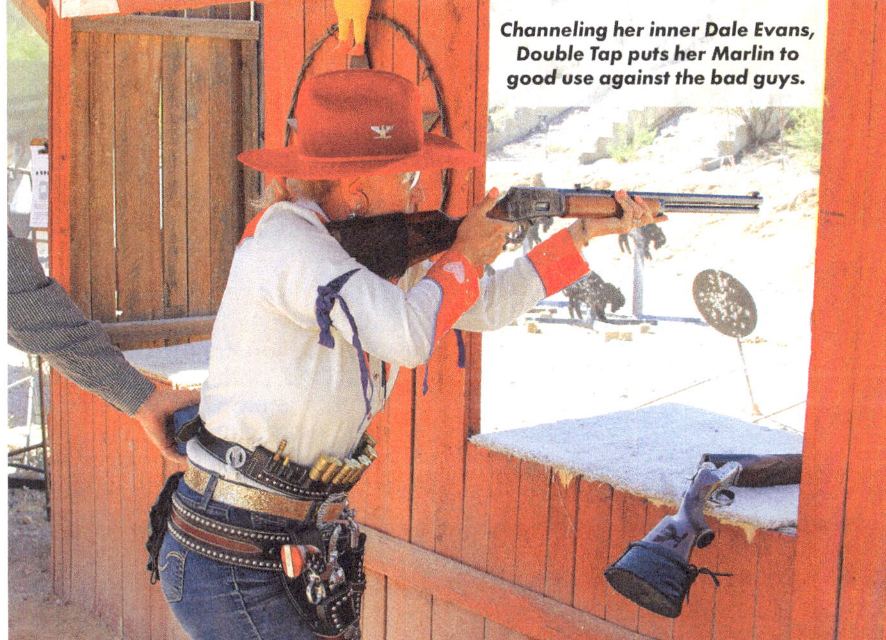

Channeling her inner Dale Evans, Double Tap puts her Marlin to good use against the bad guys.

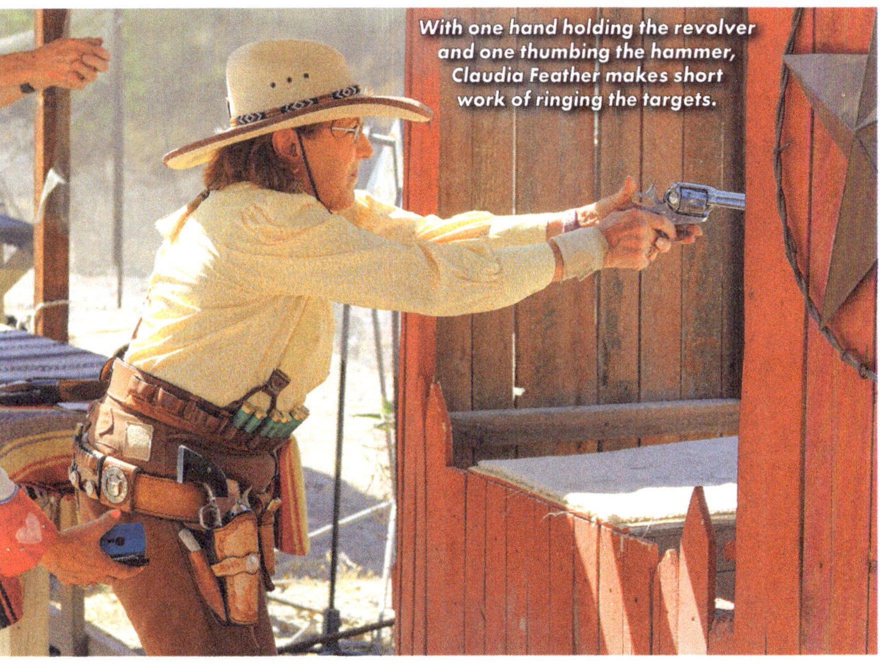

With one hand holding the revolver and one thumbing the hammer, Claudia Feather makes short work of ringing the targets.

MENTAL HEALTH: IT'S OK TO TALK ABOUT IT.

As firearms owners, we often have a tough time admitting when we need help, and that is particularly true with our psychological struggles. One great way to check in on yourself and your mental state is to take a free and anonymous screening.

Walk the Talk America is made of gun people who want to help other gun people while protecting our rights.

Take a free & anonymous screening at WTTA.org/LOVE

The rapid loading and shucking of shells from a side-by-side shotgun take practice. Scarlett Darlin' makes it look easy. Photo: Paparazzi Pahl

Waiting at the loading table, Bonnie MacFarlane and Queen of Bling focus on how they will shoot the stage.

Scarlett Darlin' was hooked on the clothing style of the B-Western category, and soon realized she could still wear the clothes and have the thrill of competing as a Lady Frontier Cartridge Gunfighter. The challenge of shooting Frontier Cartridge Gunfighter is figuring out how to shoot the targets fast, in the correct sequence, while alternating revolvers — one in each hand — and picking out the targets through the billowing clouds of gun smoke. A mental game in itself!

Scarlett also does much of her own reloading and the maintenance on her guns. She feels it helps her understand how the guns work and gets her to a place of Zen.

As a vendor, Scarlett is often dealing with new lady shooters, and her best advice is, "Call me! Do it! Find a lady shooter who will mentor you and join the fun! It is the most fun ever!"

Every woman of the SASS I interviewed agreed on those last points. Don't be intimidated. Take the first step and visit a match to see what SASS is all about. Does it look like fun? See if someone can mentor you. In many cases, club members are thrilled to help you join in the fun. Making targets ring while being dressed like Dale Evans or Sharon Stone is addicting!

Bushnell
GUNS
MAGAZINE
FREE
Digital Download with your paid order
Call (866) 820-4045
www.fmgpubs.com
($64.95 outside U.S.)
P.O. Box 460130
Escondido, CA 92046
1-YEAR PRINT
SUBSCRIPTION
ONLY $24.95!

Jeremy D. Clough

THE SHOOTER'S CASED COLT

The 2nd Generation Colt 1851 Navy

There's a fine line between resto-mod and kit car. Even if the frame and body are identical to the original, if it doesn't have a GM VIN tag, it's not quite a Corvette. In the space between these two, however, is the continuation car: bodies, chassis or even complete cars made elsewhere, but blessed by the original maker as basically restarting the interrupted manufacture of the original. And that's what the 2nd and 3rd Generation Colts are. Made from 1971 until the early 2000s, Colt reintroduced some of its most famous black-powder revolvers in three different series, giving Colt aficionados an accessible alternative to the expensive originals — one that could also be shot without worries over damage or loss of value.

Is It Real?

Candidly, there's disagreement about whether these Colts are actually, you know, Colts. It does seem clear, though, they were not made on the long-gone original tooling, but instead began with castings imported from Italy, which may have been machined, assembled and finished at Colt — or only finished there. Or only inspected. Or never saw the Colt factory at all. Mine has the lovely polish and finishing I expect from Colt, and I would love to believe it at least passed within sight of Colt's blue Onion Dome. But I strongly suspect Mike Venturino, who has forgotten more than I'll ever know, is correct, and only the specs and name were from Colt. Nonetheless, it has the name, which means Colt has decided it's a Colt.

One Strikeout, One Hit

For those with only a passing familiarity with Colt history, Samuel Colt, having conceived the idea of a handgun with revolving chambers while watching the capstan on board a ship, introduced his single-action Paterson model (named for the New Jersey town where it was made) in 1836. In all fairness, it wasn't the first revolver, and it turns out it also wasn't the first successful one. It didn't catch on and Colt went bankrupt in fairly short order.

As the story goes, the Texas Rangers, having used those early guns successfully in battle, were gearing up for an expected war with Mexico when former Ranger Samuel Walker traveled north and met with Sam Colt and spurred him on to reenter the revolver business, this time with a heavier caliber version incorporating Walker's suggested improvements. The resultant .44-caliber Walker Colt weighed some 4.5 lbs., took a charge of black powder comparable to military muskets of the day and remained the world's most powerful handgun until the advent of the .357 Magnum.

Birth of the 1851

Arriving four years later, the .36-caliber 1851 was everything the Walker was not: Long, sleek, less powerful and light enough to carry easily. Weighing nearly 2 lbs. less than the Walker, it was a far cry

Hampel's Woodland Products made an English-fitted walnut case for Jeremy's '51, complete with custom compartments for a conversion cylinder, oil bottle and nipple wrench.

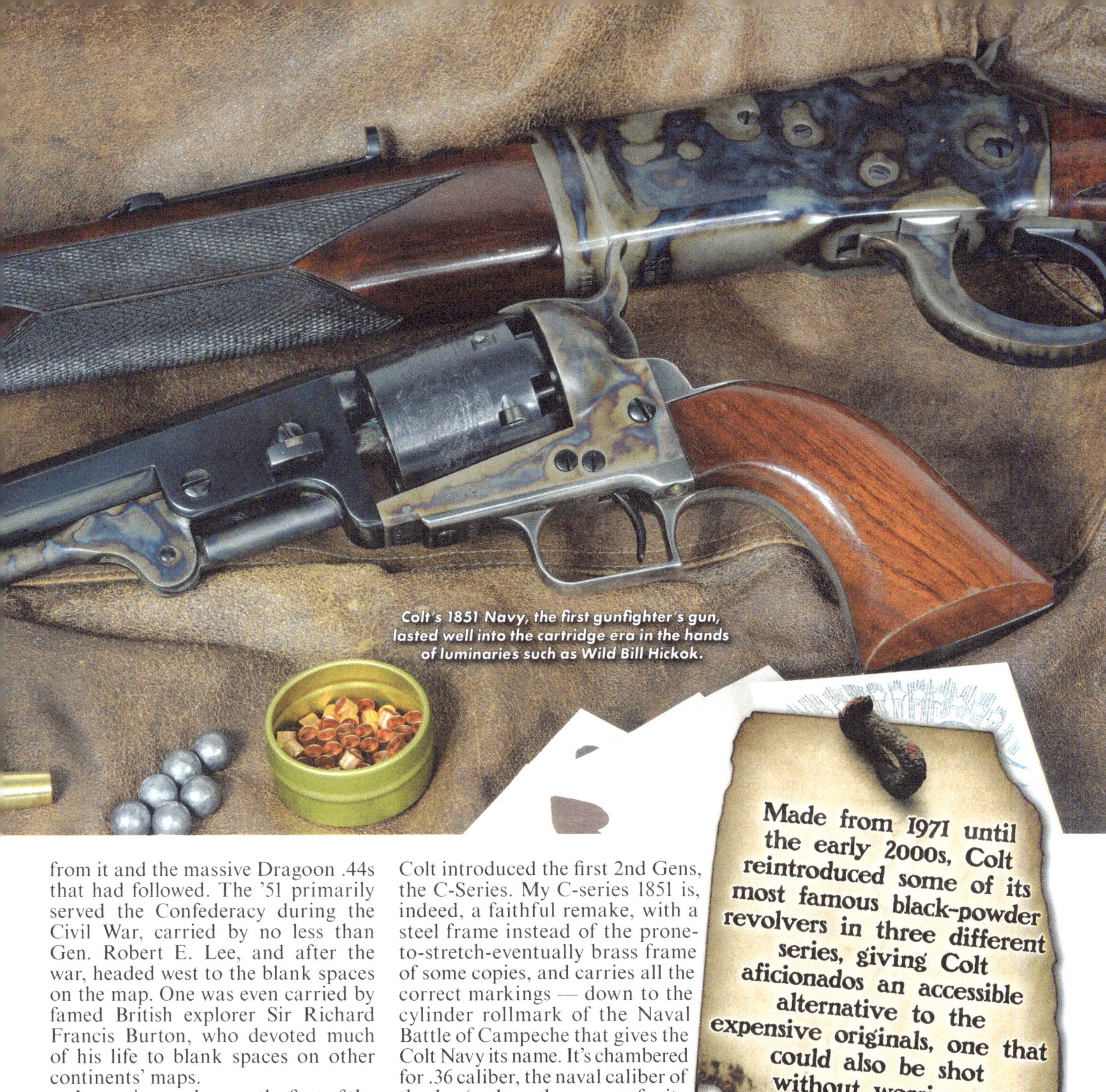

Colt's 1851 Navy, the first gunfighter's gun, lasted well into the cartridge era in the hands of luminaries such as Wild Bill Hickok.

Made from 1971 until the early 2000s, Colt reintroduced some of its most famous black-powder revolvers in three different series, giving Colt aficionados an accessible alternative to the expensive originals, one that could also be shot without worries over damage or loss of value.

from it and the massive Dragoon .44s that had followed. The '51 primarily served the Confederacy during the Civil War, carried by no less than Gen. Robert E. Lee, and after the war, headed west to the blank spaces on the map. One was even carried by famed British explorer Sir Richard Francis Burton, who devoted much of his life to blank spaces on other continents' maps.

It was, in a real sense, the first of the gunfighter's guns and was the choice of Wild Bill Hickok, who carried an ivory-handled pair of them well into the cartridge era, reputedly using one to drop an opponent at 75 yards with one shot. Production of the original guns stopped when the Single Action Army, the "Peacemaker" .45, was introduced in 1873.

Prices are what you would expect for a legendary pistol a century and a half old: They tend to start around $2,000 and move quickly into five digits for guns cased with all the required accoutrements. One of Hickok's pair recently sold at auction for a click or two over a half-million dollars.

2nd Gen C-Series

Replicas started being produced in Italy as early as the 1950s, and in 1971 Colt introduced the first 2nd Gens, the C-Series. My C-series 1851 is, indeed, a faithful remake, with a steel frame instead of the prone-to-stretch-eventually brass frame of some copies, and carries all the correct markings — down to the cylinder rollmark of the Naval Battle of Campeche that gives the Colt Navy its name. It's chambered for .36 caliber, the naval caliber of the day (and another reason for its nickname), and the long flats of its

Barrel wedges, such as on this reproduction flintlock dueling pistol, are a near-ancient way to hold a black-powder gun together. The '51 Colt used the same thing to keep the barrel and ram assembly mounted on the cylinder arbor.

Wherever they were made, the 2nd Gen Colts were color case-hardened using the traditional Colt formula, which is gorgeous and easy to distinguish from chemically colored guns.

Not only is the rear sight just a groove — fine for those of us who like fixed sight revolvers — it's a groove in the back of a moving part. Nonetheless, if you pay attention, it works.

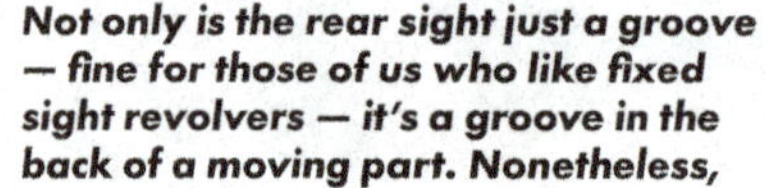

The cylinder, frame, barrel and trigger guard are all serial numbered, and three of those parts have faithful Colt markings as well, such as the "Colt's Patent" on the frame.

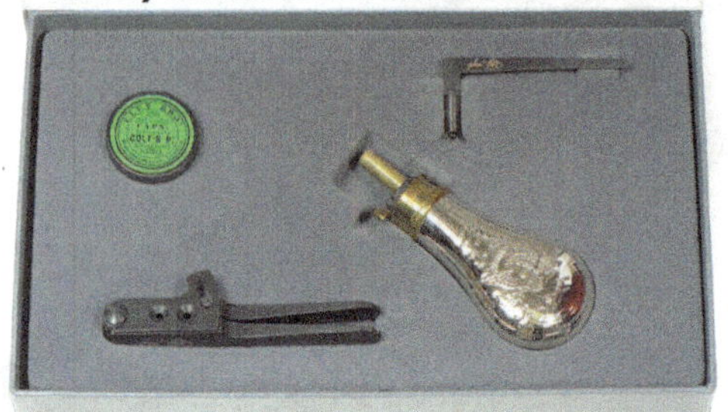

During production of Colt's resurrected black-powder line, they offered accessories kits containing a cap box, nipple wrench, appropriate powder flask and bullet mold. As the Colt kits are now quite dear to purchase, Jeremy assembled his own accoutrements.

Colt Navy sights are rudimentary at best and include this brass cone as a front sight. It's possible to do good work with it, but it ain't easy.

7 ½" octagonal barrel are beautifully polished with nary a ripple to be seen. The receiver, hammer and loading lever assembly, unlike many other replicas, are color case-hardened.

Case-hardening is a form of surface hardening that was used on earlier, softer steels that often resulted in a beautiful mix of colors ranging from straw to deep blue. While modern metallurgy has largely taken us beyond the need for the process — and modern steels are often rendered unsafely brittle from it — it's still pretty. Chemical processes can produce a similarly attractive look. Still, the Colts follow the traditional, time-consuming process of being packed with wood and bone charcoal, heated and then quenched to create the colors. Having tried my hand at it, it's quite an experience to farmer-walk a 1,000-degree steel crucible across a room to dunk its contents in cold water, but that's how it's done.

The left side of the receiver bears the "Colt's Patent" marking, as does the cylinder, and the top of the barrel is marked "Address Saml Colt New-York City." All three of those components and the silver-plated trigger guard wear the serial number. The gun is smaller than you think, with a small grip and a slenderness that makes it lively in the hand, and the hammer rolls back smoothly and assertively, with three clicks announcing the act.

Must-Have Accessories

But the gun is not enough. To shoot black powder, you need more stuff. Colt offered a finely turned out set of accoutrements to go with the 2nd Gen guns, but they're almost as expensive as the pistols, so to the Italians, long the leaders in such things, we go. While many of the accessories are a bit hard to find, they're out there if you look, and I was able to scare up a brass bullet mold and powder measure, both made by Pedersoli. I don't know that I'll be casting many balls for the '51: All my casting has been with harder lead alloys, and the brass molds are said to produce slightly undersized bullets, but the mold will look good in the case.

Hampel's Woodland Products offers black walnut cases for percussion pistols such as the '51, Remington '58 and others. Made on the English pattern, which has separated compartments instead of the tighter French fit, they closely follow the design of the original Colt cases and are shockingly affordable. Even requesting custom changes, such as compartments for another cylinder and oil bottle, the case cost about $72 shipped — about a third the price for Colt's black-powder cases in the late '90s — and arrived within the advertised 2–3-week time period. It has compartments for the pistol, mold, cap box and powder flask, perhaps the most necessary of the accoutrements.

Powder Recipes

The correct Navy-style flask has a screw-in spout marked with the number of grains of black powder it's supposed to dispense. Out of stock everywhere I looked but Cabela's, they offered a .36-caliber version with a 15-grain spout or .44 version at 24 grains. Unscrew the spout to fill the flask carefully with either FFF black powder or Pyrodex P, *using something that will not create static electricity.* Once full and with the spout reinstalled, put your finger over the spout, turn the flask upside down and depress the lever, so powder flows into the spout. Release the lever and turn the flask right side up. The spout should be full.

This measures powder by volume, not weight: My RCBS scale says the 15-grain spout dispenses about 12.5 grains of GOEX FFF. Similarly, a 20-grain spout dispensed just under 20, while a 25 threw just over 20 grains. If I find a charge weight the gun likes better than what the spout throws now, I'll shorten a longer spout until it dispenses that amount.

Load and Shoot

The loading process starts with the hammer at half cock so the cylinder can rotate. Carefully pour in a spoutfull of powder, add a ball and ram it into place, loading one charge hole at a time to avoid an accidental double charge. The charge hole also needs to be sealed for lubrication purposes and to reduce the risks of a dangerous chain fire, where sparks cause all the charges to go off at once. You can do

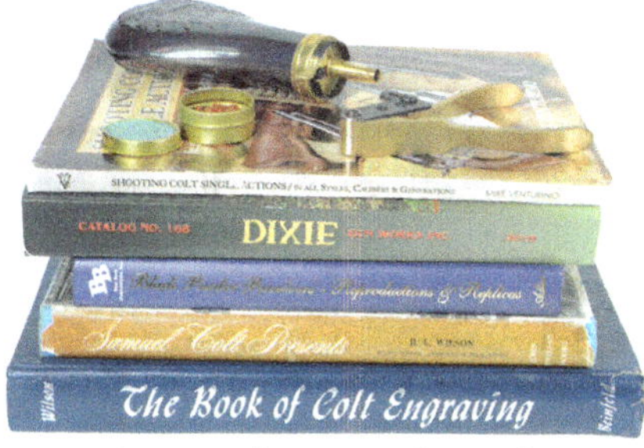

No less than Sir Richard Francis Burton, the greatest traveler of all time, carried a Colt 1851 Navy. Burton spoke dozens of languages, sought the source of the Nile and made the pilgrimage to Mecca at a time when discovery would have meant certain death. And survived being speared through the face while in Africa.

Putting together a cased set takes a bit of homework: The two bottom Colt books show what one should look like, the Adler and Venturino books tell you what to do with the gun and Dixie Gun Works, along with Track of the Wolf, is one of the primary sources for black powder supplies of all kinds.

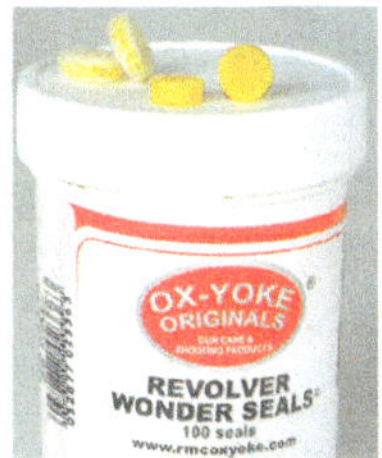

Black-powder revolvers require the end of the cylinder to be sealed to avoid chain firing. You can do this with Crisco, but the easier way is using either an over-powder wad from Ox-Yoke or one of their seals placed over the ball and spread by the ram.

CCI caps come in a neat little tin, but don't look right in a fitted case. Track of the Wolf, Dixie Gun Works and others offer reproductions of the Eley Colt cap tin or similar silver-plated tins that look even classier and work for seals or spare nipples.

Cased sets typically contain a bullet mold, with the classic one being all brass and casting both a round ball and a conical one. While functional, the brass handles will get very hot and reportedly produce slightly undersized projectiles that suffer from suboptimal accuracy.

The powder flask is a critical accessory, as it measures the correct amount of powder for each shot. Different spouts are available and are marked for the amount of powder they're intended to dispense. Jeremy found the accuracy varied.

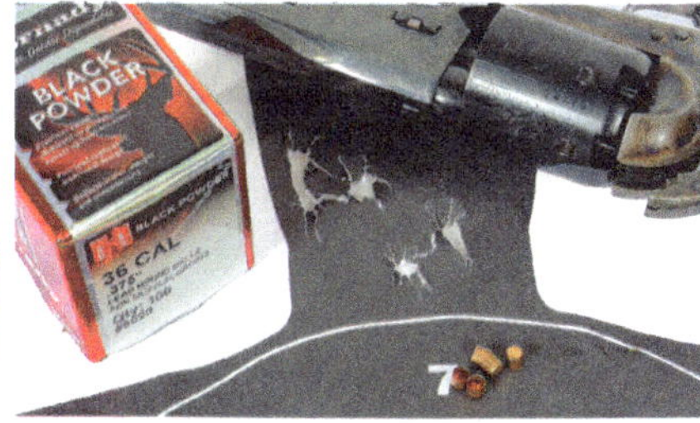

The sights are difficult but not impossible: Jeremy put five of his six rounds into less than 2" at 25 yards shooting with his hands rested.

this with a wad rammed into place between the powder and ball, such as Ox-Yoke's Wonder Wad or the Wonder Seal by the same company, that goes over the ball and is spread out by the ram until it oozes from the front of the cylinder. Or smear the front of the charge hole with Crisco or Vaseline. It all works and also reduces leading and keeps powder fouling soft and easier to clean. And clean you will, since it's all terribly messy and letting it sit dirty is inviting disaster.

Once charged, cap each nipple, which I did with CCI #11 caps. It should go without saying, but if the gun is going to be carried around, only

five should be loaded, so the hammer stays down on an empty chamber. Roll the hammer back, so the notch in the top presents itself as your rear sight, and do your best to line it up with the conical brass front. With such a light charge, there's a puff of white and a low boom, minimal recoil and the ball rips a ragged hole, 6" or more high at 25 yards. High, but tight: I put five of six balls into only 2", resting my hands.

I bet Hickok did hit that guy at 75.

For more info: DixieGunWorks.com, HampelsWoodlandProducts.com, TrackOfTheWolf.com

ENTER TO WIN!

RANGER II MINI REVOLVER PACKAGE

RANGER II (NAA-22MC-R)

Manufacturer: North American Arms
(801) 374-9990
NorthAmericanArms.com

Caliber: .22 Magnum/.22 LR **Capacity:** 5
Barrel Length: 1.6" **OAL:** 5.16" **Weight:** 7.4 oz.

Value: $600

Total Value: $804.99

ENTER ONLINE:
GUNSMagazine.com/giveaways

ENTRY DEADLINE: December 31, 2022

ROADRUNNER

Manufacturer:
Finch Knife Co.
FinchKnifeCo.com

Value: $145

FEDERAL AMMUNITION: THE FIRST HUNDRED YEARS

Manufacturer: Federal Premium
FederalPremium.com
(800) 379-1732

Value: $59.99

Our premier prize for this *Old West Special Edition* is North American Arms' *Ranger II* (NAA-22MC-R). This mini revolver is like a two-in-one gun. It includes two cylinders, one in .22 Magnum and another in .22 LR. It has a 5-shot capacity, break-open cylinder, star extractor, a 1.6", full-ribbed barrel, bead sight and rosewood bird's head grip.

The roadrunner is a fast-running bird with long legs popularized in cartoons being chased by a coyote. The *Roadrunner* from Finch Knife Co. is also fast! To deploy, that is. Its 3.4" lean stiletto blade is made of 154CM steel with a satin finish. OAL is 7.75"; weight is 4.5 oz.

Federal Ammunition: The First Hundred Years highlights Federal's vast history of cartridge production and innovation over the past century. Broken down by decade, each section of the book covers the historical achievements by Federal through rich historical photos, vintage packaging, marketing materials and unique company images.

A mini revolver that reminds us of the Old West, a coffee table book highlighting the achievements of an ammunition company and a fast-to-deploy knife are all prizes you're sure to cherish. Join the giveaway for a chance to win! Go to GUNSMagazine.com/giveaways or mail a postcard!
— *Jazz Jimenez*

WINNERS CHOSEN BY RANDOM DRAWING. To protect the privacy and security of winners, their names will NOT be made public. Contest void where prohibited by law. Winners may undergo a background check and comply with all other federal, state and local laws. Taxes and fees will be the responsibility of the winner. Contest open to U.S. residents only. Employees and agents of Publishers' Development Corp. are not eligible. No purchase necessary. Winners will be notified by certified mail on official letterhead. Attention deployed military: Use stateside address! Giveaway guns and accessories may have evidence of being test fired or exhibit minor handling marks. Factory warranties may apply in some cases. Winner must undergo a background check (if needed) and comply with all other federal, state and local laws. Prizes will not be awarded if the firearm presented is illegal in the jurisdiction of the winner. An alternate, authorized winner will be selected. No substitutions or transfers to a third party are allowed.

If you are unable to enter online, mail a postcard with your name and address (no envelopes, please) to GUNS Magazine, Old West Vol. 90, P.O. Box 488, Escondido, CA 92033. Entries must be received by December 31, 2022. Limit one entry per household.

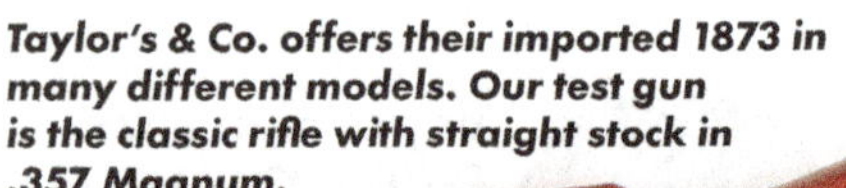

Taylor's & Co. offers their imported 1873 in many different models. Our test gun is the classic rifle with straight stock in .357 Magnum.

TAYLOR'S & CO.

A Modern .357 Take On Old West Style

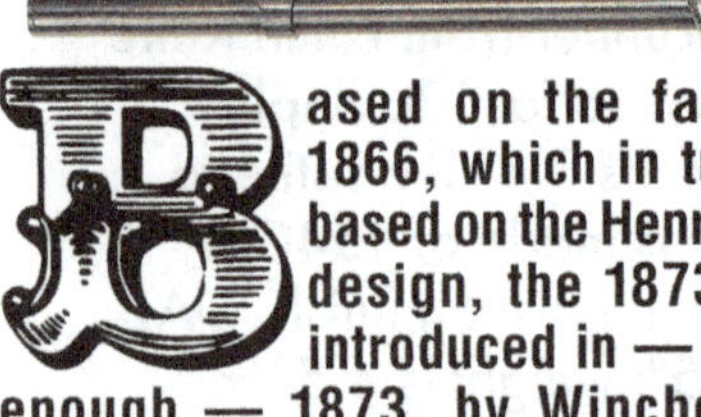

Based on the famous 1866, which in turn is based on the Henry rifle design, the 1873 was introduced in — oddly enough — 1873, by Winchester. Oliver Winchester had bought out the insolvent Volcanic Repeating Arms Company, reorganized things and then renamed the new company the New Haven Arms Company in 1857. After the Civil War, Oliver retitled the company Winchester, and introduced the Model 1866, which used the same .44 Rimfire round as the old Henry. The '66 added a wooden forearm and the same bronze-alloy frame as the Henry, but added an improved magazine system. I'd call it the first "modern" lever action and the beginning of an iconic style. A favorite name for it is "Yellowboy," due to the color of the receiver.

A profile anyone in the Old West would instantly recognize.

To keep up with demand for a more powerful cartridge, when Winchester introduced the iron-framed 1873, the default cartridge was the .44-40 — a centerfire round. The .44 Rimfire tossed a 200-grain bullet at about 1,100 fps, while the new cartridge managed 1,300 fps with a similar RNFP bullet, upping the ante a good deal. It was an instant hit and Winchester later billed it as "The Rifle That Won the West." Some might say big-bore "Buffalo Rifles" won the West, but that's a discussion for another time.

The "One of One Thousand" series of hand-selected "extra-accurate" rifles of the time have become the stuff of legend too, only adding to the mystique of the 1873. Jimmy Stewart's *Winchester '73* movie centered around adventures with his own "One Of One Thousand" certainly helped things along in more modern times.

Built from 1873 to 1923, the '73 was chambered in .38-40, .32-20 and even .22 LR — but never in .45 Colt. Surprised? The rim of the .45 Colt rounds produced then didn't have enough "meat" to allow reliable extraction. A Colt single-action revolver knocked empties out with the ejector rod, not relying on a fragile extractor. Today's ammo with wider rims, however, allows the .45 Colt chambering.

Originally, you could get a 20" carbine, a 24" "rifle" and a "musket" (full-stock) geared toward military sales. In total, some 720,000 Model 1873s were crafted before production stopped, making them still very common on the used/collectible gun market from "affordable" — for a beater — to tens of thousands for a minty one.

A Modern Take

With the explosion of interest in Cowboy shooting, Uberti of Italy jumped on the bandwagon decades ago, and today, thanks to companies like Taylor's & Company, shooters

The ".357 Magnum" barrel marking sets this Smoke Wagon apart from its big-bore brethren. Roy found it easy and fun to shoot and as accurate as they come.

Pairing a revolver with a lever action in the same caliber made perfect sense in the field. The 1873 at top and 1873 SAA below, both in .357 Magnum, would have caused any cowboy to grin.

can relive the Old West with modern, well-made guns. The Taylor's & Co. guns have always caught my eye at the annual SHOT Show I attend, and for good reasons. It seems they always have interesting, innovative designs based on the classics. Some are essentially mirror images of the originals, while others, based on, say, an 1873 revolver, offer new barrel lengths, grip styles and other features never available on the originals. Taylor's also works closely with the Italian maker to constantly improve and hone the designs and manufacturing of the models imported.

Founded in 1988 by Sue Hawkins McFarland and her daughter, Taylor's & Company's intent was — and still is — to deliver the best quality firearms possible, while maintaining classic Old West flavor and history. More than three decades later, they're still at it and their products continue to grow in every category.

I've handled many guns from them over the years and each has been historically accurate while showing an attention to fit and detail often missing on many of the imported Italian "Cowboy" guns. I think the family's personal commitment to quality control — and endorsing modern manufacturing methods with old-time designs — helps to make Taylor's & Co. guns standouts.

Smoke Wagon

The single action here is Taylor's "Smoke Wagon" model in a non-traditional .357 Magnum chambering, with their "Taylor Tuned" custom touches to the action. Gunsmiths at Taylor's use custom spring sets and careful hand polishing to smooth a gun's action, tuning any gun in the lineup to meet a customer's needs. Think of it as a custom action job, but offered by Taylor's in-house staff.

Here, the lifter/ejector has placed a .357 round in place and when the lever is run forward, the bolt will push the cartridge into the chamber while the lifter drops down, out of the way.

Branded "The Smoke Wagon," Taylor's 5.5" SAA is classic Old West but in .357 Magnum persuasion. The "Navy" grips were a nice touch as well as being more slender than standard SAA grips.

All is tidy here. The lifter is dropped and the bolt is home against the base of the cartridge in the chamber. The next sound will be that round going off!

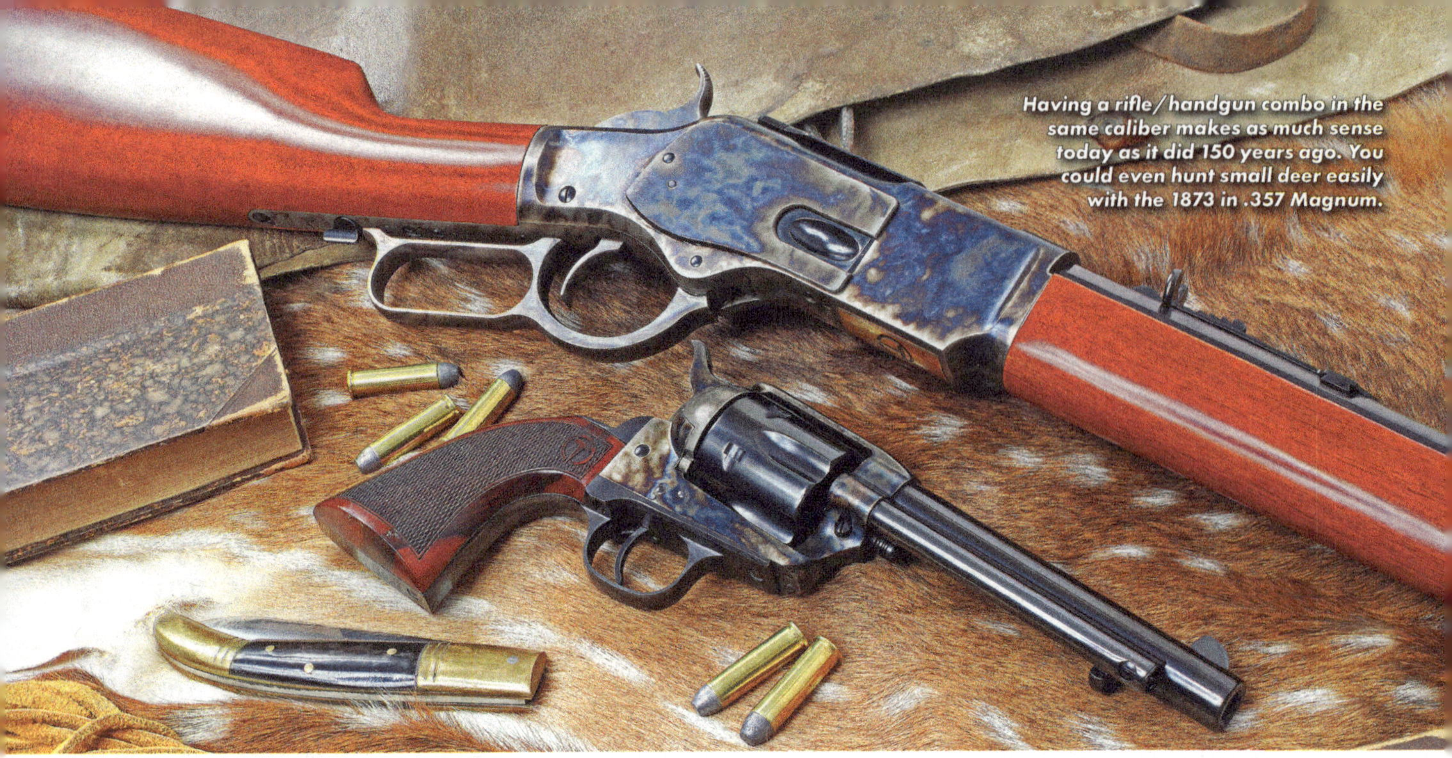

Having a rifle/handgun combo in the same caliber makes as much sense today as it did 150 years ago. You could even hunt small deer easily with the 1873 in .357 Magnum.

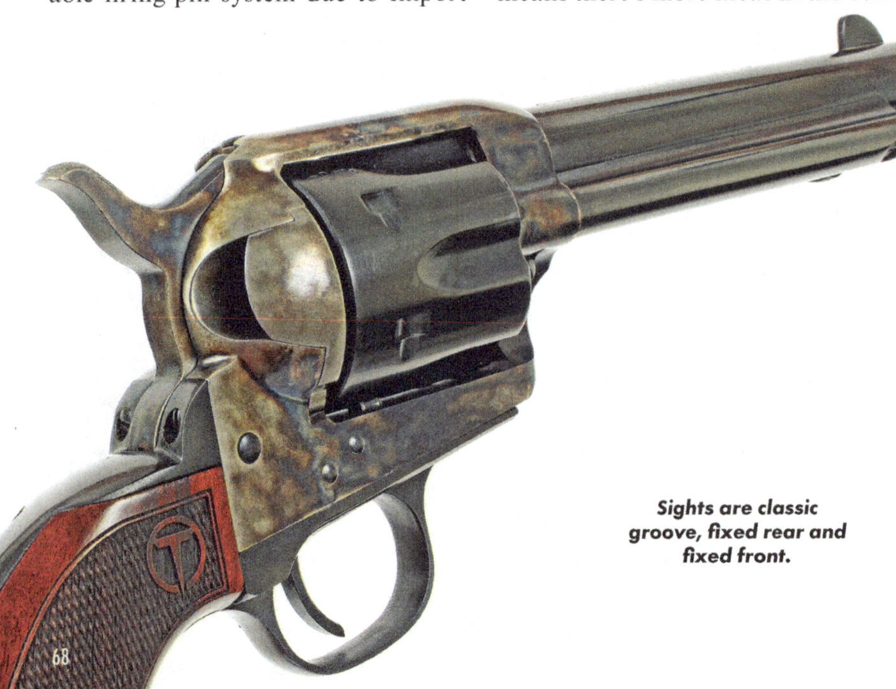

The Smoke Wagon model I shot has a 5.5" barrel, which I think is the perfect size for an SAA. The barrel is long enough to stabilize things when shooting, providing a slightly longer sight picture too, but is also short enough to holster easily and carry comfortably. The gun is essentially a classic "Colt" single action, and has Taylor's "Short Stroke" action, with a slightly abbreviated hammer throw for faster, more comfortable shooting.

The Navy-sized grip frame gives you a bit more purchase, while the slim grips really feel good in your hand. I have small- to medium-sized hands and even classic Colt-style SAA grips can feel a bit large. No issues with the Smoke Wagon though, and I found it hard to put down.

Some newer models have a retractable firing-pin system due to import regulations, but Taylor's sells parts to convert the gun "back" to four-click operation, rather than the three-click safety system. But the safety system doesn't interfere with operation and frankly, there's no real reason to change things other than if you're picky for originality.

Our test gun has a forged, color case-hardened steel frame, blued steel parts, checkered Navy-sized grips (with that thinner profile) and with the Taylor Tuned action is smooth and reliable. The loading gate opens easily, which is nice as some imports are "crunchy" when you open the gate, cock them and run the ejector rod.

The only odd thing I experienced is the fact the gun handles slightly differently than one chambered in .45 Colt or .44-40. The .357 chambering means there's more meat in the barrel and cylinder, adding some ounces to the weight. I'm not sure quite how much as I didn't have a matching 5.5" barreled gun in .45 Colt to weigh. But it's enough to subtly influence the "feel" as you manipulate, holster, unholster and shoot it. After a while, you get used to it and it doesn't really affect anything. But when you transition back to a bigger-bore model, it does feel "lighter" and sort of "faster" for a while. It's a bit like wearing ankle weights; when you take them off, you feel lighter and faster until you get used to it again.

The MSRP on my test gun is $804.18, about middle of the road for a modern import.

The 1873

"Back in the day," the 1873 was really the first lever action you could order with different options. With a Henry or 1866, you got what the factory sent out. Taylor's continues in that spirit, offering a pretty broad range of 1873 models. You can get a straight stock, pistol grip, checkered straight stock and a half-round barrel. There are also lots of finishing options, including "in the white" and antiqued.

They also offer two custom-action options on all 1873 models. The "Comanchero" work includes a custom short-stroke action, lightened hammer and trigger pull, butt cover, a lever wrap and gold bead front sight. The Taylor Tuned option delivers a custom action — with hand polishing, custom hammer and lever springs, custom magazine tube spring — and an overall lightened action.

My test gun, also in .357 Magnum in the spirit of "one cartridge for both guns," is a straight-stocked,

Sights are classic groove, fixed rear and fixed front.

At full open in the cycle, the dust cover has been pushed back by the action and the brass lifter is doing its job having just ejected a spent case.

The "innards" of the Taylor's & Co. 1873 mirror the original, but use modern steels and manufacturing techniques.

The ".357 Mag." label looks right at home on the Taylor's & Co. 1873. Note the classic Buckhorn rear sight.

Classic SAA design is in evidence on the Smoke Wagon, including the loading gate, full-length ejector rod and color case-hardening.

non-checkered model and has the Taylor Tuned feature. I have to admit; it is one of the slickest running lever actions I've ever handled. I've worked on the actions of dozens of Model '92s, a few '73s and lots of '94s over the years — stoning, changing springs, polishing and such — and truly, the work Taylor's has done would be very hard to improve upon. It's stunning and worth the extra money for the option. I'd opt for it for sure.

If you're not familiar with the 1873, it uses a toggle-action system feeling much different from an 1886, '92 or '94. On a smooth rifle, you can almost "flick" the lever to operate it on a '73, while the others require a more methodical movement. The downside is the '73 design is less robust than the others as it was made for the early pistol-caliber cartridges, and you should never "load

My test gun, also in .357 Magnum in the spirit of "one cartridge for both guns," is a straight-stocked, non-checkered model, has the Taylor Tuned feature and I have to admit, is one of the slickest running lever actions I've ever handled.

up." Staying at standard-velocity loads is critical. Having said this, the modern '73 can safely handle factory .357 loads, but if it was my gun, I wouldn't push things.

The test rifle has a 24.25" octagonal barrel and classically curved buttplate. It also has the small rotating lever at the rear of the action lever. Rotated toward the lip on the lever disengages the trigger and locks the lever down. This prevents the hammer from being cocked or the gun from firing. At the time, I'm betting it made perfect sense in a rifle carried in a saddle scabbard or across a pommel. But later designs by Browning (the '86, '92, etc.) did away with it due to action changes. I think it's more of a tribute to the original design than anything actually needed today.

I found the '73 to handle like any classic lever action, and the unique feel of the lever and "clacky-clack" of the action is distinctive to the model.

A .357 COWBOY GUN?

I've been surprised by some push back when I mention enjoying lever actions and single actions in .357 Magnum. The purists cry foul, while the shooters simply smile and go shooting. While the .357 may not have existed in the Old West, Colt certainly chambered the Peacemaker in .357 in the last century, and thousands of Model '92 Winchesters were converted to .357 by gunsmiths in the 1940s through the 1960s. So, the idea is both sound and not new at all.

For the purists, I say we let them grumble and point their fingers. But if you like to shoot, a lever-action or single-action revolver in .357 opens some interesting doors. From mild target wadcutters (in revolvers) to 180-grain fire-breathing .357 loads, versatility is the name of the game when it comes to the .357 Magnum in these classic guns. Do you like to load the .38 Special? Have at it and enjoy single-action or lever-action shooting at a bargain price.

If you're a Cowboy Action shooter, the .357 offers low recoil (.38 Specials or down-loaded .357 loads), accuracy, reliability and is soft-shooting for new shooters, old-timers and kids. Plus, any of the guns can perform reliable double-duty as home protection guns, trail guns, plinkers, casual target guns or just looking good hung on the wall in the home office.

I'm betting had the .357 been around in 1873, guess which guns would have been chambered in it — *and* been hugely popular?

You're looking at them.

The flash of brass as the cartridge carrier does its job and that slender bolt running home puts you back on the wide-open range fending off attackers or hunting for the camp pot. Sometimes just the feel of it all is worth the price of admission. MSRP is $1,314 and seems fair for this exceptionally nice rifle.

Shooting

This was my first experience with a '73 in .357 Magnum, but I've been around single actions in .357 before. I found the '73 to load, feed and eject just fine and the smaller cartridges changed the lever feel, making it very easy to manipulate. The "ka-chunk" of a .45 Colt or .44-40 as they transition from the mag tube feels different, and I really enjoyed just how easy the .357 rounds fed and ejected. The sliding dust cover is also fun to use and to watch move neatly out of the way when the action is cycled.

Interestingly, it also handled .38 Specials well, much to my delight. However, you do need to keep the overall length at about that of a .357 load or you might get some feeding issues as rounds transition from the mag tube into the carrier. Roundnose flat-point (RNFP) bullets work great, but a jacketed hollowpoint (JHP) can also work fine, too. Semi-wadcutters might hang up due to their sharp shoulder angles.

As expected, velocities were higher in the rifle than the revolver. Some examples were: 1,731 fps with Federal Premium .357 with the 140-grain Barnes Expander bullet (1,307 fps in the revolver); an old box of PMC cowboy .357 delivered 1,043 fps with a 158 RNFP and did 803 fps in the revolver. Black Hills 125-grain JHP .38 Specials clocked 1,151 fps (977 in the revolver) and just for fun, their 148-grain full

Everything fed and ran just fine in the 1873. Modern steels means .357 Magnum loads are safe in the '73 action.

The all-steel Smoke Wagon SAA (5.5" barrel) handled any .357 load Roy tried. It proved accurate and reliable. Velocity suffered from the shorter barrel, but 1,200 fps was reached by some loads.

wadcutter (single-loaded) delivered a blazing 715 fps in the rifle — or 747 fps in the revolver. I've found this before with wadcutters. They seem to reach terminal velocities in pistol-length barrels and often "slow down" in rifle barrels due to friction.

I shot a few more loads, but this gives an idea of rough velocities. With a hot 125-grain .357 you can chase 2,000 fps if you really need to. As far as accuracy goes, that Federal .357 load hovered in 2" or a tad more at 50 yards, which surprised me. I suspect with better sights it would shoot even better. I have a torso gong set up here at 80 yards and it was very easy to keep centered chest hits with the rifle off-hand with that load. With upward of 12 or 13 rounds in the magazine, it'd be pretty easy to keep the scoundrels off your trail if needed. The '73 was also fast to shoot at a bank of falling plates, and the light recoil of the .357 in this 8-lbs.-plus rifle made it easy and fun to shoot, even for novices.

The single-action Smoke Wagon proved reliable and great fun to shoot.

The Black Hills target wadcutter load cut ragged one-hole groups at 15 yards (a bit low on the target) and at 25, using my "good glasses," I could chase 2.5" or so. That's plenty of accuracy for Cowboy shooting, plinking, a trail gun or even defensive use if things were pressing. Once I got the sight hold correct, I was able to clang that 80-yard gong with .357 loads as well as .38s. As a sheer fun gun, the Smoke Wagon works just fine.

A Pair To Draw To

Both guns, I might add, showed outstanding fit and finish and would become immediate family heirlooms in any household. If you're a Cowboy shooter looking to lighten your load from a .45 Colt or .44-40, this is a natural step for you. All the mechanics are the same, just less recoil, muzzleblast and loading costs. If you just like Old West guns because of what they are and what they represent, Taylor's & Co. can deliver the goods.

For more info: TaylorsFirearms.com

Frank Jardim

EMF/PIETTA .50 SMITH CARBINE REPLICA

Unique in its Time and Fun Today

Contemporary engraving of the pandemonium that erupted in the streets around the Northfield Bank on September 7, 1876. The artist may have intended the shooter in the window on the left to be Henry Wheeler, but the arrangement of the buildings isn't quite accurate.

A view of the town from the bridge showing the Dampier Hotel on the left and the bank on the right.

The Dampier Hotel occupied the upper two stories of this building. Wheeler fired from a top-floor window.

In this contemporary photo, the relationship of the Dampier Hotel to the bank can be seen.

On September 7, 1876, the James-Younger Gang rode into Northfield, Minn., intent on robbing the First National Bank of Northfield. They never expected the town's citizens to challenge their plans. The Northfield Bank Robbery went down in history as an extraordinary example of spontaneous, massive and successful civilian resistance to the forces of lawlessness and chaos that plagued the small, civilized communities that were sprouting up across the American West.

Shots Fired

Edward Dampier owned the Dampier Hotel in Northfield. In the Civil War, he served in Hatch's Independent Battalion, Company F of Minnesota's volunteer cavalry, where he was issued

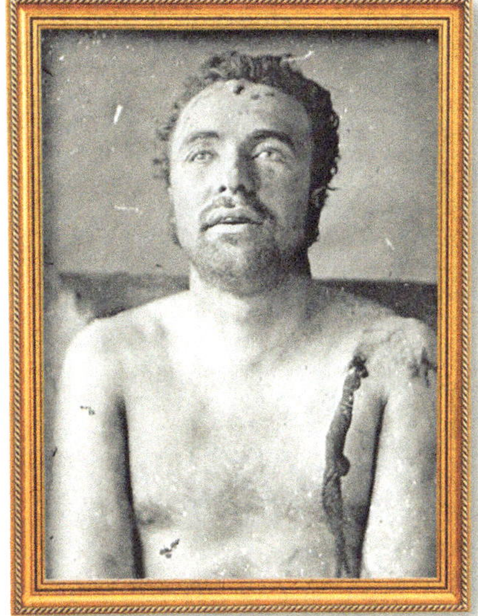

Outlaw Clell Miller was shot dead by Henry Miller from the third-floor window of the Dampier Hotel with a borrowed Smith carbine.

Edward Dampier owned the Dampier Hotel in Northfield. In the Civil War, he served in Hatch's Independent Battalion, Company F of Minnesota's volunteer cavalry, where he was issued a Smith Carbine. He took the carbine West with him after the war and still had it at his hotel the day the James-Younger Gang rode into town.

a Smith Carbine. He took the carbine West with him after the war and still had it at his hotel the day the James-Younger Gang rode into town. As such, it was handy when Henry Wheeler, a friend of Dampier's son and fellow medical student at the University of Michigan, came running into the hotel to the sounds of gunshots and shouting from the street. Wheeler was an eye-witness and participant who contested the gang's escape. He wasn't alone, but he is credited with killing gang member Clell Miller and wounding Bob Younger badly enough to take him out of the fight, making him the most effective marksman of the engagement.

Wheeler's Account

In 1926, on the 50th anniversary of the robbery, he dictated an account of his role in defense of Northfield.

"At the time of the Northfield bank raid, Thursday, Sept. 7, 1876, I was a student in medicine and home in Northfield for my holidays. I was sitting on the sidewalk, in front of father's drug store, nearly opposite the bank about half-past one or two in the afternoon when I saw three men ride up the street, tie their horses, and go into the bank. I thought they were cattlemen. Two more men came riding up the street and stopped in front of the bank. One of them dismounted, looked through the bank door, and then remained outside.

"I was beginning to get suspicious, rose from my chair and moved up the street until I was directly oppo-site the bank. J.S. Allen approached the bank and attempted to enter but received a blow from the horseman, which sent him spinning down the street. I shouted, 'Robbery! They are robbing the bank,' with the result that

EMF/Pietta Smith Carbine (Artillery Model tested)

Caliber: .50 bullet fired from a reusable plastic or turned brass case

Barrel: 21 5/8"

OAL: 38 7/8"

Weight: 7.5 lbs.

Stock: Walnut

Action: Break Open

Finish: Color case-hardened & Blued

Capacity: 1

MSRP: $1,305

For more info: EMF-Company.com, Lodgewood.com

The EMF Smith carbine, made by Pietta in Italy, and an original cavalry model.

Rare photo of a Civil War cavalryman armed with a Smith. Note the distinctive spring latch behind the rear sight.

the man in front of the bank turned immediately and fired at me, but the shot went over my head. 'Get back, or I'll kill you,'" he shouted.

"I ran into the drug store, thinking to get my gun, which I generally kept there, but I had lent it to someone who had returned it to the house. I made for the Dampier Hotel, where I knew there was a gun, asked the clerk for ammunition, and he got me four cartridges from the storeroom. I ran upstairs to a bedroom on the third floor, facing the bank. As I approached the window, three more men on horseback came riding up across the bridge square, shooting. I shot at one of them but missed him. I reloaded.

"The man who had fired at me before had got into the saddle and was bending down adjusting the left stirrup. I got a rest for the gun in a corner of the window, aimed low and shot him through the chest. In the meantime, A.R. Manning had come up to the corner on the other side of the street, shot one of the horses, behind which some of the bandits were sheltering themselves, and had also shot one of the men.

"Bob Younger had come out of the bank and was having a revolver duel with Manning. I took a shot at Bob, breaking his right elbow. My fourth cartridge had fallen from the bed to the floor, breaking the tissue paper forming the cartridge, and the powder had escaped, so my ammunition was exhausted. I watched two bandits come out of the bank, mount their horses, and ride away with the others. At the time, the clerk came with more cartridges for me, but he was too late.

"When the excitement had died down, it was found that the robbers had made away with about $290, which they took from the till on the counter, but Heywood had refused

to open the safe, declaring there was a time lock on it, which he could not open. They shot him thru the head, killing him instantly, but were afraid to go into the vault."

The Smith Carbine

The .50-caliber Smith Carbine Henry Wheeler used still exists today and is on display at the Northfield Historical Society. Though the Northfield Robbery might be considered the Smith's "15 Minutes of Fame" in the Wild West, it deserves a much closer examination.

On the eve of the Civil War, when the muzzle-loading military rifle was at the apex of its development, the U.S. government took an interest in a unique breech-loading .50-caliber carbine invented by Gilbert Smith.

Smith was an upstate New York doctor with a penchant for firearms design. His new carbine was a single shot, hinged break-open action, with a conventional external hammer and percussion cap ignition, but with a rubber cartridge case to contain the powder and bullet. The unique rubber cartridge was easy to handle, durable, fairly moisture resistant and created an excellent gas seal where the carbine's breech locked together. By the time the war was over, the army had bought just over 30,000 carbines and nearly 14 million rounds of ammunition.

Cartridge Troubles

Though the Smith was the fourth most numerous breech-loading carbine of the Civil War, it did not earn the praise of the troops that Sharps and Spencer carbines did. The Smith's unique cartridge was the root of the trouble and caused more serious problems than it solved. For one thing, rubber had to be imported from South America and was an expensive

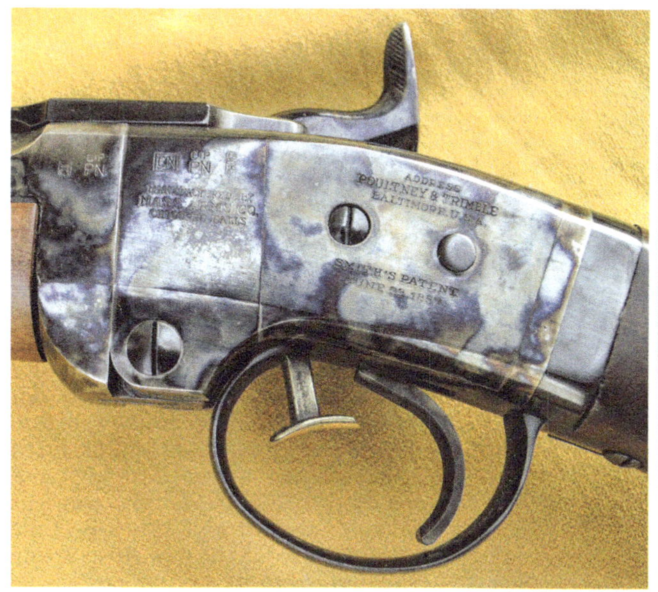

The markings are well executed on the reproduction, as you can see by comparison to the original.

commodity. Cases could also be made from gutta-percha (a form of natural, plant-derived thermo-plastic), but this also had to be imported. Alternative cartridges were made of rolled foil, paper and even thin metal.

Reports from the battlefront say the Smith's chamber was susceptible to fouling from the cartridge casing materials and would have to be cleaned after firing a few dozen rounds. Ironically, the Smith carbine is much more popular among modern shooters than it ever was in its day. Modern plastic makes a near-perfect and reusable cartridge that doesn't gum up the chamber.

Early Modern Firearms/Pietta Replica

Early Modern Firearms (EMF) in Los Angeles, Calif., imports an excellent replica of the 1857 patent Smith Carbine made by Italian gun maker F. LLI Pietta. EMF specialized in historic reproduction American firearms back in 1956 and remained an industry leader in the field. No company has played a more significant role in raising the authenticity bar on 1873 Colt replicas than EMF. Late president Boyd Davis played a significant role in founding and cultivating the Single Action Shooting Society (SASS) too.

EMF's close relationship with Pietta has resulted in a number of really well-executed replicas and the Smith Carbine I examined and tested was no exception. I compared it with original guns and found Pietta's attention to detail was excellent, including even the font style and stamping of the markings.

Smith Action

The operation of the Smith is simple. A heavy milled spring on top of the action bridges the barrel and receiver and connects them by snapping over

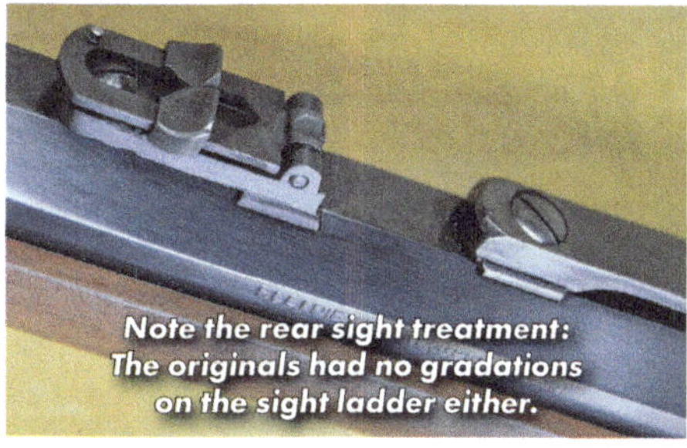

Pietta sought to recreate the style of the serial number markings on the receiver and barrel assembly.

Note the rear sight treatment: The originals had no gradations on the sight ladder either.

Note the attention to detail in the reproduction receiver.

a precisely machined square boss on the top of each part. The Pietta replica locked up like a bank vault. To open the action for loading/unloading, the spring is lifted off the boss on the receiver by pressing the brass finger plunger inside the trigger guard in front of the trigger. The big spring on top of the action is the only thing holding it closed, and it takes some strength to push it up with the finger plunger. Once a fresh round is loaded into the barrel, the action is snapped closed, the spring popping over the boss on the receiver to lock it shut.

With the action open, you can see that about a quarter of the chamber is recessed into the receiver. Having a quarter of the cartridge sticking up from the barrel gave the shooter some purchase when pulling out the spent case. Inside the chamber,

The front sight is a brass plate sandwiched and pinned into a steel base, a complex feature Pietta took the time to reproduce accurately.

Rear sight, raised position.

The Smith's chamber was sealed by the rubber cartridge case, not the raised metal lip. Firing loose powder and ball resulted in gas leakage but could be done in a pinch.

Pressing the brass finger plate inside the trigger guard raises the rear of the latch to open the action.

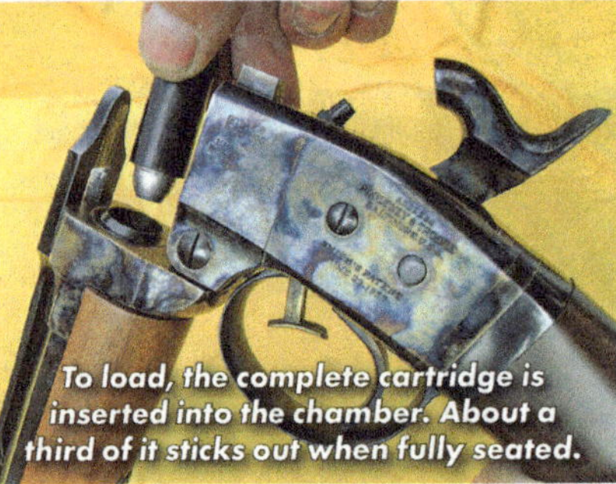

To load, the complete cartridge is inserted into the chamber. About a third of it sticks out when fully seated.

The spring is a fairly massive affair, and there seems to be no chance of accidentally opening it.

Removing the side panel on the action reveals the simple sear and trigger spring. When the trigger pull weight is excessive, look first for an overly heavy hammer spring.

there's a thick shoulder where the cartridge case headspaces. The chamber mouth on the barrel has a tapered male flange that mates with a corresponding female bevel on the receiver to form a mechanical gas seal.

The high degree of machining precision needed to create a perfect gas seal was impractical in the mid-19th century, but the rubber cartridge case did a good job of taking up the slack. I noted no gas leakage on the Pietta Smith during testing. I didn't shoot it like a muzzleloader, with loose powder and ball, as the Confederates were said to have utilized captured Smiths. Fired in that manner, a spent cartridge case was used to seal the action from gas leakage. Even without it, I suspect the gas leakage would be more distracting than dangerous to the shooter.

The Smith's 21 $^5/_8$" barrel is rifled with three broad lands and grooves and slugged at 0.507" from land to groove, with all surfaces of the bullet showing contact with the bore. The twist rate is 1:66" and the sights are faithful to the original. The front sight is a brass blade, and the rear is a "V" notch ladder-type without graduations but adjustable for windage by virtue of its dovetail mounting to the barrel. When folded down, the battle sight notch gave me a 50-yard point of impact about 11" higher than my point of aim. I found the sights easy to use; perhaps the short sight radius (only 16") made them easier for my old eyes to focus on.

Fit and Finish

Overall, the Pietta replica is a great-looking gun showing nice metal-to-metal and wood-to-metal fitting. The walnut stocks look to be sealed with a satin polyurethane, which is great for weather resistance but fills in the grain's texture. If you don't like it, there's nothing stopping you from stripping it off.

The receiver, trigger and hammer are color case-hardened and the balance of the metal is blued nearly black. They also went through the trouble of reproducing by stamping the patent, manufacturer and distributor markings on the left side of the receiver.

During the war, three companies made the Smith. The Pietta replica is stamped "MASS. ARMS. CO. /

CHICOPEE FALLS," representing the Massachusetts Arms Company. Poultney and Trimble of Baltimore, Md., managed the military sales.

Carbines were issued to cavalry and artillery units. The cavalry model had a single sling attachment ring attached to the receiver by a metal bar. The artillery model had conventional oblong sling swivels on the buttstock and foregrip.

Very few Smiths were sold to private citizens before and during the war. After the war, it was apparent the brass cartridge case was the future of ammunition, not the Smith's rubber cartridge, so there was no peacetime demand for new Smiths. On top of that, the military sold off its inventory as surplus, and many went West with the settlers.

Modern Applications

Smiths got a reputation for ease of use and accuracy among contemporary shooters in the North-South Skirmish Association (NSSA) and reproductions were being made by the early '70s as they became popular among competitors. Their break-open action makes them extremely easy to clean too.

Lodgewood Manufacturing specializes in U.S. martial arms and parts from 1750–1899. They stock authentic-looking black plastic cartridge cases ($0.40 each) that you can easily push a bullet into with just thumb pressure. The mouth holds the bullet tight and should last for years if you don't store them loaded for long periods and stretch out the necks.

Lodgewood also has a heavy lathe-turned brass case ($3.25 each) that got my attention. Some Smith reproductions had overly large flash holes that burned up the vent hole in the back of the plastic cases and ruined them in short order. For those guns, a brass case was the best option. The brass cases required a little bit of fitting to my test gun before the action would close fully. All that was needed was to remove a few thousandths of an inch from the mouth of the case to reduce its overall length. This was easily done with a few passes across a sheet of 220-grit sandpaper laid on a flat surface. The brass cases also hold less powder than the black plastic cases do. The plastic ones seem to hold about 35 grains of FFFG powder, while the maximum for the brass ones is about 27.5 grains of FFFG, which is a recommended target load. The inside diameters of the brass cases are 0.515", making larger bullets hard to push in. Lodgewood sells a handheld seating tool ($40) that allows you to press the bullets straight down into the case with just hand pressure.

Will Dabbs, MD

157 YEARS LATE

The Final Shot of the American Civil War

CSA Colonel Rip Ford commanded the Confederates at the Battle of Palmito Ranch in 1865.

Union Colonel Theodore Barrett commanded Federal troops during the last serious combat engagement of the American Civil War.

Colonel Ford went on to a distinguished career with the Texas Rangers after the war.

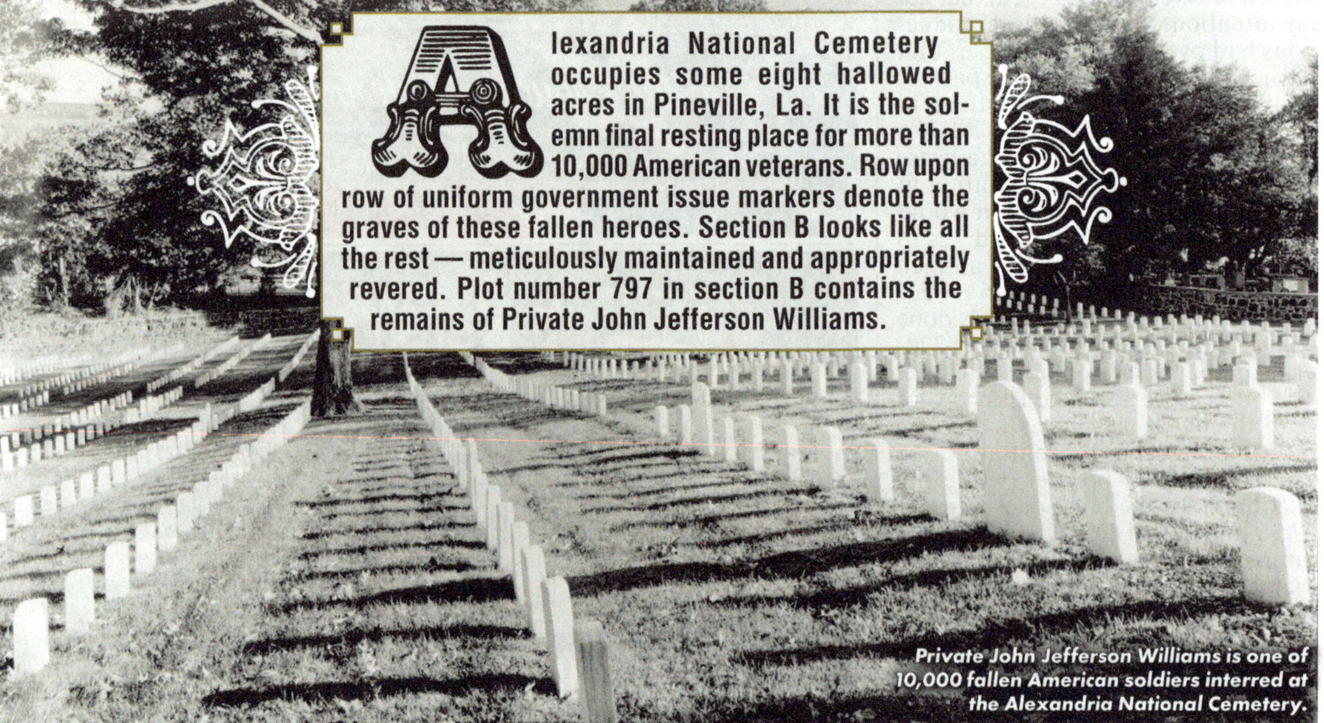

Alexandria National Cemetery occupies some eight hallowed acres in Pineville, La. It is the solemn final resting place for more than 10,000 American veterans. Row upon row of uniform government issue markers denote the graves of these fallen heroes. Section B looks like all the rest — meticulously maintained and appropriately revered. Plot number 797 in section B contains the remains of Private John Jefferson Williams.

Private John Jefferson Williams is one of 10,000 fallen American soldiers interred at the Alexandria National Cemetery.

Private Williams was born in 1843 in Jay County, Ind. He enlisted in the Federal Army in September 1863, and originally learned to drill at Camp Joe Holt in Jeffersonville, Ind. Williams spent most of the Civil War pulling garrison duties and getting bored in the Western Theatre. After a stint in New Orleans, Private Williams accompanied his regiment for the invasion and occupation of Texas in early 1865. His first and last combat engagement was the Battle of Palmito Ranch outside Brownsville, Texas, on May 13, 1865.

Palmito Ranch was a curious fight. General Robert E. Lee had inked the general surrender of Confederate forces at Appomattox Court House more than a month earlier. Across the war-torn South, troops from both sides were demobilizing and heading home. However, arrayed on the banks of the Rio Grande, roughly 500 Federal troops serving under Colonel Theodore Barrett found themselves in a meeting engagement with 300 Rebels under Colonel John "Rip" Ford.

Ford's Confederates seized the initiative and, backed by half a dozen field guns purportedly provided by the French Army garrison at nearby Matamoros, routed the Federals into disarray. In the final tally, Barrett's Federals had four killed, 101 captured and a dozen wounded. The Rebels had six wounded and three captured. Private John Jefferson Williams was the last man to fall that day. While some historians dispute the details, Pvt. Williams was likely the last soldier to die due to direct enemy action in the American Civil War.

Modern Treatment

As I sit typing these words, it has been nearly 157 years since Private Williams breathed his last on that torrid

Texas battlefield. There is a modest government marker commemorating the spot today. The guns have been silent for more than a century and a half. However, using some precious original Civil War-era black powder, we wanted to try to fire one last round.

My goal was to fire the last shot of the American Civil War, not become its final casualty, so I took pains to do this safely. I used a Pietta 1858 Remington .44-caliber pistol from Dixie Gun Works as a vehicle. Dixie Gun Works is one-stop shopping for cool reproduction Civil War-era firearms. The 1858 Remington, with its steel top strap, doesn't have quite the dashing lines of the svelte Colt Navy, but it is the more rugged gun. Additionally, these reproductions are cut from modern quality steel. I surmised this manly pistol could easily handle the stress

of firing 157-year-old black powder harvested from a Yankee cannonball.

The Gun

The designation Model 1858 is technically a misnomer. The gun we call the Model 1858 first saw large-scale production in 1861. However, the patent date stamped into the barrel was "SEPT 14, 1858," so the name stuck.

In 1861 Samuel Remington offered his 1858 pistols to Uncle Sam for the princely sum of $15 apiece. That was 10 bucks less than Colt's offerings, and about $421 in today's money. However, by March 1862, the Army had only purchased 8,200 copies in all configurations.

Samuel Colt was the Tony Stark of his era, a gifted war profiteer whose creations spilt a veritable ocean of blood on both sides of the line. His 1851 and 1860 models were the stan-

The Bormann fuze was typically formed from pewter or zinc and was a simple powder train.

Both of these cannonballs were recovered near Will's home. The one on the right is a piece of solid shot.

dard Federal handguns. However, a factory fire in 1864 set production back. Where the Model 1858 had been a secondary supplemental issue weapon, it now had its time to shine.

The Model 1858 came in three broad flavors and both .36 and .44 calibers. The .36 was called the Navy, while the .44 was referred to as the Army Model. All the versions were quite similar.

The Model 1858 was a single-action design wildly overbuilt. It was, in general, a sturdier, more efficient design when compared to the Colt offerings. To take the gun down, one just broke open the rammer, extracted the cylinder-retaining pin, retracted the hammer slightly and dropped the cylinder out the side. Colt pistols were a bit tougher to maintain.

The Colt utilized separate screws for the trigger and cylinder stop. These two components of the Model 1858 shared a common screw. Unlike that of the Colt models, the barrel of the Model 1858 was fixed and not removable. This made cleaning a bit more onerous, but not by much.

The sights on the Model 1858 consisted of a groove in the top strap and a simple forward post. There were

UNOBTAINIUM

So, where does one come by original Civil War-era black powder? As you might imagine, it's not the sort of stuff you pick up in 5-lb. kegs at your local Cabela's. In our case, it began with a squirrel hunting trip.

My dad was out shooting tree rats on the wet side of the levee in the Mississippi Delta south of Friars Point. Friars Point is all but a ghost town today, but it was quite the happening burg during the American Civil War. The largest trans-shipment point for Delta cotton south of Memphis, Friars Point had some real strategic value in the 1860s. This attracted the attention of Federal troops.

The Federals landed December 21, 1862, backed by a modest flotilla of gunboats. One of these magnificent vessels, the *USS Cairo*, is preserved and on display at the military park in Vicksburg today. It's definitely worth a visit if you're ever passing through.

It was rumored the locals had put a Union sympathizer in a barrel and rolled him into the Mississippi River. The 83rd Ohio Infantry disembarked looking for some payback. The Yankees burned much of the town along with all of the churches for some unfathomable reason. The locals subsequently started taking potshots at the gunboats set at anchor nearby. The Federals responded by raking the surrounding tree lines with cannon fire. Now hold that thought.

Dad was traipsing about the woods stalking squirrels when he spotted what he thought to be a piece of half-buried fruit. Being a man, he naturally wandered over and kicked it. He was surprised to find the offending item to be quite substantial. Dad then recognized the cannonball for what it was and pried it out of the ground with a stick.

Dad hefted the little bomb onto his shoulder and headed home. Once there, he buried the old cannonball in a pickle bucket filled with sand in the backyard and called me. Dad later told me he wondered what might happen should the piece of dud ordnance detonate while he was carrying it. He presumed someone would eventually trip over his smoldering boots and simply assume he had spontaneously exploded while out walking in the woods.

This ball was equipped with a Bormann time fuze. This thing was designed by the Belgian Army Captain Charles Bormann and looked like a clock face. Before firing, the artilleryman punched through the desired number with an awl and loaded the ball, fuze forward. Blowby from the propellant charge should theoretically ignite the exposed powder chain and set the ball off after the desired time delay. The Bormann fuze had a 50% failure rate in combat. So long as we didn't toss it into a fire, that fuze should be thoroughly inert by now.

It should go without saying, but don't try this at home. Drawing on my vast well of experience as both a military veteran and a gun writer, I obtained a drill press, an old tabletop and three 100' orange extension cords. Thusly equipped, Dad and I exhumed the bomb and trundled out to the levee in the family RV, itself big enough to warrant its own zip code. Both my mom and my wife inexplicably stayed home.

We arranged the rig 300' out into the woods and tied a long piece of trotline to the drill press handle. We set the ball in a big rubber gasket from Home Depot in the bottom of the pickle bucket. We then filled the bucket with water up to the top of the ball to serve as a heat sink. With the RV generator driving the whole shebang, we both crouched behind a big log and commenced tugging gently on the trotline.

It was then the local game warden drove up in his big green cop truck.

"What you boys doing?" he inquired amicably.

I looked at Dad. Dad looked at me.

"Drilling a hole in an old cannonball, sir," I replied. They say honesty is the best policy.

The longsuffering law enforcement officer verified we weren't hunting or camping on the levee and left us to our devices with a helpful, "Y'all have a great day. Don't blow yourselves up."

An hour later, the cannonball was inert, and I had harvested about a quarter pound of fresh dry Yankee black powder that I transferred to a Tupperware container. Amongst many extraordinary adventures, that day ranks among the best father-son experiences my dad and I have ever had.

Oh, how I do love the Deep South.

notches located between the nipples on the cylinder that allowed the gun to be carried with the hammer down for greater safety than might otherwise be the case. A great many folks, myself included, cannot bring themselves to pack these old guns with all six chambers loaded. I'm happier to leave the hammer down over a dead chamber. However, were I relying upon this weapon in combat, I could likely get over my anxiety in that regard.

Starting in 1868, Remington began offering a five-shot cartridge conversion for the Model 1858 chambered in .46 rimfire. One of the nifty aspects of the design was cylinders could be rapidly exchanged on the fly. Though the Army never issued the Model 1858 with a spare cylinder, civilian shooters often carried an extra that could be quickly exchanged as the need arose.

The Parting Shot

On the appointed day, I cleaned the pistol, fired a cap through a random chamber to clear the nipple and carefully measured out a fixed charge of 25 grains from my modest stockpile of irreplaceable Civil War powder. I picked through the powder stash with a toothpick to exclude any irregular chunks. What I had left was a decent approximation of FFFg black powder. I meticulously charged the cylinder and seated a .44-cal. lead ball using the pistol's rammer before mounting a cap.

Despite its age, Will's vintage Civil War-era black powder remained plenty spunky to do the job.

With the camera running and my eye and ear protection checked for the nth time, I thumbed the big hammer back and drew a careful bead on a BulletSafe armored vest to catch the ball. With some trepidation, I gently squeezed the trigger. My efforts were rewarded with a wonderfully satisfying cloud of rancid white smoke and a proper shove. The 157-year-old powder pushed that 141-grain ball hard enough to flatten it on the vest. Even after a century and a half, this stuff would still quite handily kill you.

Denouement

The American Civil War was the bloodiest conflict in our history. This was our first taste of warfare on an industrial scale, and everyone who perished was obviously an American. The North had more than 365,000 dead, while some 290,000 Southerners fell. Add in roughly 50,000 civilians and another 80,000 slaves, and you get nearly a million American deaths over four years and 27 days. We modern folk honestly cannot imagine such a river of blood.

In the spring of 1865, the country breathed a collective sigh of relief as the guns finally fell silent. Troops went home to grow crops, rebuild homes, raise families and get about the business of living. Now 157 years later, we have had the privilege of firing one last round. What a blast.

For more info:
DixieGunWorks.com

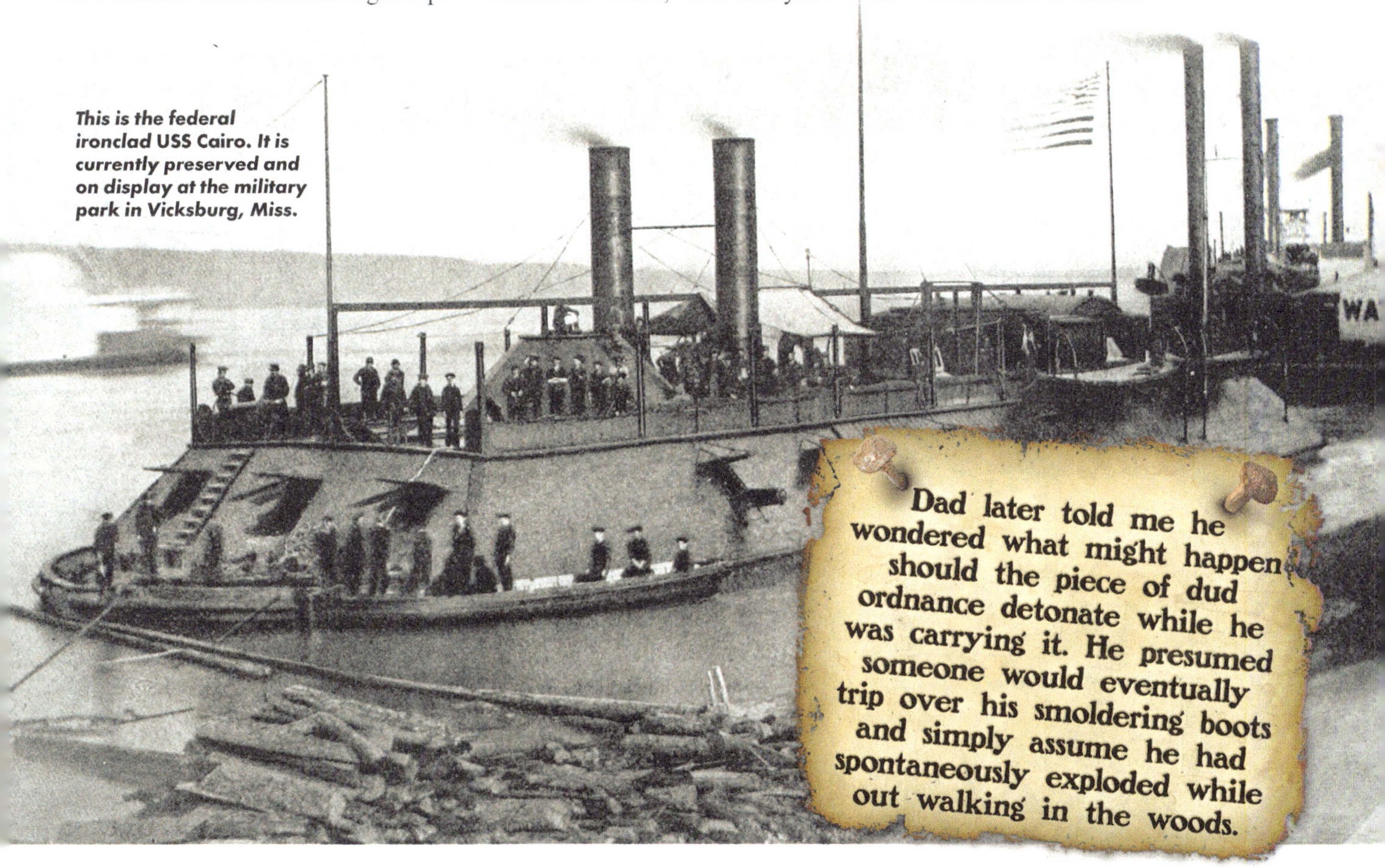

This is the federal ironclad USS Cairo. It is currently preserved and on display at the military park in Vicksburg, Miss.

 Mike "Duke" Venturino · Photos: Yvonne Venturino 

SCATTERGUN TO TACK DRIVER

Rediscovering the .32–20

ver 40 years ago, I got mad at a Colt Single Action Army revolver caliber with good reason. My first SAA .32 WCF (aka .32-20) delivered pitiful groups. Despite a bright shiny bore, the best clusters at 25 yards were in the 4" range. I thought it should have fired near one-hole groups. Finally, I slugged its barrel and each chamber mouth. The problem became apparent. The barrel measured 0.314" across its grooves, but all chambers were uniformly 0.310". Bullets were swaged down, going through those tight chamber mouths and then wobbling through the oversize barrel.

In disgust, I sold or traded that Colt — I don't even remember which — and I vowed never to buy another Colt SAA .32-20. About 20 years later, I did give an Italian single action .32-20 a try. It shot nicely but not being a "real" Colt, it didn't stick. Also, I had a Browning Model 53 .32-20 lever-action rifle. It was a fine shooter, but someone made an offer I couldn't refuse.

A Second Try

Attitudes soften with time, so in 2021, upon spotting a 3rd Generation SAA .32-20 for sale on the internet, I captured it. What tripped my trigger was its price, plus the fact it was wearing a 7 ½" barrel — my favorite. Back in the 1st Generation run of SAA production, the .32-20 was the fourth most popular in terms of numbers produced, with 43,102 inclusive of standard SAAs, Bisley and Target Models or both. No .32-20s were

These are Duke's trio of new .32-20s. Carbine is Cimarron Model 1873; both revolvers are Colt SAAs made in the 21st century with barrel lengths of 5 ½" and 7 ½".

made in the 2nd Generation lasting from 1956 to 1974. With the impetus of Cowboy Action competitions, Colt started offering SAA .32-20s again around 2004. Evidently, they didn't sell many, for the caliber was dropped again about 10 years later. So far, Colt has released no data on exactly how many 3rd Generation .32-20s were made. Nowadays, they are relatively hard to find — and high-priced!

As I said, the low price was my primary reason for buying this .32-20. It was price tagged at about half what others were going for, plus it wore a 7 ½" barrel. It's the first and only 3rd Generation .32-20 with that length I've seen. As to its price, here's what the seller related to me. When he originally purchased it, upon opening the plastic factory case, he found its color case hardened frame had light surface rust all over. Left alone, that rust would have deepened into pitting. His solution was to remove the case colors

chemically, leaving the finish a sort of mottled gray. The rest of the revolver, i.e., all blued parts, were still perfect. Being currently nigh-on obsessed with SAAs, my thought was to buy the long-barreled .32-20 and, after a hiatus of 25 years, begin reloading .32-20s again.

Better Luck!

If it shot as poorly as my first SAA .32-20, I'd pass the good price on to someone else, but if it shot to my expectation, I'd have it re-color case hardened. As for shooting much more accurately even than my expectations? It did! It is likely due to its barrel groove diameter of 0.310" with 0.313" chamber mouths. And have it recolored I did also! The Colt was sent to Bill Fuchs DBA Spring Creek Armory in Ten Sleep, Wyo. Bill specializes in single-action work and soon sent back to me a beautifully color case-hardened Colt. Furthermore, I'd asked that he fit it with a set of extra fancy one-piece style walnut grips. And I hit the jackpot there, as the photos show.

Nothing Is Easy

Not everything went perfectly afterward. A few glitches popped up in my plan. On my reloading bench were a set of never used RCBS "Cowboy" .32-20 dies, but my first problem was finding .32-20 brass in this age of component shortages. Some of my hard-earned

gun'riter bucks saved by the new Colt's low price were consumed in finding on Gunbroker.com a couple of 100-round bags of Starline brass. To my surprise and pleasure, I discovered in my storage shed plastic bags holding 500 Oregon Trail 115-grain roundnose/flatpoint (RN/FP) bullets and 100 of Missouri Bullet Company's coated version of the same weight and shape. My second glitch came with bullet molds. I knew for sure there was a #RCBS #32-98SWC mold on my shelves along with a Lyman mold #311008. They were gone! And I have no recollection of selling or loaning them.

An Alternative Molds Find

As with components, reloading tools were in very short supply in 2021. Neither of the two mentioned bullet molds happened to be in stock from their original manufacturers. My recourse was to order some similar ones from custom makers. This required more of the cash saved from buying the "inexpensive" .32-20.

Arsenal Molds of Utah has one .32 mold advertised as a clone to the RCBS #32-98SWC. It was offered in brass and aluminum. I ordered brass with four cavities. Shortly before this time, I had discovered MP Molds located in Slovenia. The company may be in Europe, but several molds I've ordered from them have all arrived in about a week. Their website lists a rather ingenious option for some molds. By means of a

This is the Cimarron Model 1873 .32-20 "Short Rifle" Duke ordered by mistake. Although a fine shooter, it was sold because he favored the carbine.

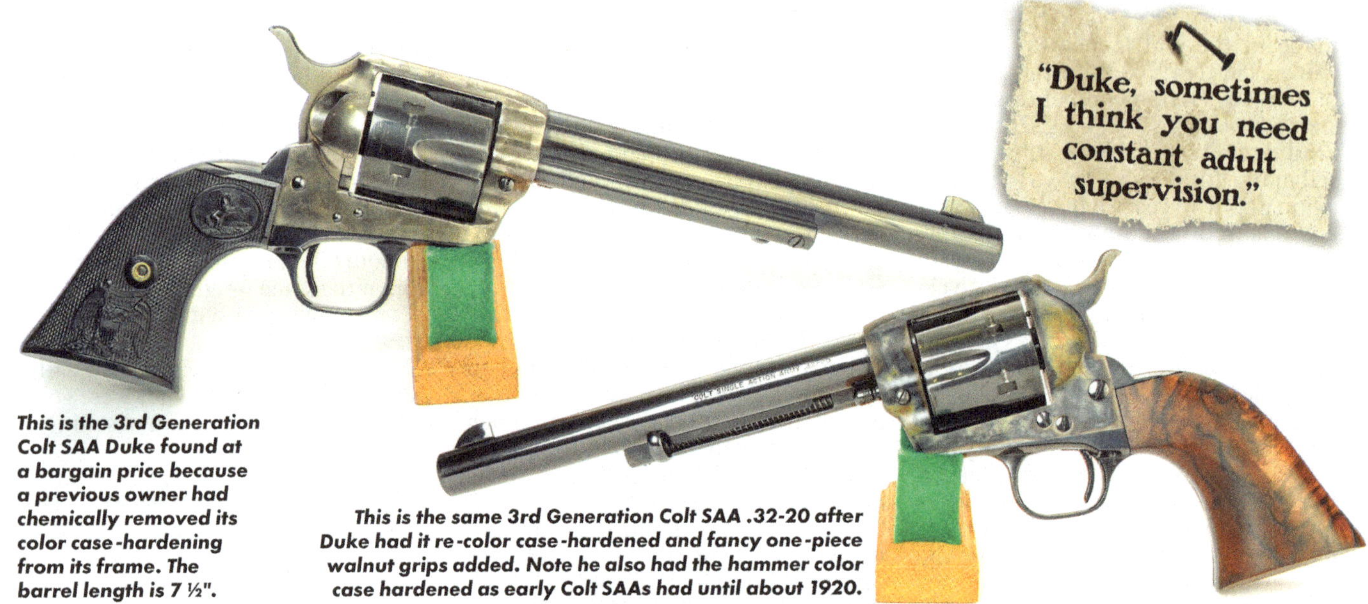

This is the 3rd Generation Colt SAA Duke found at a bargain price because a previous owner had chemically removed its color case-hardening from its frame. The barrel length is 7 ½".

This is the same 3rd Generation Colt SAA .32-20 after Duke had it re-color case-hardened and fancy one-piece walnut grips added. Note he also had the hammer color case hardened as early Colt SAAs had until about 1920.

set of pins and plugs, select MP molds can be converted from dropping standard solid bullets to either hollowpoint (HP) or hollowbase (HB) designs. I ordered their #314-640-115HP, also in brass blocks with four cavities. From my one-part tin to 20 parts lead alloy blend, the MP mold dropped 120-grain solid RN/FPs and 115-grain HPs of the same shape. Of that same alloy, Arsenal Mold's bullets weighed 100 grains. All bullets cast by me or the commercial ones were sized 0.313". I lubed mine with DGL lube from Idaho. Oregon Trails' .32-20 bullets carried a hard lube and Missouri Bullet Company's .32-20s were coated.

Range Performance

Coupling those cast bullets with Bullseye, Titegroup, W231 and Unique powders gave fine results from my 3rd Generation .32-20. The mildest loads chronographed at about 850 fps, which gave low noise and recoil for just plain fun shooting. Due to the .32-20s smaller bore and chambers, it weighs a full 8 oz. more than a .45 with the same barrel length. The hottest loads tried exceeded 1,000 fps and would be perfect for small game

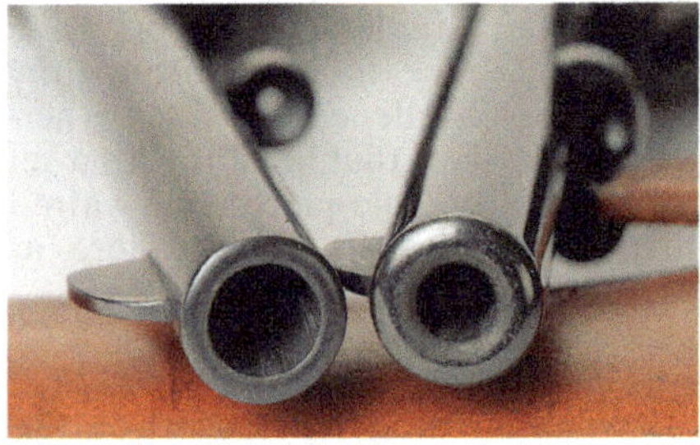

This photo shows why .32-20 SAAs are about 8 oz. heavier than big bore ones.

or varmints. All loads gave decent groups, and some bordered on great. My load testing was over a sandbag rest at 25 yards and I'm not world-class at that endeavor.

One problem occurred. The Colt's firing pin punched through some of the Winchester small pistol primers. A steady course of that will erode both the firing pin and its corresponding hole in the revolver's frame. Those were the only brand of small pistol primers I had on hand, and as stated above, components were difficult to find. A little-known reloading fact is that although large pistol and large rifle primers differ dimensionally along with cartridge case primer pockets, small pistol and small rifle

primers are identical, as are their cartridge case pockets. A switch to small rifle primers solved the punctured primer problem. Chronograph figures remained essentially the same.

.32-20 ... Forgiven

About this time, some readers are thinking, "Old Duke" is about to wrap up this .32-20 story. Not hardly! My positive experience must have touched some long-dormant nerve in my psyche. I've become a dyed-in-the-wool .32-20 shooter. Following that first Colt, I've purchased a 5 ½", 3rd Generation .32-20. It was new in the box and the premium price paid for it completely wiped out all the savings from buying the 7 ½" one. I can't help it; I'm hooked! I slugged its barrel and measured a 0.310" groove diameter. Five of the six chambers measured 0.313," but the sixth was a tight 0.312". This doesn't seem to have affected its grouping ability. My chronograph showed about a 50 to 60 fps velocity loss with the 2" shorter barrel.

Long(er) Guns

But that's not all. I've added a 19" barreled Cimarron Model 1873 .32-20

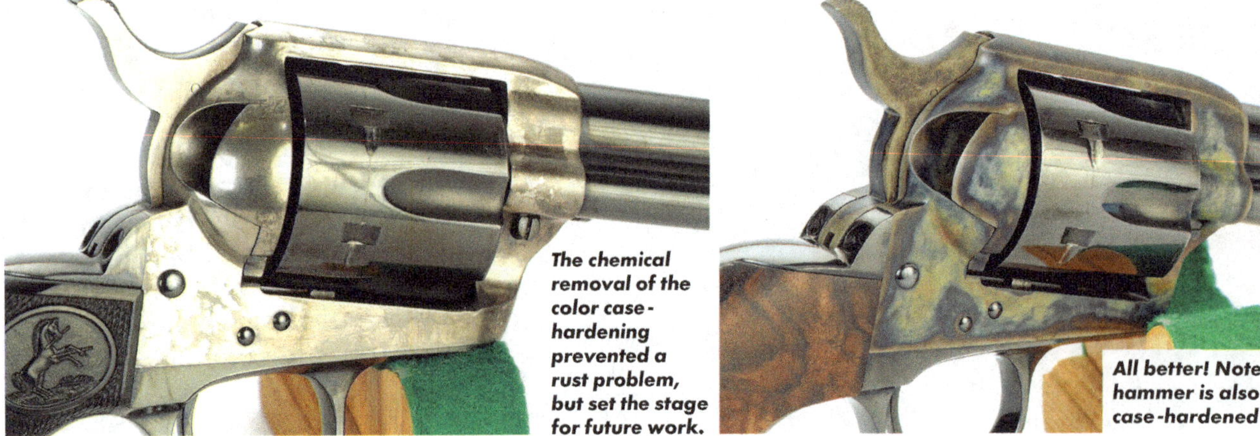

The chemical removal of the color case-hardening prevented a rust problem, but set the stage for future work.

All better! Note the hammer is also color case-hardened now.

These are the three bullets Duke settled upon for shooting in all three of his new .32-20s. The blue lubed bullet is from Oregon Trail Company. It weighs 115 grains. At the far left is 100-grain MP Molds' HP and in the middle is MP Molds' 105-grain solid.

Duke's first .32-20 MP Molds was set up for 115-grain HP bullets and 115-grain solids. When crimped properly, overall cartridge length is too long for .32-20 lever guns but fine for revolvers.

This is the Accurate Molds version of RCBS bullet #32-98-SWC.

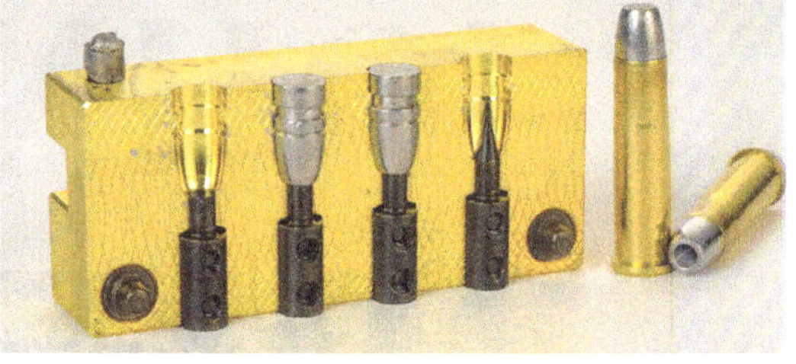

This is the MP Molds set up for casting both hollow point and solid bullets at the same time.

saddle ring carbine (SRC) to my rifle racks. Its story is sort of comical if you want to make fun of me. While waiting in a parking lot for Yvonne to shop, I browsed my iPad for .32-20 lever guns. Sure enough, I found a .32-20 Cimmaron "Saddle Ring Carbine," whipped out my credit card and bought it. When it arrived, I was disappointed to find a 20" barreled Cimarron '73 "Short Rifle" in the box. Rechecking my invoice, that's exactly what I ordered! Evidently, I needed a new set of reading glasses. Never fear; again, out came the credit card, and this time a proper Cimarron SRC arrived soon. Yvonne said, "Duke, sometimes I think you need constant adult supervision." After plenty of shooting, I sold the "Short Rifle" but kept the carbine.

Guess what was the first thing I learned about my new lever-action Cimarron .32-20? It would not feed any of the handloads I made for the 3rd Generation SAAs. A little measuring with a caliper showed my revolver loads all measured over 1.60," but Winchester lever guns will not feed rounds with an overall loaded length exceeding 1.592". Naturally,

my first correction was a fizzle. I tried seating bullets just a mite deeper and putting a heavy crimp into the bullet. Nope, won't work. The '73's tubular magazine spring pressure pushed all bullets back inside the cases. Not a good thing.

This is where MP Molds' ability to quickly get a proper bullet mold in my hands was comforting. I ordered another convertible version of .314-640-100HP, dropping 105-grain solid RN/FPs and 100-grain HPs. Their crimp grooves are perfectly placed for less than 1.592" overall cartridge lengths. And they shot beautifully from both my Cimarron .32-20 SRC and both revolvers. By the way, when the carbine arrived, I was out of Missouri Bullet Company's coated 115-grain RN/FPs but still had some of Oregon Trail's 115-grain commercially cast RN/FPs, so at least I was able to shoot it before the new mold arrived.

Arguably the most accurate handload tried in the revolvers had Arsenal Molds' 100-grain SWCs over 3.0 grains of Bullseye. However, those rounds are unsuitable for lever guns due to the overall length problem. Therefore, my favored handload meant for both types

of .32-20s has MP Molds' 105-grain RN/FP substituted over a 3.0-grain Bullseye charge. If shooting at the "gophers," which periodically try to invade Yvonne's hayfield, a switch to the MP Molds' 100-grain HP is more destructive. If I'm too lazy to cast for myself, Oregon Trail's 115-grain RN/FP over 3.5 grains of Titegroup is fine for all three of my .32-20s. By the way, the 19" barrel of the '73 Cimarron carbine added about 200 to 250 fps muzzle velocity and it proved a truly fine shooter. Groups at 25 yards sometimes have been as small as half an inch.

In my old age with arthritic hands, the gentle recoil and very mild muzzle blast of .32-20s is a welcome change from many firearms I use for other purposes. What I thought was a great deal on one .32-20 actually became a money pit when counting in the Cimarron carbine, the second Colt SAA and the several bullet molds. I don't regret a cent spent. 🔫

For more info: Cimarron-Firearms. com, MP-Molds.com, ArsenalMolds. com, OregonTrailBullets.com, MissouriBullet.com

These are the four powders Duke found best results with for reloading .32-20s in both long guns and revolvers.

Duke used a brand-new set of RCBS "Cowboy" dies, and due to primer punctures, he switched from small pistol to small rifle primers.

Alan Garbers

LET LOOSE YOUR INNER JOHN WAYNE!

Cowboy Action Shooting 101

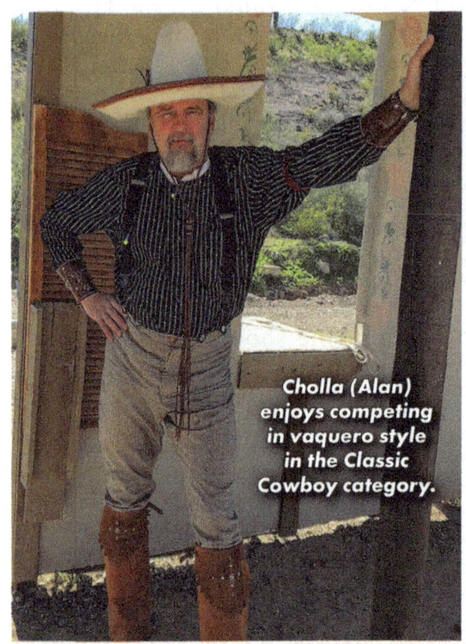
Cholla (Alan) enjoys competing in vaquero style in the Classic Cowboy category.

Barbwire is like a coiled rattlesnake waiting to strike at the sound of the buzzer. Her experience and dedication make her a fierce competitor.

My spurs jingle as my heels drum on the wooden floor. The sound of gunfire echos down the cactus-studded canyon walls. I steel myself for what is about to happen. Glancing out a window, I sigh and nod to a man watching. Then, like a coiled spring, I draw a pistol and start firing, a shot here, two there. Pulling the next revolver, I blaze away, then grab the rifle. It spews fire and lead like a demon until empty. I shove two rounds into the shotgun and fire. Shucking the empties, I load and cock the hammers again. As the stock hits my cheek, I let loose the dogs of hell. Then it is over.

Cowtown, near Peoria, Ariz., is one of the original Cowboy Action Shooting venues and draws competitors worldwide.

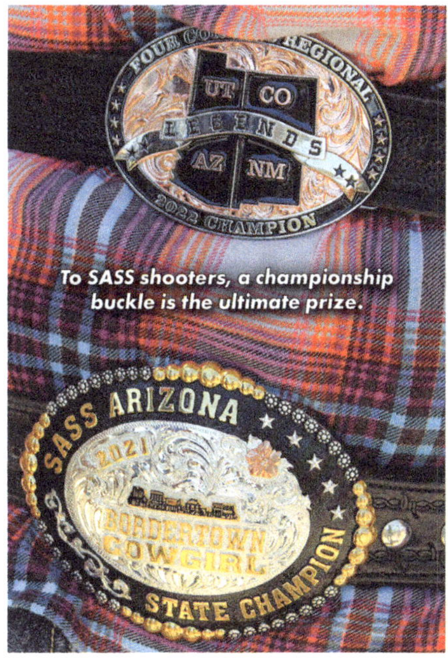

To SASS shooters, a championship buckle is the ultimate prize.

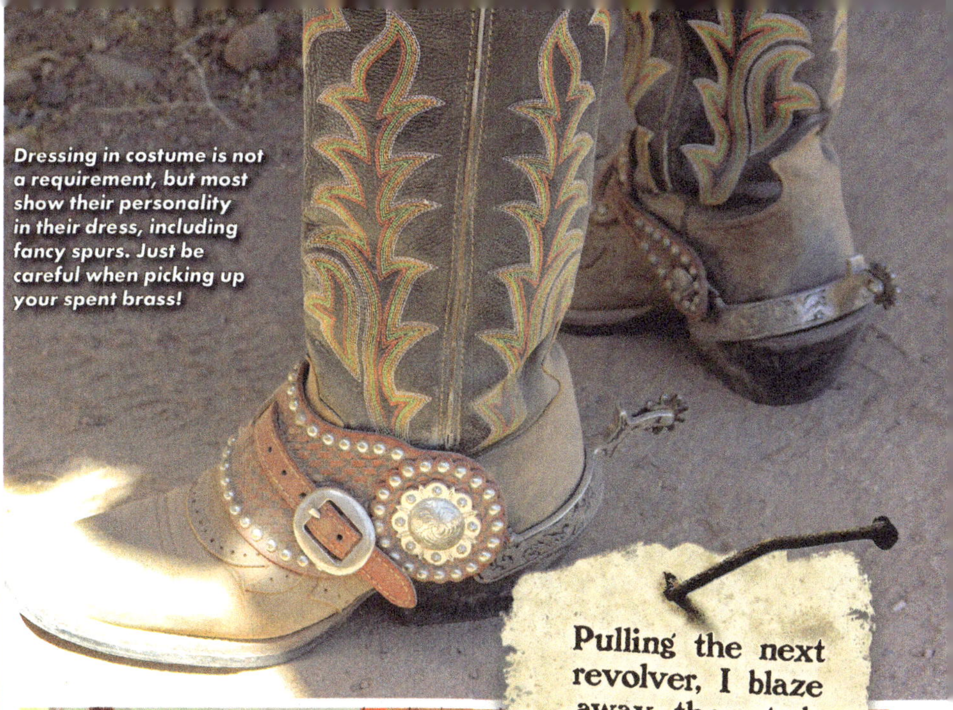

While all of this sounds campy, it is meant to entertain, just like Cowboy Action Shooting (CAS) entertains. Seriously, if you're not wearing a smile and laughing at a CAS match, you're doing it wrong!

Cowboy Action Shooting is a relatively unknown shooting sport, yet it attracts shooters of all ages, literally from 9 to 90. But what is CAS?

Cowboy Tactical … with Friends

Some call it "cowboy tactical," shooting four guns at large and close steel targets while being timed. But it's more, much more.

Like other shooting sports, it's a competition. Unlike other shooting sports, there are no monetary prizes, no sponsorships and no reason not to help fellow shooters.With nothing on the line, top shooters mentor slower shooters to improve their game. Champions shoot with rookies. Older shooters help younger shooters. Often, entire families shoot together, urging each other to do their best. Old friends have rivalries, driving them to get better for the next match.

For many, it's a way of life, a creed, a return to simpler times. It's called *The Cowboy Way.* The old but true Single Action Shooting Society (SASS) motto is: Come for the shooting, stay for the friendships. In many cases, shooters have lifelong bonds. Honesty and integrity are revered values.

Just so you don't get any unsafe notions, we don't spin our rifles like Rooster Cogburn. We don't do trick shooting or spin pistols like Brett Maverick. While we try to get into action fast, it is not a fast-draw competition. *Gun safety is of paramount importance, and rules are strictly enforced.*

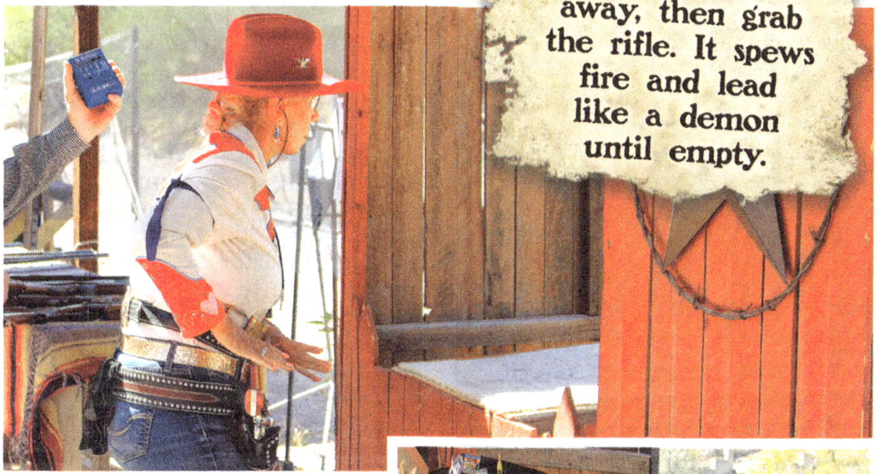

Double Tap enjoys competing in the B-Western category and was top in her class at the SASS world championships, End of Trail 2022.

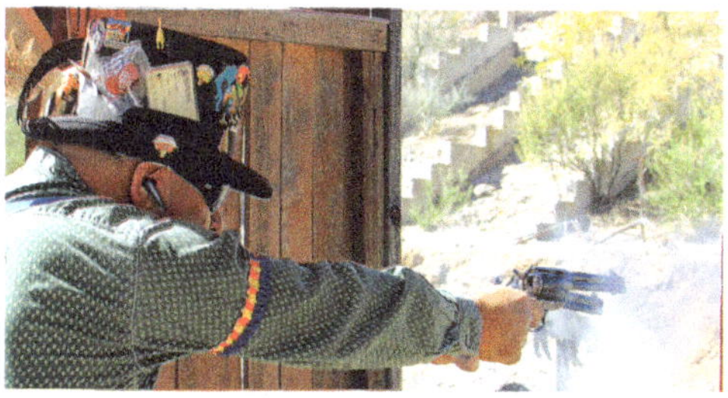

Dry Gulch Johnny excels in the Frontier Cartridge Gunfighter category, alternating shots from his brace of revolvers. The clouds of black powder smoke make seeing the targets challenging.

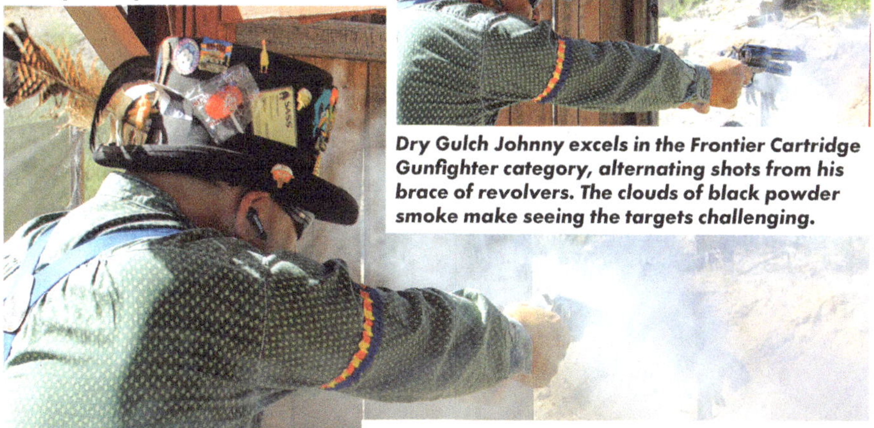

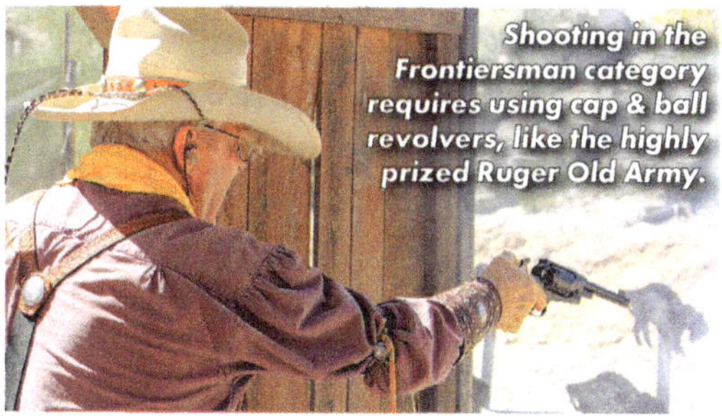

While CAS is predominantly older shooters emulating their TV heroes, younger shooters are serious competitors and blazing fast. Photo: Paparazzi Pahl

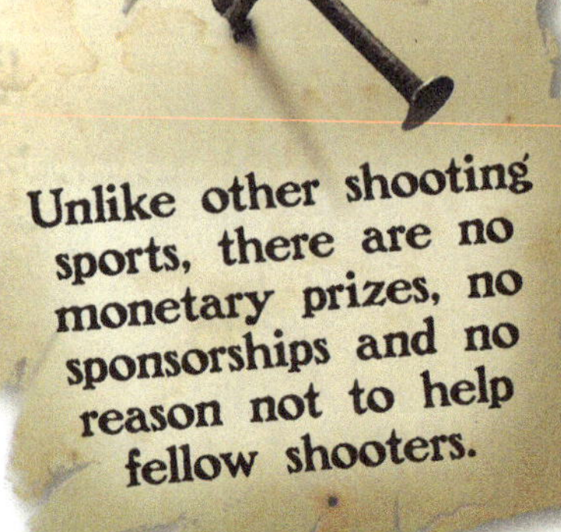

Unlike other shooting sports, there are no monetary prizes, no sponsorships and no reason not to help fellow shooters.

Match Structure

A match is usually made up of six stages. A stage is a series of targets to be shot in a specific order with specific guns: two revolvers, a rifle and a shotgun. The stage is timed, with the time being the score. Any misses are penalized by adding time to the stage. Not hitting the targets in the specified order or with the specified guns will result in a procedural penalty which adds more time to the score. Champion shooters can clear a stage in 12 to 15 seconds. Shooters like me enjoy the stage a little longer, but with just as much passion!

The targets are big and close, but once the timer buzzes, it's incredible how easy they are to miss, even with shotguns! Trust me when I say a clean match with no misses or errors is rare.

Unlike other tactical shooting sports, CAS has minimal movement, so shooters from young to elderly have no issues moving through the stage. If a shooter has physical challenges, stages can be shot "stand and deliver" — meaning no movement.

The rule is for shooters of all ages and skill levels to have fun.

Larger events such as regionals, state or special matches generally have 10 to 12 stages and are shot over a weekend or even a week.

Larger events may also have "extras" like long-range matches, pocket-pistol matches, derringer matches, cap & ball revolver matches and shotgun matches. The general overlying rule is that all guns must be single action and designed before 1899. There are exceptions, but let's not get too deep in the weeds in this article. To clarify, single-action guns are manually cocked before they can be fired.

Laws of the Land

There are two major organizations in the CAS world: the Single Action Shooting Society and the National Congress of Old West Shootists (NCOWS). The two are more alike than different, with the most significant differences being authenticity in dress and gun modifications.

SASS allows guns mimicking the style of the Old West, while NCOWS only allows original firearms or accurate reproductions. SASS allows modifications to make guns operate faster while NCOWS does not.

The SASS category matrix can be confusing for new shooters. Categories are divided based on age, shooting style and costuming. There is too much information to go through here, but I highly recommend starting in an age-based category. Once you see what other shooters are shooting and how they are shooting it, decide if you want to try something different.

Accoutrements

Costuming is a significant component of CAS. NCOWS strives for historical accuracy, and often members participate in historical enactments. SASS embraces anything portrayed on the silver screen, from authentic clothing to B-Western outfits; some even choose steampunk garb. (If you have enjoyed the *Wild Wild West* movie with Will Smith and Kevin Kline, you know what steampunk is.) While a shooter doesn't have to dress up, they do have to dress in simple Western style and use eye and ear protection.

The most important thing you should take away is this: before buying anything — guns, leather or clothing — attend a match or two to see what shooters are using. Those in the game quickly learn what works and what doesn't. Some, like myself, like to shoot in the Classic Cowboy category, which means we have to dress the part and shoot specific guns in specific calibers. Some like to dress the part of Roy Rogers, Hopalong Cassidy or Gene Autry, so they compete in B-Western. Still others like to shoot in a specific manner, such as Gunfighter, Duelist or Double Duelist. You decide how you want to play the game to have the most fun.

The Guns of CAS

While an authentic Colt Single Action Army is highly desirable, it has a price tag to match. Shooters find they can shoot just as well with the less expensive Uberti or Pietta reproductions. The hands-down favorite revolver in CAS is the Ruger Vaquero. It follows the tradition of the Colt SAA, but its internal design is much more robust and reliable.

Main match rifles must use a pistol caliber, the .38 Special being the most popular. The .45 Colt is next in popularity. There are exceptions for youth and physically challenged shooters allowing the .22 rimfire. Rifles in .30-30, .45-70 and similar are reserved for long-range matches only.

Rifles can vary from the Winchester '66 to a Marlin '94, from the 1860 Henry to the Winchester '92. Far and away, the most popular gun is one of the many Winchester '73 variations. *I strongly recommend avoiding any rifle without a side-loading gate.*

Almost any side-by-side shotgun made in the last 100 years will work for CAS, but most shooters use a coach gun with 20" barrels. Many models are available, but some are of low quality. Baikal shotguns are pop-

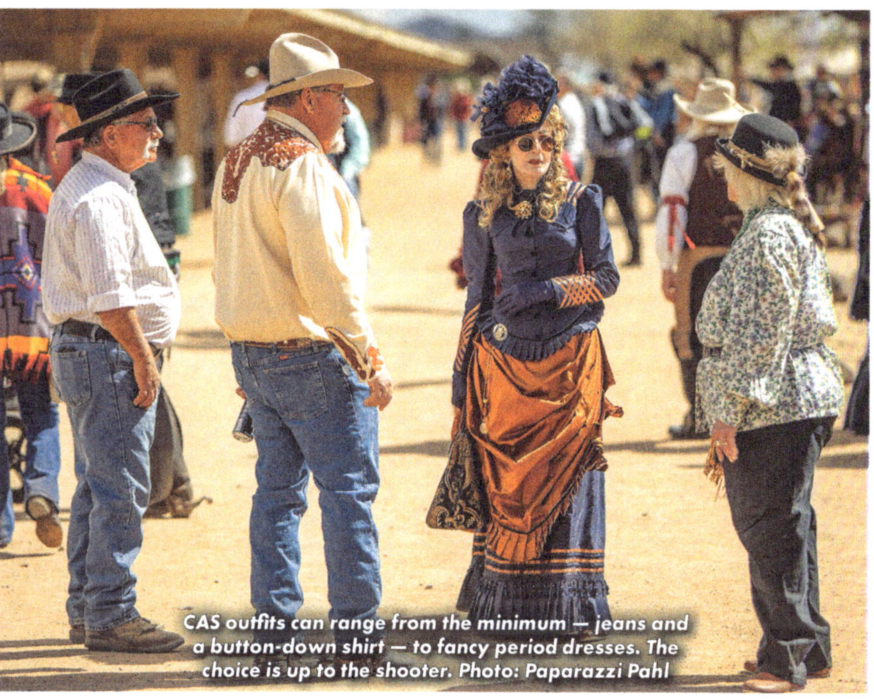

CAS outfits can range from the minimum — jeans and a button-down shirt — to fancy period dresses. The choice is up to the shooter. Photo: Paparazzi Pahl

ular, reliable and inexpensive. The single-trigger SKB is highly sought after by champions.

Terminator fans will be happy to know they can use the Winchester Model '87. Nothing says "cowboy" more than the '87 lever-action shotgun.

The Winchester Model 97 pump shotgun is very popular with CAS shooters. They were used by the U.S. military and produced into the 1950s. There are reproductions, but their quality ranges from excellent to poor.

Many new shooters go high-end on their rifles and pistols, then go cheap on their shotgun. A match is won or lost with the shotgun, so see what works for you and buy the best you can afford. It's genuinely a buy once, cry once situation.

Ammo and Feeding

With monthly matches consuming 120 rounds or more, it is wise to reload. Commerical CAS ammunition from Black Hills Ammunition and others are available, but costs can quickly exceed $100 per match. Reloading cuts those costs significantly. Casting bullets can reduce expenses even further.

Among shooters who attend a match every weekend, reloading is a must. Add shooting practice to increase speed and muscle memory, and the savings from reloading become clear.

Before you rush out and buy ammunition, realize CAS main match ammunition must be lead with no copper jackets and must be below 1,000 fps from a handgun. Shotgun ammunition must be lead shot. Low-recoil rounds are best.

There are many more aspects of CAS we don't have space to cover. One essential thing is the selection of an alias. Many use something catchy, a play on words, a character on the silver screen, someone in history or even honor a past family member. Once you pay your dues, the alias is yours as long as you are a member.

So, if you binge-watch *Gunsmoke*, wonder how Hopalong Cassidy snuck up on anyone using spurs, quote John Wayne, have all 100-plus Louis L'Amour novels or think *Tombstone* is the best movie ever made, you should check out SASS or NCOWS.

If we meet someday at a match, my alias is Cholla.

Jeremy D. Clough

NOT TO BE MISSED

Ruger's Birdshead Wrangler .22

By now, you've probably seen a bit about the Ruger Wrangler, which seems to be everywhere since its introduction in 2019. With a street price of just under $200, the little rimfire sixgun is no departure from Ruger's legacy of reasonable pricing and making innovative single-action revolvers.

Ruger's Sixgun Story

Ruger's story doesn't start with sixguns, but you can't tell it without them. After Colt announced in 1947 it would not be continuing to produce the Single Action Army, Bill Ruger's fertile mind looked beyond his successful Standard Model .22 pistol — now in its fifth iteration as the MkIV — to reintroducing the cowboy gun. The .22 caliber Single Six, along with the Corvette, made its debut in 1953 to the great fanfare you would expect of a country well and truly enamored of TV and movie Westerns.

The .357 Blackhawk followed it two years later, and on its heels a .44 Magnum version, a coup in which Bill Ruger didn't necessarily steal S&W's thunder about the cartridge they'd been secretly designing with Remington, but certainly appropriated a fair amount of it. A downsized companion piece to the Single Six, the Bearcat (which, like the Blackhawk, shared its namesake with a Stutz car) appeared in 1958. Perhaps this was intended symbolically, as while the Single Six was patterned after the Colt SAA, the Bearcat followed the lines of the 1858 Remington single action, down to its brass-colored trigger guard.

Intended to be less expensive to produce, the Bearcat did nothing to push out the Single Six, which added an alloy version in 1956, and had its drift-adjustable fixed sight replaced with a true adjustable in '64. In '73, it got the transfer bar safety, making it safe to carry fully loaded. A .22 Magnum version appeared, and development continued to today's line of six, seven, nine and 10-shot

small-caliber revolvers. As the options and refinement increased, so did the list price, which now hovers around $800, creating a prime market for a simpler, less expensive sixgun … which Ruger then filled with the Wrangler, now in a ridiculously cool birdshead version.

Similar in size to the birdshead Vaquero, the Wrangler shares its 3 ¾" barrel and general *je ne sais quoi*. Belligerence, if you prefer. In place of the finely finished steel of the Single Six, it has an aluminum frame and a trigger housing made from a zinc alloy that, while less expensive than steel, maintains its heft, with the gun weighing in at 1 lb., 11 oz.

Simplicity Drives Out Cost

While the unfluted cylinder (a throwback to the Bearcat and .44 Super

Ruger was built on .22s, including the Standard auto, now in its fifth version, the MkIV, and the Single Six, of which the birdshead Wrangler is only the latest derivation.

Ruger's birdshead version of its popular Wrangler .22 is near-perfectly proportioned. It handles well, shoots well and with a street price of a little over $200, you're not likely to find more gun for the money anywhere else.

The Wrangler is a simplified, much less expensive derivation of Ruger's venerable Single Six. The price reduction comes from changes in materials and finish, which is Cerakote rather than the usual polish and blued finish.

The Wrangler's rear sight is pure cowboy, a groove machined in the top strap of the receiver. Changes like this make the gun less expensive to produce than the Single Six, with its adjustable rear sight.

The front sight also follows the traditional lines with a rounded blade.

The rear sight is a traditional square notch found on the Vaquero and SAA before it. The bronze Cerakote gives the sights enough contrast to be easily picked up.

The birdshead Wrangler pairs nicely with this Ranger model holster from Mike "Doc" Barranti, initially made for a .45 Vaquero.

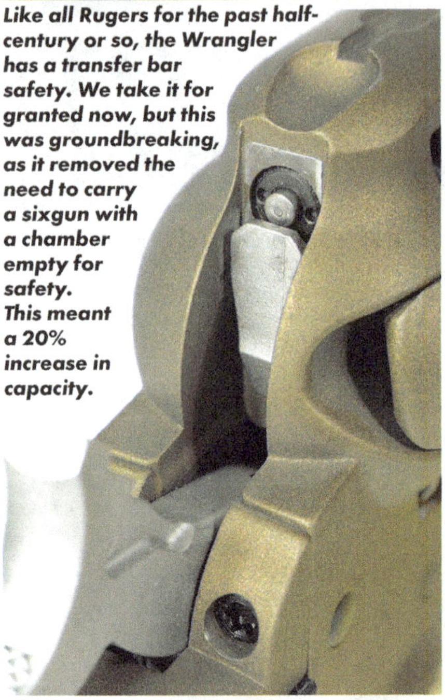

Like all Rugers for the past half-century or so, the Wrangler has a transfer bar safety. We take it for granted now, but this was groundbreaking, as it removed the need to carry a sixgun with a chamber empty for safety. This meant a 20% increase in capacity.

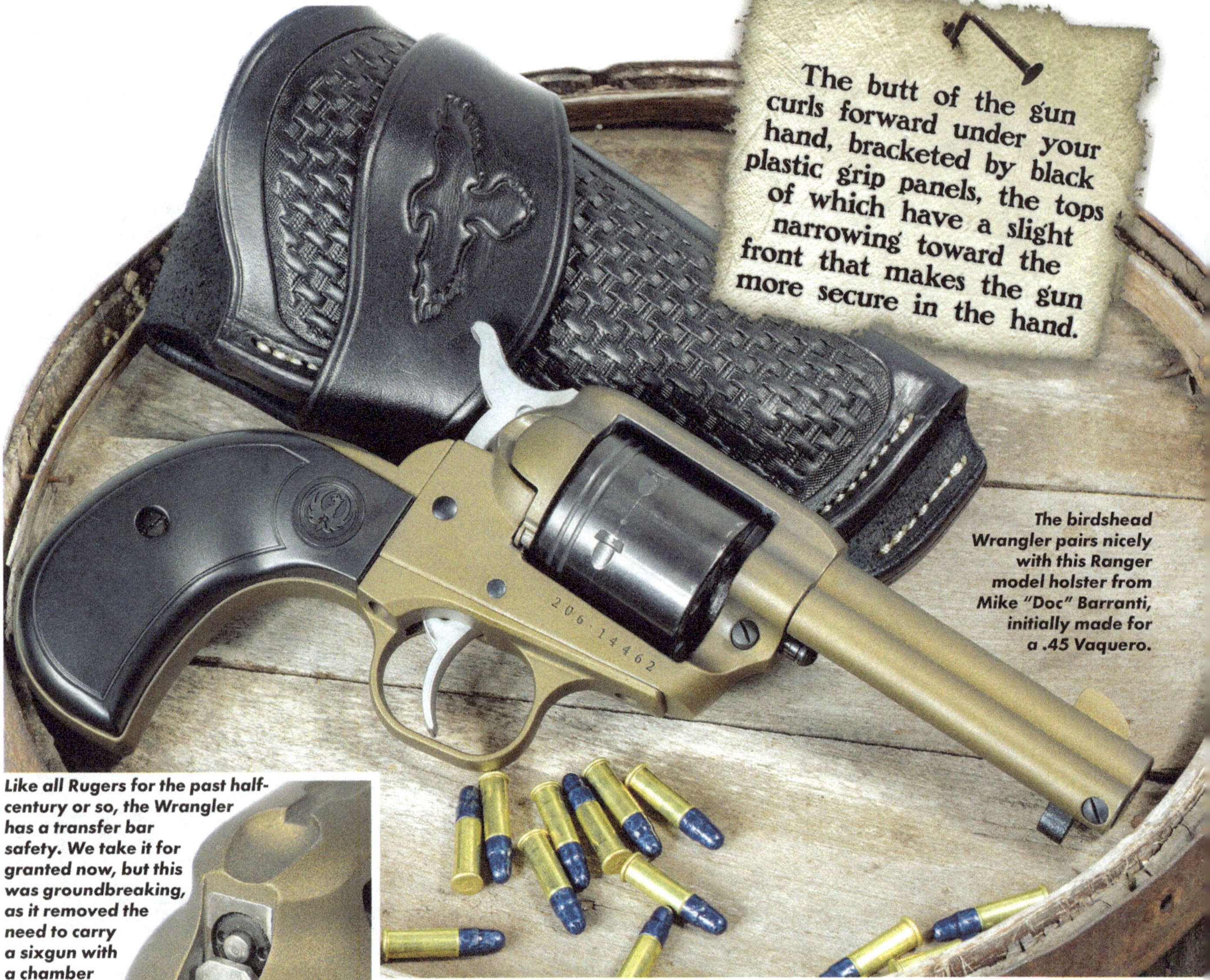

The short little head on the cylinder pin is part of how you get a long ejector stroke: The longer the head is, the less travel there is available for the ejector.

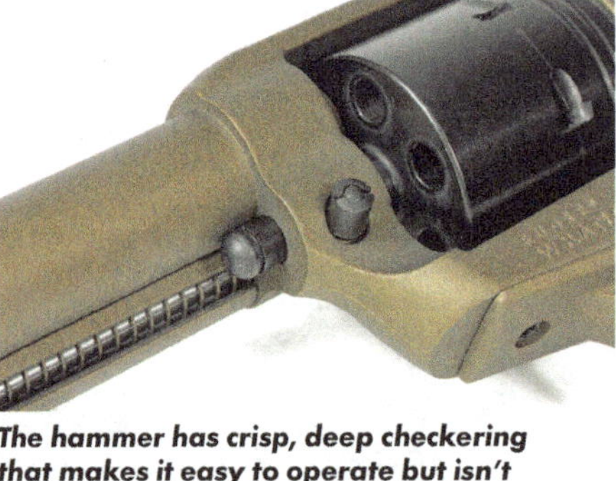

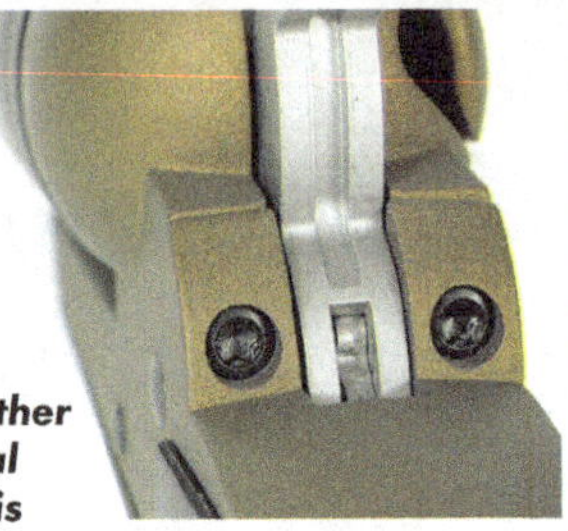

The hammer has crisp, deep checkering that makes it easy to operate but isn't sharp enough to abrade your thumb. Cocking the hammer with the off-hand is preferable, and this technique works well with the birdshead Wrangler.

The zinc alloy grip frame is attached to the aluminum receiver with Torx screws rather than traditional slot screws. This will be greatly appreciated by anyone who takes the gun apart, as they're much less likely to get burred up in the process.

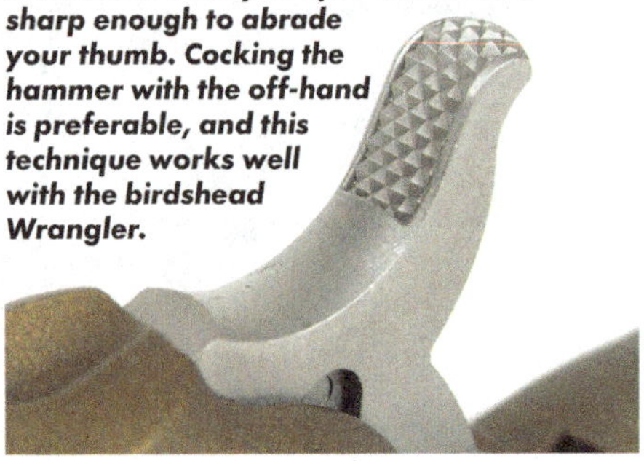

Blackhawk) appears to be blued, the rest of the gun is finished in Cerakote in a vast panoply of colors from black and silver to bronze, green and purple. This is more than aesthetics: Metal finishing takes time and production time costs money. Media blast followed by a spray-on finish, neither of which requires polishing, accounts for some of the cost savings and makes it easier to provide a consistent color with the different materials used in the gun.

The Wrangler is also a simpler gun. Gone are the adjustable sights, even the early dovetailed rear notch, in place of the traditional groove in the top strap and a rounded blade up front. Think Vaquero as opposed to Blackhawk and you've got it.

The test gun arrived finished in Burnt Bronze, with a black cylinder and silver trigger and hammer. The hammer has particularly crisp, deep checkering in it, which is positive enough to cock easily but not so sharp as to make you cringe when you do it. The usual legal notice has been thoughtfully placed on the bottom

Jeremy put over 650 rounds through the little Wrangler, a mix of bulk ammo from Winchester and Federal and premium rounds like Stingers and Silvertips. It hit 3" to 4" to the right but was accurate enough to hit steel out to 80 yards.

Jeremy was taught at Gunsite to "shoot one, load one." Take the gun in your left hand, using your thumb to roll the cylinder around and your index finger to pull the ejector rod back to eject the empty, then immediately replace it with a live cartridge using your right hand.

Despite the shortish 3 ¾" barrel, there's still enough room for an ejector rod long enough to easily kick out empties. The ejector rod head isn't sharp but do it enough, and it can get uncomfortable. On the other hand, a more rounded one wouldn't be as easy to use.

The distinctive feature of the birdshead Wrangler is its eponymous grip frame, which feels good and just looks cool. The top of the grip panels narrows toward the front, which helps the gun sit well in the hand.

To load, flip open the loading gate and insert a cartridge. There's no need to put the hammer at half cock — it doesn't have one — and the cylinder spins freely, so if you miss a chamber, there's no need to rotate it all the way back around.

of the barrel next to the ejector rod housing rather than proudly emblazoned on the top as it was on my first Vaquero. The butt of the gun curls forward under your hand, bracketed by black plastic grip panels, the tops of which have a slight narrowing toward the front that makes the gun more secure in the hand.

Slow and Steady

The vice of the single action is how long it takes to load and unload, but this is its virtue as well. It stretches out your ammo a bit further. More importantly, it makes you slow down and pay attention to what you're doing and avoid the temptation to just hose bullets at the target. With only six, you tend to pay attention to each one, making it useful as a teaching tool, or just for those of us who benefit from getting back to the basics of sight picture and trigger control. That's all of us, by the way.

That said, there's no reason not to be efficient in your gunhandling. I was taught at Gunsite to "shoot one, load one" with a single action, so one quick way to reload is to take the gun in your left hand, using your thumb to roll the cylinder around and your index finger to pull the ejector rod back to eject the empty, then immediately replace it with a live cartridge using your right hand. Since it's a better practice to have rounds back in the gun as quickly as possible, it's my preferred method, but you can also roll the cylinder with your thumb and rapidly plunge all six out with your right hand, then reload all six once the gun is empty.

For those of us used to bigger calibers, it can be a bit fiddly to get those little .22 LRs lined up correctly to go into the chambers — .45 Colts they ain't — and the chamber mouths seemed to have a bit of a sharp edge on the test gun. As I'm keeping this one, I'll likely use my Brownells chamfering tool to barely break that edge to make reloading a little smoother. There's no need to use half-cock to open the loading gate (the Wrangler doesn't even have a half-cock notch), as on earlier single-action designs, so just flip it open. Thankfully, the cylinder spins freely, rather than just in one direction, so if you miss a chamber, you can roll it back rather than having to go all the way around. Despite the shortish barrel, which means less room for an ejector rod, the rod is plenty long enough to clear empty brass. If you want to be particularly neat with your shooting, it's easy enough to stroke the empties out into the palm of the hand holding the gun.

Home on the Range

The trigger breaks at 4 lbs., 12 oz., as measured by my Lyman digital scale with noticeable creep, and while the traditional sighting groove can cause problems on some revolvers, especially highly polished stainless ones, the metallic bronze color of the sights creates a nice contrast, making it easy to see them.

I put over 650 rounds through the little Wrangler, a mix of bulk ammo from Winchester and Federal and premium rounds like Stingers and Silvertips. There was exactly one malfunction, a round that took two hits to go off, which basically just confirms I was shooting .22 ammo. While all the rounds I used hit about 3" to 4" to the right of point of aim, once I adjusted to that, it was easy to make good hits. My best 25-yard group, fired with rested hands, was with CCI's polymer-coated Clean-22, and measured about 1.65", more than acceptable for a gun that'll get mostly plinking duties.

It was particularly fun to shoot at steel: A pair of 4"x8" plates were there for the picking, just aim at the left edge and bang-ping, bang-ping, bang-shoot, bang-ping to your heart's content. I also used the Wrangler in a walkback exercise with a 14" round plate. Starting a little farther back than 25 yards, I shot until I got all six rounds in the cylinder on steel, then backed up and started again from the new distance. I made it to 80 yards, but at that range, I couldn't seem to do better than 4 or 5 rounds on steel.

Yes, I said 80 yards with a 3 ¾" fixed sighted .22. It'll do it if you will.

It's accurate and dead simple, and while I try not to enthuse too much in print, there are reasons you hear all of us at *Handgunner* raving about the Wrangler. As I mentioned earlier, I'll be buying this one, partially because I already have a birdshead Vaquero in .45, and it'll be a nice understudy gun, but also because it is just so much fun to shoot. The birdshead guns cost about a box of ammo more than the regular Wrangler, and for the price, it's hard to imagine where you can get more gun for the money.

For more info: Ruger.com, BarrantiLeather.com

Frank Jardim

HIGH-CAPACITY IN THE SIDE-BY-SIDE ERA

Chiappa's Replica 1887 Winchester Shotgun

The lever-action Model 1887 Winchester shotgun is often referred to as the first successful repeating shotgun, but it was by no means the first repeating shotgun. The four-shot Roper repeater was patented in 1866 and sold for a decade. The Spencer repeating pump-action (often called slide action) shotgun first appeared in 1884 with a sliding front grip (mounted around the magazine tube) and remains the archetype of all pump actions to this day. All of these shotguns had some commercial success, just nothing close to the popularity of the Winchester Model 1887.

The Model 1887 was the first American lever-action shotgun. Though it looks strange to our eyes, it was

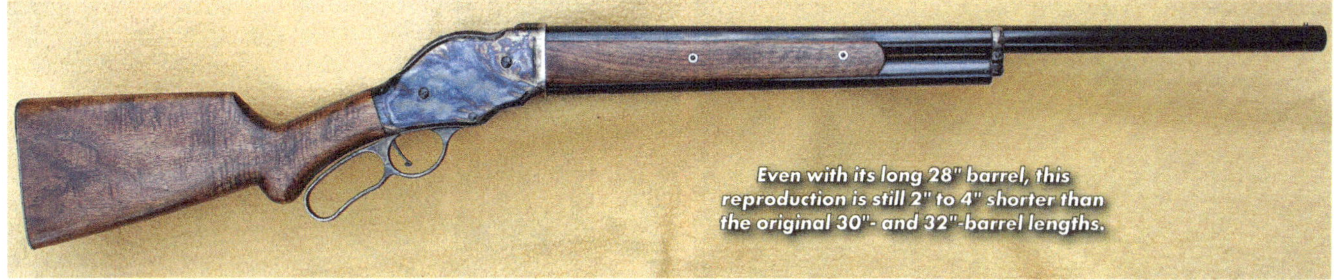

no weirder in its day than any of its contemporaries. By design, it resembled the excellent lever-action rifles Winchester built their reputation on. From a marketing standpoint, that was worth a lot. They sold 51,355 Model 1887 shotguns by 1901 in 12 and 10 gauge.

The Master's Hand

The weapon's success owes much to the ruggedness and simplicity of its design that were hallmarks of the man Winchester commissioned to create it. That man was John Browning. He wasn't wildly enthusiastic about the concept of a lever-action shotgun because he already had ideas for a slide action he believed was far superior. However, Winchester was a paying customer, and it was in Browning's business interest to make the shotgun his customer wanted. Browning designed a lever-action gun, specifically a lever-operated rolling block action, and sold Winchester the patent. Then he went off to do missionary work for the Mormon Church.

The first time he actually saw a production gun was on the shelf in a general store he happened to be walking by. When he finished his patents for his new slide-action shotgun, Winchester realized its merits and bought those too. That decision was the doom of the lever-action Model 1887. Winchester gradually phased the lever-action design out of production so as not to compete with itself. In 1901 they dropped the 12-gauge version and re-engineered the 10-gauge model to handle the new and more powerful smokeless powder cartridges destined to replace black powder. The Model 1901 ceased production in 1920 with another 13,500 units, so the sun set on the Model 1887.

A Unique Chiappa Creation

Renewed collector and shooter interest led Chiappa to reproduce this unique design in various forms, traditional and modern. Curiously, lever-action shotguns have had a limited renaissance recently in the form of .410-bore models made by Henry and Winchester, the latter based on the Model 94. Several Turkish-made lever-action 12-gauge models are now available from various importers like Landor and Black Aces, but they are nothing like the Model 1887. That gun is unique.

Hefty Firepower

When you first see an original Model 1887, the thing that grabs your attention is the long barrel and the height of the receiver in profile. It has a hefty appearance. The most common barrel lengths were the standard 30" and 32". Long barrels were needed to maximize the burn of the black powder for maximum velocity. Smokeless powder ammunition made those long barrels generally unnecessary, which is why you don't see them today. One aspect of the rolling-block action is it's significantly shorter than slide actions. A few inches less steel saved weight and length in the 1887, but it was still longer and heavier than the break-open action shotguns ubiquitous at the time.

By far, the most important features of the Model 1887 were its seven-round capacity (five in the magazine, one in the carrier and one in the chamber), the speed it could be fired effectively and it was about half the price of its closest competitor, the

Only the higher-grade Winchesters had color case-hardened receivers. Chiappa chose to go the high-grade route with this model. It is beautiful.

Chiappa greatly enhanced the versatility of this gun by threading the bore for modern screw-in chokes.

Spencer Repeating Shotgun. Only the slide-action Spencer, in its death throes as a company in 1887, could compare in terms of firepower, but the cheapest-grade Spencer cost $45 compared to $25 for the Winchester.

The Model 1887 was a more practical gun than the Spencer in several respects, which also helped its commercial success. The Winchester was simpler to make and operate. The motion needed to cycle the action on the Model 1887's lever action was less disruptive to aim than stroking the Spencer's slide action (and probably any slide action for that matter), which gave the Winchester the advantage for staying on target in rapid shooting. Both guns ejected from the top, but the Spencer's action blocked the shooter's sight line until the slide was pushed forward, further slowing down follow-up shots. Both were equally clumsy to load by modern standards. By the end of 1887, the first year the Winchester Model 1887 shotgun was produced, over 7,000 were sold. That was over twice the total sales of Spencer slide actions since production began in 1884!

Fit and Finish

The Chiappa reproduction Model 1887 is beautifully finished and wood-to-metal fit is excellent. The stocks on the one I examined for this article were a striking striped walnut. They were finished in a low-gloss sealant leaving the grain of the wood visible, so it looks like wood and not plastic. The receiver, lever, barrel band and buttplate are color case-hardened. The barrel, magazine and trigger are blued steel. Those familiar with the 1887 will notice the stylized Winchester logo is conspicuously absent from the left side of the receiver. It is evident the maker took care to avoid marking up this gun and spoiling its historic character. The only markings I could find were "Chiappa Firearms Italy 12-ga. 2 ¾" – 12/70" along the top of the barrel, the serial number laser engraved in the same spot Winchester did on the bottom of the receiver, the barely noticeable proof markings that are very discreetly applied to the lower left side of the receiver and to my surprise, a 1 ⅛" diameter "CF" logo in the middle of the smooth buttplate. I can forgive the logo. If I made a shotgun this fine, I'd want to put my name on it too.

Close examination of the major components showed they were cast and then machined and polished to final dimension. Unless you open the action and look at the inside of the lever, one might never notice this. I found only a few tiny imperfections in the polishing where the rough surface of the casting showed through. It did not detract from the overall impression of the gun.

Sighting

The 28" barrel model I tested had a nice brass front side bead 0.150" wide and came with three screw-in choke tubes and a wrench. The full choke measured 0.685", the modified choke was 0.701" and the cylinder was 0.734". They installed and came out with ease. Chiappa warns not to

The magazine tube held five 2 ¾" shells.

The front handguard treatment of the 1887 was minimalist, perhaps more for aesthetics than anything else.

The Winchester Model 1901 shotgun shown here was mechanically the same as the 1887 but was chambered in 10 gauge only and had a new hinged lever for great leverage when working the action.

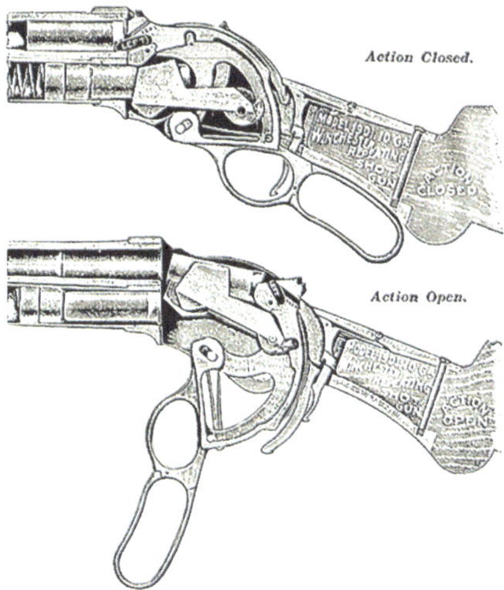

go crazy over-tightening them lest you end up getting them stuck. Also included were some mounting screws for a removable sling.

1887 Operation

The instruction manual is a must-read if you are not entirely familiar with this model. Don't be embarrassed about this because it includes just about everyone. The 1887 is a unique design and back in the olden times, there was a basic expectation people would exercise good common sense. Old technology can hurt you if you are not careful. For example, this model never had a safety other than a half cock notch on the hammer. The hammer's thumbpiece is pretty darn small. I would not recommend attempting to lower the hammer to the half-cock position over a loaded chamber. It wouldn't take much for it to slip from under your thumb despite the checkering Chiappa wisely cast into the surface.

Shooting the 1887 requires you to discard all your pump shotgun muscle memory and get into the lever-action mindset of the 19th century. It didn't take me long to get the hang of it. Despite its ungainly appearance, this gun is very fast. I loaded five shots in the magazine tube, one in the carrier and another in the chamber, for a total of seven shots. I got off seven aimed hits on water jugs in a bit less than seven seconds and I'm fairly ham-handed. A skilled hunter could bring home a lot more birds with this gun than a double barrel. Arizona Ranger Clarence Beatty was partial to a sawed-off 10 gauge '87, which he claimed to be able to shoot from the hip so fast it was like an automatic. He used it to break up ambushers and rioters.

Here, the carrier is down, and you can see the pivoting lever resting on the tip of the magazine follower. The end of that lever is what holds the shells in the magazine.

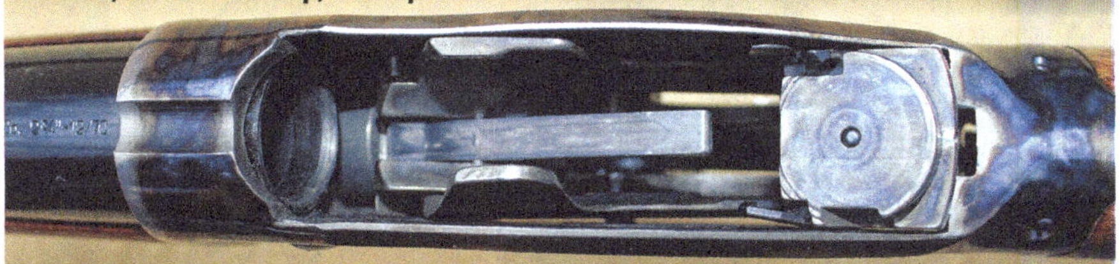

Here, the carrier is up, in the position it would be in to load a round in the chamber.

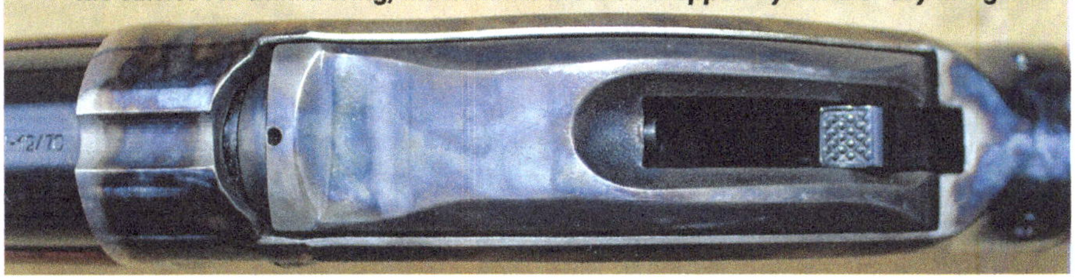

Here, the action is closed and the hammer cocked. To get a round from the magazine to the carrier for chambering, the hammer must be dropped by hand or dry firing.

The stock on this gun, which wasn't a special order, had beautiful striping in the wood. The steel buttplate isn't checkered like the original, but is one of the only places that the replica diverges.

The Chiappa reproduction Model 1887 is beautifully finished, and wood to metal fit is excellent. The stocks on the one I examined for this article were a striking striped walnut.

Like many Browning designs, a lot comes out of the 1887's action when you cycle it. It is a lever-operated rolling block.

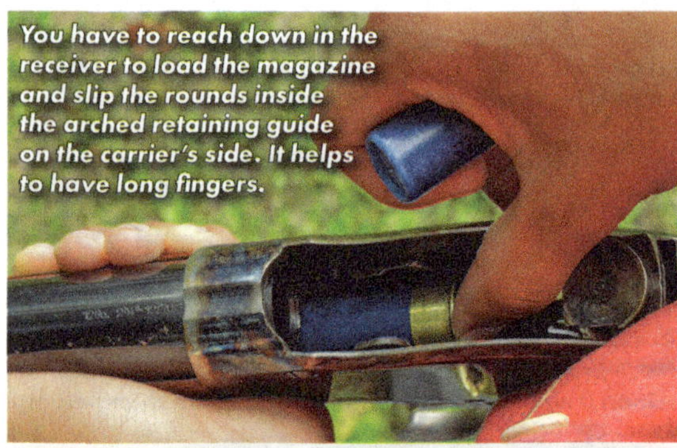

Probably to avoid trademark infringement, Chiappa did not attempt to reproduce the original marking on the tangs and the left side of the receiver.

The operation of the action out of the box was alright, but it got smoother the more I used it, and it was great fun to shoot. Like most lever actions, it works best when worked briskly. At 9 lbs., it requires some upper body strength to swing it around, but the weight does soak up a lot of the recoil.

Loading

Loading the 1887 takes a little more dexterity than a modern pump shotgun. You push the shells deep into the receiver from the top and then slide them forward with the tip of your thumb into the magazine tube by the top edge or their rim. The front edge of the pivoting carrier holds the shells in the magazine tube. This is why you need to push them

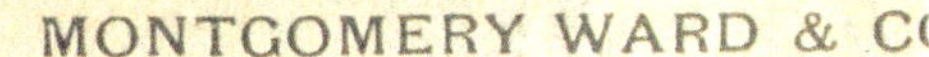

In 1895, Montgomery Ward advertised the Model 1887 for $16.88. At that time, Winchester was still competing with the Spencer Repeater, which was selling for about the same price since Francis Bannerman bought out and reorganized the company.

Remington is making Peter's Premium Blue paper hull shotshells again, and for at least a while, they can be had in boxes replicating the look of those from 100 years ago. Paper hull shells and 19th-century shotguns go hand-in-hand, as does a leather shell belt like this # 70 from Triple K. It is American made from American leather tanned in American tanneries.

Legendary lawman John Slaughter with what we could assume is his personal hunting Model 1887.

in by the uppermost edge of their rim. That way you don't accidentally depress the carrier, preventing it from catching and holding the bottom edge of the shell's rim … and ejecting the rounds you previously loaded! It helps to point the barrel downward while you load too.

I found I could load a round in the cartridge carrier and another in the chamber for a total of seven rounds. Even today, that's respectable fire-power. However, unlike a modern bottom-loading pump shotgun, the 1887's magazine is more complicated to top off if the shotgun is partially loaded. Every time you work the lever, another round pops from the magazine into the cartridge guides and pushes the empty shell being extracted from the chamber out of the top of the action. To load more shells into the magazine, you would need to first push the round in the guides back down and forward into the magazine tube before you could load any additional rounds. This was not a bad tradeoff for the firepower in an age of side-by-sides.

Legendary Arizona Sheriff John Slaughter was said to favor a short 12-gauge double barrel during his law enforcement career, but at least two photos show him armed with an 1887 just like this one. Chiappa has done a fine job in recapturing the character of this classic Old West repeater while discreetly improving it. This is the best replica of this model on the market right now and probably ever.

For more info: ChiappaFirearms.com, TripleK.com

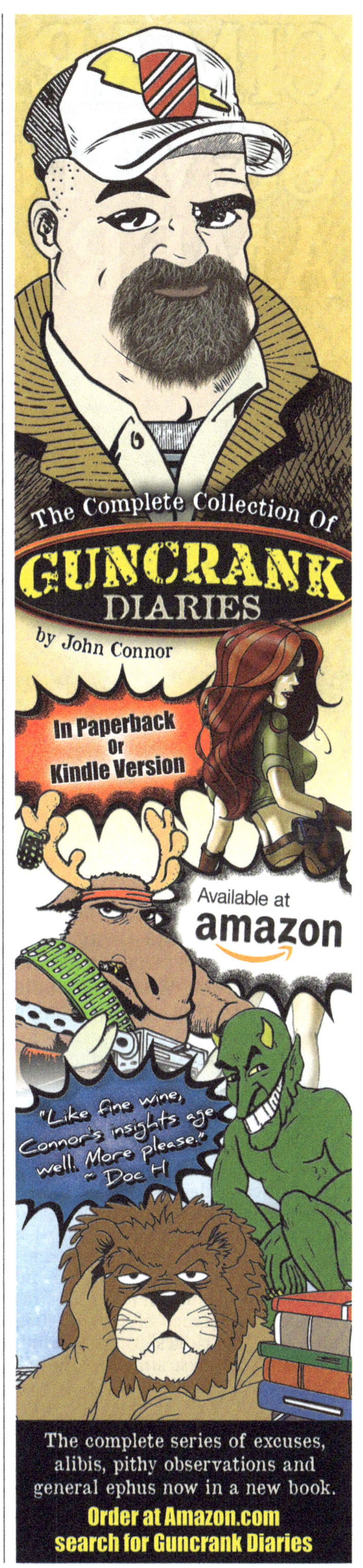

CIMARRON S&W NO. 3 AMERICAN

Roy Huntington
Photos: Rob Jones/The Imagesmith, LLC

Historically Accurate, Impeccably Crafted .45 Colt

The 8" barrel of the No. 3 lends a certain steadiness when aimed single-handed — as all proper pistols should be fired.

uick … The first big bore, cartridge-firing center-fire sixgun in the Old West. What gun would you think of? Why, the Colt Single Action of course.

And you'd be wrong, of course. Here's why.

History at S&W had them developing the No. 1 revolver in 1859 using the ground-breaking .22 Short RF cartridge. This was the first time a metallic cartridge was chambered in a bored-through cylinder and it was an instant hit. The idea of a .22 Short as a defensive gun seems quaint today, but think about it — no muzzle loading chores, fewer misfires and the convenience of easy loading and more "cartridges" right at hand. Thousands of these unique "upward tilting barrel" revolvers were carried in the Civil War as backup guns, also finding their ways into the coat pockets of countless civilians.

As time passed the public wanted a bigger caliber and eventually the No. 2 Army, a sort of biggie-sized No. 1, was developed chambered in .32 RF. It also had the tilting barrel feature.

But if you squint your eyes a bit, you can see the beginnings of the outlines of the No. 3 lurking in plain sight.

Then, in 1870, S&W introduced the No. 3 in .44 American and presto, Western history was destined to be changed. The U.S. Army awarded a contract to S&W for the gun, and Russia also bought some 41,000 chambered in what was called the ".44 Russian" to differentiate it from the .44 American. Sales were brisk. The No. 3 was eventually chambered in .44 Henry, .44-40, .32-44, .38-40 and .45 Schofield.

Army Changes

The various No. 3 Models can be confusing but if you think of them as being the same gun with very minor changes, it can calm the nerves somewhat. A big change involved the ones designed by Major George Schofield (there's the name) in 1875, consisting of changes he felt were needed to make it a more battlefield-worthy revolver. One change allowed a cavalryman to open the revolver with one hand and tilt the barrel by flipping it, ejecting the empties. Then a reload, and you're back in the fight. The standard No. 3 requires two hands to unlock and open the action.

The Army also wanted S&W to chamber the "Schofield" in .45 Colt but alas, the cylinder wasn't long enough for the full-size Colt cartridge. S&W instead offered a ".45 Schofield" (.45 S&W) cartridge — a shortened .45 Colt. But alas, with so many Colt SAA revolvers in use chambering the full-sized round, and the fact the Colts could shoot either, the Army eventually dropped the Schofield design from general issue use. It might interest you to know the wholesale price at the time was about $14, or $278 in today's money.

Many of these military guns were sold and became very popular with both the good guys and the bad guys, while the military still kept many in stock for backup issue. These were used in the Spanish-American War and the Philippine-American War.

Names like Jesse James, Bob Ford, John Wesley Hardin, Pat Garrett, Theodore Roosevelt, Virgil and Wyatt Earp, Billy the Kid and others carried No. 3 revolvers. We're pretty sure Wyatt and Virgil had No. 3s at "That Gunfight" in Tombstone. Wells Fargo and Com-

Cimarron lengthened the No. 3's cylinder a tad to accommodate the longer .45 Colt cartridge. Originals were .44 American and .44 Russian.

pany bought thousands of the surplus Schofields, cutting the 7" barrels to 5" and re-stamping them with "W.F. & C" turning them into instant collectibles today. But, alas, beware of fakes.

Believe it or not, production of the No. 3 variants continued until 1915. Before the advent of general sales of the Colt Single Action, the No. 3 was clearly the best game in town, which may explain its long legs.

Perhaps one of the biggest legacies of the No. 3 design is the fathering of the first big-bore DA sixgun for S&W, the famous top-break S&W .44 Double Action First Model. Able to be fired single or double action, the top-break design, external hammer, well-shaped grip and .44 Russian and .44-40 chambering introduced the first high-quality, big-bore DA revolver for the brand. The rest is history and we owe all of the famous S&W DA revolvers we love today to that gun. And perhaps, in due course, to the No. 3.

Cimarron

It simply gives me no end of genuine pleasure to talk about this fine company and the people behind it. Mike Harvey, owner and president, started with a modest gun store in Texas and during a turn in business, discovered the imports from Italy replicating famous Old West firearms. But Mike being Mike, his penchant for authenticity drove him to Italy where he met and befriended Aldo Uberti. Since the beginning, Mike and the team at Uberti worked hard to properly replicate the original design, feel and quality of the various classic Old West designs. It sounds easy but it wasn't.

Mike's personal collection of authentic Old West firearms paved the way for Uberti to bring in the first truly authentic Colt Model P (SAA). The Italian "clones" of the time (in the early 1980s) looked generally like a Colt Single Action, but there were serious flaws in cosmetics, design and engineering. The top straps were much too thick, almost twice those of an original Colt and the flats, curves and evidence of the delicate hand workmanship of the original Colt artisans was often lacking. While the Uberti team was excellent, they simply had no experience with the originals.

Mike fixed that. He made sure Uberti was able to reverse-engineer one of Mike's very early Colts down to the last pin. Since then, Mike has made countless trips to Italy to meet, work with and help them hone the many models Cimarron has introduced over the years — he even has his own desk at their factory!

Mike's passion for the old guns and keeping his products as authentic as possible essentially helped change the way Americans see the Italian guns. Mike's demand for high quality, authentic builds and correct finishes pushed other companies here and in Italy to up their game. I have no issue at all saying if it wasn't for Mike's personal commitment, today the rich round-up of high-quality imported guns like Cimarron's simply wouldn't exist. Mike doesn't just "buy what's there" and import it — he continues to work with a broad cross section of companies outside the U.S. to assure the various models he offers are all correct in every respect.

As proof, you only have to look at movies like the *True Grit* remake, *Unforgiven, Lonesome Dove, The Lone Ranger, Young Guns II* — and too many others to list — to see Cimarron gets it right. If you're like me, when I see a movie showing guns out of sync for the times,

CIMARRON
S&W NO. 3
AMERICAN

Minuscule sights mirror the originals and are part of the cylinder latch. The later Schofield based on the No. 3 had a redesigned latch enabling a galloping cavalry soldier to work the latch and eject empties with one hand.

it takes away from the whole experience. Cimarron's lineup makes it easy for history to repeat itself — correctly.

Our No. 3 American

Think of our test gun as a first generation No. 3 but with a couple of slight changes to accommodate the .45 Colt cartridge. Under Mike's close watch, Uberti has replicated the original as closely as possible while lengthening the cylinder to handle the longer .45 Colt round, as well as the original .44-40, .44 S&W and Russian and the .44 Special. From looking, I believe they didn't lengthen the cylinder "window" but shortened the bushing flange or ring at the front of the cylinder to fit inside.

Details include period correct color case hardening on the hammer, top latch and trigger guard. The original-style grip frame and accurate two-piece walnut grip is here too. You can also get one with correct markings for a military-issue version. The finish is a deep, rich bluing coming out more black and looking like minty originals I've seen. Nickel is also offered and was very popular in the day due to the black powder cartridges used and the tough life on the trail.

Barrel lengths are 8" (our test gun) and a very handy-to-tote 5" model. I wanted first-model authenticity so I asked for the longer barrel, but a shorter one may be in the cards too. I also think they're particularly handsome and fierce-looking with a 3.5" barrel. Mike, are you listening?

One of the nearly miraculous things Mike accomplished is to figure out ways to keep the myriad of mandated Italian proof marks out of sight, or at least as much as possible. Early imports were littered with the "approval" stamps from a dozen or more tests the revolvers had to pass in order to be approved for sale. I've seen those guns and it often looked like some kid got a metal stamp kit and went to work with crowns, swords, letters and numbers. Mike's methods to hide these hideous attacks on the glory of these designs pays dividends in personal enjoyment for us. When

The magic of the design is the fact it was not only the first large-bore centerfire cartridge revolver in the U.S., but it ejected the empties simultaneously, making loading fast and easy too.

you hold any Cimarron firearm you have to peer very hard in order to decide if what you're holding is a rare and wonderous original — or an authentic reproduction.

Sheer Delight

Shooting something like the No. 3 is the whole thing, isn't it? To hold it, cock it and touch it off is to relive a past still very much alive in our history, legends and just plain wishful thinking. The click of the hammer engaging the sear, the cold trigger against your finger, the heft lent by the long barrel and the easy rolling in your hand when the big bullet leaves the barrel — all grabs at the heart. If you don't feel it, I'm sorry for you.

This gun was never meant to shoot tiny groups on targets way out there. Although, even with the minuscule original-style sights — complete with sun glaring off them — I was able to coax 1.75" groups to appear at 25 yards. In all honesty, if I had better eyes and it had better sights, who knows what this amazing gun could

do? I had not planned on targeting this very much, mostly just wanging at steel, but this changes everything as they say. It's also all modern steel, so as long as you don't get silly, you could certainly load it with ammo suitable to protect your skin or to shoot a wily pig or three. But do carry it with five and then hammer down on an empty chamber!

Suffice to say, when this No. 3 sits on my desk, I feel like I need to pick it up, point it with a fierce scowl and cry out, "Unhand her, you ruffian, or I shall have to shoot!" No … really. You will too. I feel a new cowboy Slim Jim holster in my future. I live in Missouri, and, well, Jesse James "worked" here and loved his No. 3, and … and … and.

Call this a collaboration of American entrepreneurship striving for excellence and joining forces with talented gun builders from around the world. If you're smart, you'll also call one yours soon.

Cimarron-Firearms.com
Black-Hills.com

Safety first … carrying with an empty chamber under the hammer is the proper way for the No. 3 — just like the original.

Will Dabbs, MD

THE HOWDAH PISTOL

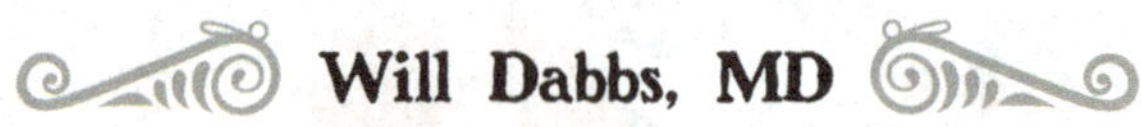

The howdah pistol was a curiously powerful 19th-century handgun.

This particular example is more than 150 years old and shows its age. The twin triggers and accompanying lockwork are not as reliable as was once the case.

When new, this old gun was nicely engraved. The years have taken a toll.

There is a nifty compartment in the butt for caps and patches. Will pulled a couple of century-old greasy patches out of the gun when he first cleaned it.

Ethnocentricity is the technical appellation. This is the characterization one's particular group or tribe is innately superior to some other. A corollary is the concept of American Exceptionalism. American Exceptionalism postulates the United States is inherently different from other, lesser nations.

These two interrelated concepts were once quite in vogue. We actually believed so strongly in ideas like Manifest Destiny that we seized the American West from its previous inhabitants by force of arms and the surgical application of genocide. I'm not here to debate the finer points or moral implications. Human beings are tribal. Failure to believe your tribe is the best embraces institutional weakness.

Over on this side of the pond, most can agree we Yanks have raised ethnocentricity to an art form. After all, we gifted the world with the microchip, the internet, the atomic bomb, the ThighMaster, silicone breast implants, woke-ism, Miley Cyrus and Paris Hilton. To the rest of the planet, you're welcome, by the way.

As it relates to our discussion today, folks of my generation raised on serialized Westerns and Louis L'Amour novels could be understandably forgiven for believing that wandering the untamed wilds subsistence hunting amidst massive, deadly predators is

This percussion howdah pistol features dual triggers and over-and-under matched barrels. It represented the apex in handheld firepower for its era.

The gun's ramrod is secured along the left side of the weapon.

Will has absolutely no idea what this mark is, but he thought it cool enough to photograph.

a uniquely American phenomenon. The graphic depiction of the desperate cowboy wielding a lever-action rifle to face down a hungry grizzly ultimately became an advertising trope that sold quite a few Winchesters. However, in other parts of the world, hard men were also making their way into strange lands red in tooth and claw. One of those rugged spaces was the Indian subcontinent.

Hunting dangerous game has held an allure since man first fashioned a stone-tipped spear and sallied forth for mastodon. Implicit in this practice is the quickening of one's manhood and the necessity of obtaining comestibles. Where American frontiersmen hunted from horseback, their counterparts in India frequently stalked massive tigers for sport atop elephants. Engaging in close-quarters battle with an enraged Bengal tiger weighing a quarter ton required some specialized tools. If the tiger successfully ascended the pachyderm, these well-heeled gentlemen hunters often availed themselves of a howdah pistol. Those early howdahs were massive handheld howitzers designed to offer maximum firepower in a stubby, maneuverable, man-portable package.

War Story

Michael Carsten was a man in search of a war. Spawning from old English money, Carsten embarked for the subcontinent in 1853 in the service of the East India Company (EIC). Initially chartered in 1600 as the "Governor and Company of Merchants of London Trading into the East-Indies," by the early 19th century, the EIC accounted for fully half the world's trade. Michael Carsten's mission was to spread the Pax Britannia to the savages. What Carsten and the rest of England failed to appreciate was that most of the savages would sooner determine their own governance.

Prior to his departure, Carsten's wealthy aunt bestowed upon him a most unique pistol. Made in Belgium, this massive double-barrel hand cannon was colloquially referred to as a howdah. Carsten had a custom holster maker craft a belt rig for his colossal handgun and wore it regularly on his many forays around the EIC holdings.

By the mid-1850s, the British East India Company maintained one of the largest private armies in human history: 50,000 British troops, along with some 300,000 Indian sepoys, served the company ensign. In 1857 the situation in India had reached a boiling point. Curiously, the final straw stemmed from the way the British packaged ammunition for the issue Enfield Pattern 1853 rifled muskets of the day.

These advanced weapons fired Minie balls that came in prepackaged paper cartridges greased with either beef fat or pork lard. To fire these rounds, the soldier had to bite the end off of the paper cartridge prior to loading. As Hindus venerated cows and Muslims

The Pedersoli 20-gauge howdah is a fun range toy for guys like Will who don't take themselves too seriously. You could conceivably hunt deer or pigs with it if you really felt froggy.

despised pigs, these greased cartridges were viewed as offensive to most of India's sundry religions. Eventually, being British in India constituted a fairly hazardous undertaking. Some 6,000 Englishmen ultimately perished in the resulting Indian Rebellion.

Though he did bag three tigers from atop an elephant, Carsten never had need of his howdah for its intended purpose. However, just having the big pistol perched on his hip projected an air of authority that sometimes defused a potentially unpleasant situation before it became truly pear-shaped. By the time Carsten returned to London, he was introspective, wise and tired; the very personification of declining Victorian-era British power projection.

Origin Story

The term *howdah* literally translates to "bed carried by a camel." Also spelled *houdah* or *hawdaj*, the word became most intimately associated with the same contrivance mounted atop an elephant. This removable carriage strapped to a pachyderm accommodated mounted hunters.

Well-heeled tiger hunters in India would use beaters to drive tigers forward until they could be engaged with rifles from the relative safety of the howdah. However, sometimes the tiger failed to get the memo. For those times when an enraged 500-lb. jungle predator leapt up on the elephant to torment the tormentors, they desired something stubbier and more maneuverable than the full-sized sporting rifles of the day.

A variety of 19th century European gunmakers produced an array of large-bore multi-barrel handguns for this purpose. Early versions were fired by either flintlock or percussion mechanisms. Later versions accepted cased ammunition and were

Tiger hunting from elephants was a popular pursuit for wealthy expats on the Indian subcontinent in the mid-1800s.

frequently little more than cut-down versions of corresponding rifles. They all yielded brutal recoil, but offered inimitable firepower in the close fight.

A Peculiar Example

I found this particular howdah for sale on GunBroker.com. It is coincidentally the same model gun used in the epic 1996 movie *The Ghost and the Darkness. The Ghost and the Darkness* was a piece of historical fiction that chronicled the hunt for the man-eaters of Tsavo, a pair of maneless male African lions that ultimately accounted for as many as 135 human victims.

The big-bore howdah pistol was the purview of well-heeled English big-game hunters of the 19th century. Though they were likely seldom used for their intended purpose, these howdahs nonetheless offered inimitable close-range firepower. As an aside, Will's 13-year-old buddy, William, owned the hat and bandoleer, so it seemed appropriate to have him model the gear. His dad offered the mustache to add an air of sophistication.

The howdah in the movie has a curious folding knife blade installed underneath the weapon but seems otherwise identical to mine.

This howdah is a muzzleloading over-and-under design with twin triggers driving separate hammers. The bore is roughly 28 gauge or half an inch. The finish is badly worn, but the gun originally sported some nice engraving. The ramrod is retained along the left side of the barrel assembly, and there is a cool little compartment in the grip to hold caps or patches.

This howdah is expectedly heavy, but would indeed offer some serious firepower at a time when close-range firepower was tough to come by. Reloading would have been typically laborious, but the gun's ample payload would give pause to predators whether they crept about on two legs or four. The gun would also invariably make a statement strapped to the hip of a swashbuckling 19th-century Englishman questing for adventure.

An Odd Encounter

The British-made Lancaster pistol was likely the most popular howdah. While I have found several references to the howdah and its use in Europe, Africa and India, I have never seen anything in print concerning the operational use of such a weapon in North America. However, I did actually find a physical example among a group of Civil War-era arms being sold at an antique store many years ago.

I was a married medical student with three children, so I had absolutely no discretionary cash. My family and I were exploring Vicksburg, Miss., and soaking up its inimitable Civil War history. After exploring the local military park and the superb old courthouse museum, we wandered downtown into an antique store. This establishment offered a wide array of Civil War-era artifacts along with several period firearms. Among them was a stubby over-and-under muzzleloading howdah pistol similar to this one.

The price was $400, and I was indeed enraptured. However, short of hocking a kidney, there was just no way I could swing that purchase. The proprietor explained the gun came from a local collection along with several other vintage pieces. He stated it should have indeed been field-used during the Civil War.

I don't recall any specific markings. I couldn't afford a cell phone at the time, either, so I couldn't take any pictures. I had searched for a howdah of my own ever since. In retrospect, maybe I would have been better off without the kidney. Why else might God have given me a spare?

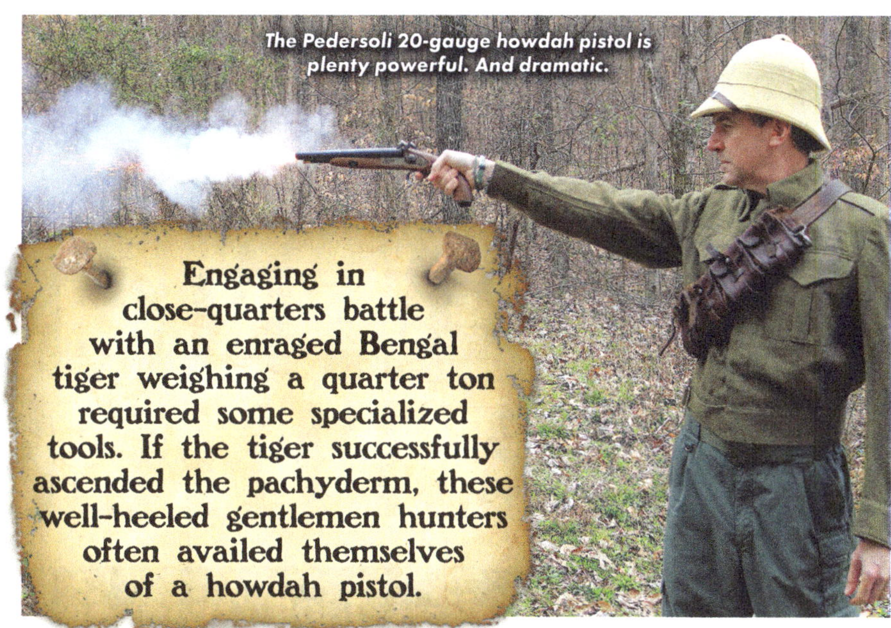

The Pedersoli 20-gauge howdah pistol is plenty powerful. And dramatic.

Engaging in close-quarters battle with an enraged Bengal tiger weighing a quarter ton required some specialized tools. If the tiger successfully ascended the pachyderm, these well-heeled gentlemen hunters often availed themselves of a howdah pistol.

Denouement

The howdah pistol was a curious footnote in the pantheon of 19th-century working guns. Bulky, heavy, slow to reload and undeniably mean, the howdah nonetheless offered peace of mind in the dark places where death could come snarling out of the tall grass with no notice. Nowadays, Pedersoli offers side-by-side modern reproduction howdahs with either flintlock or caplock firing mechanisms you can safely shoot. These guns are available in .50, .58 and 20 gauge from Dixie Gun Works.

This deep into the Information Age, the big cats have been radically culled in the wild. Today we have much more to fear from human predators than the furry sort. However, a vintage howdah pistol still adds an extra layer of cool to even the most seasoned gun collection. It hearkens back to the days when a level head, a sure eye and an implacable resolve were what kept a man alive in a world awash in proper peril. Makes me wistfully nostalgic just thinking about it.

For more info: DixieGunWorks.com

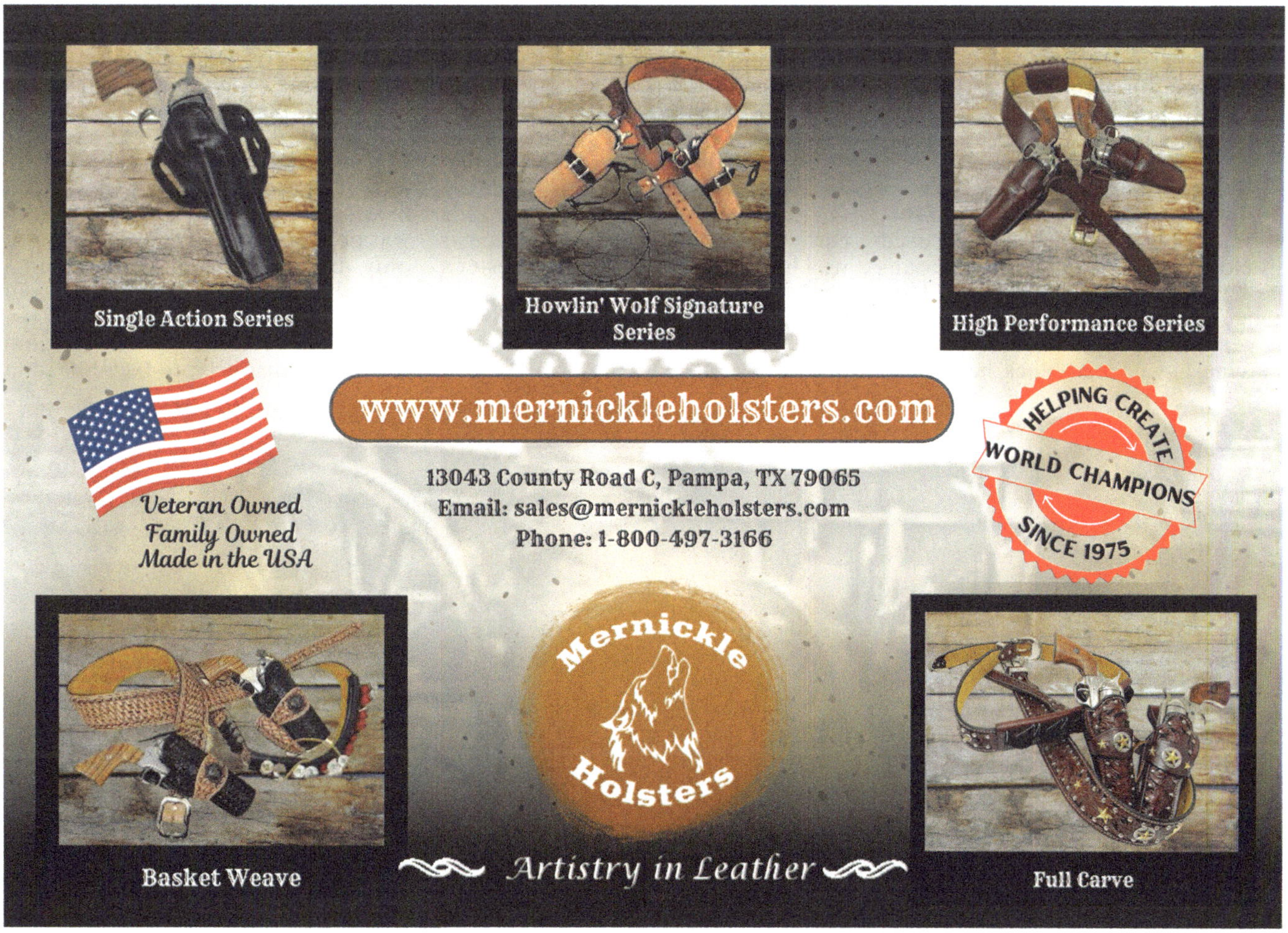
Single Action Series
Howlin' Wolf Signature Series
High Performance Series
www.mernickleholsters.com
Helping Create World Champions Since 1975
Veteran Owned
Family Owned
Made in the USA
13043 County Road C, Pampa, TX 79065
Email: sales@mernickleholsters.com
Phone: 1-800-497-3166
Mernickle Holsters
Basket Weave
Artistry in Leather
Full Carve

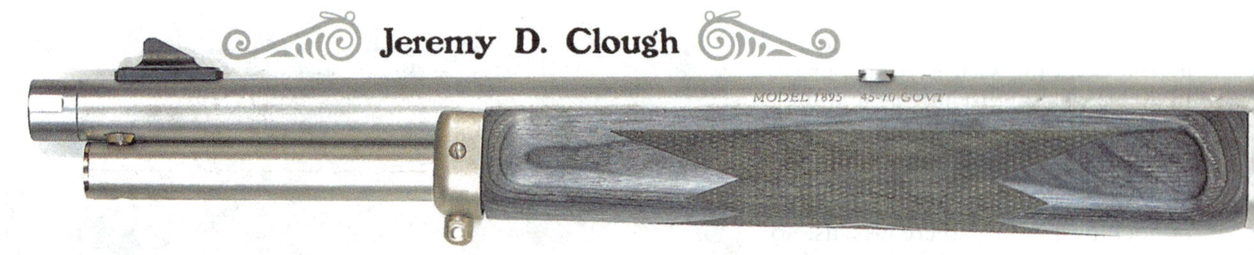

Jeremy D. Clough

THE TICKET FOR THICKETS

My introduction to short-barrel lever guns was over 20 years ago, shortly after Marlin announced its ported 18½" Guide Gun in .45/70. Someone showed up with one at the Forest Service range in Tennessee where I was shooting, and no one was prepared for its ferocity. We were in awe. One poor sap who hadn't bothered to bring ear protection started stuffing cigarette butts in his ears.

Short, powerful rifles to be used in close quarters against large, dangerous game were not a new idea. They remain important today and can also have some application for self-defense. Having twice faced black bears with a large-caliber Ruger revolver in my hand, I would have felt much better doing it with a big-bore rifle — but we're getting ahead of ourselves.

Marlin's Story

The original Guide Gun, like the newly introduced Trapper version, was based on an improved version of Marlin's 1895 lever gun. While most of us think of Winchester as the gun that "Won the West," it wasn't alone. Marlin's history goes back to 1881, when it introduced its first lever-action rifle. Available in large calibers, including .45/70, it didn't beat the Henry or earlier Winchesters to market, but it was five years ahead of Winchester's Browning-designed 1886. Its successor, the 1895, also came in .45/70, .45/90 and other heavy calibers. It was produced until 1917, during which time Marlin was producing machine guns in support of the U.S. war effort.

A later version introduced in the early '70s — the one we know now — was based on a modified version of the 336 action, a pattern Marlin had followed a decade earlier when it upgraded that action to take the potent .444 Marlin. A pistol-grip version of the 1895 (which I prefer to the straight-grip style) came in 1980 and a crossbolt safety three years later.

A Comfortable Home

Once the oldest family-owned firearms company in the U.S., Marlin was purchased by Remington in 2007, only to be sold again after Remington's bankruptcy. They landed in a soft place: Now owned by Ruger, Marlin has retained its character and remains a distinct product line, but

The Ruger-made Marlin Trapper .45/70 retains everything good about the earlier Marlin Guide Gun in an even more compact package. For those going into harm's way with big animals in small places, it'll get it done.

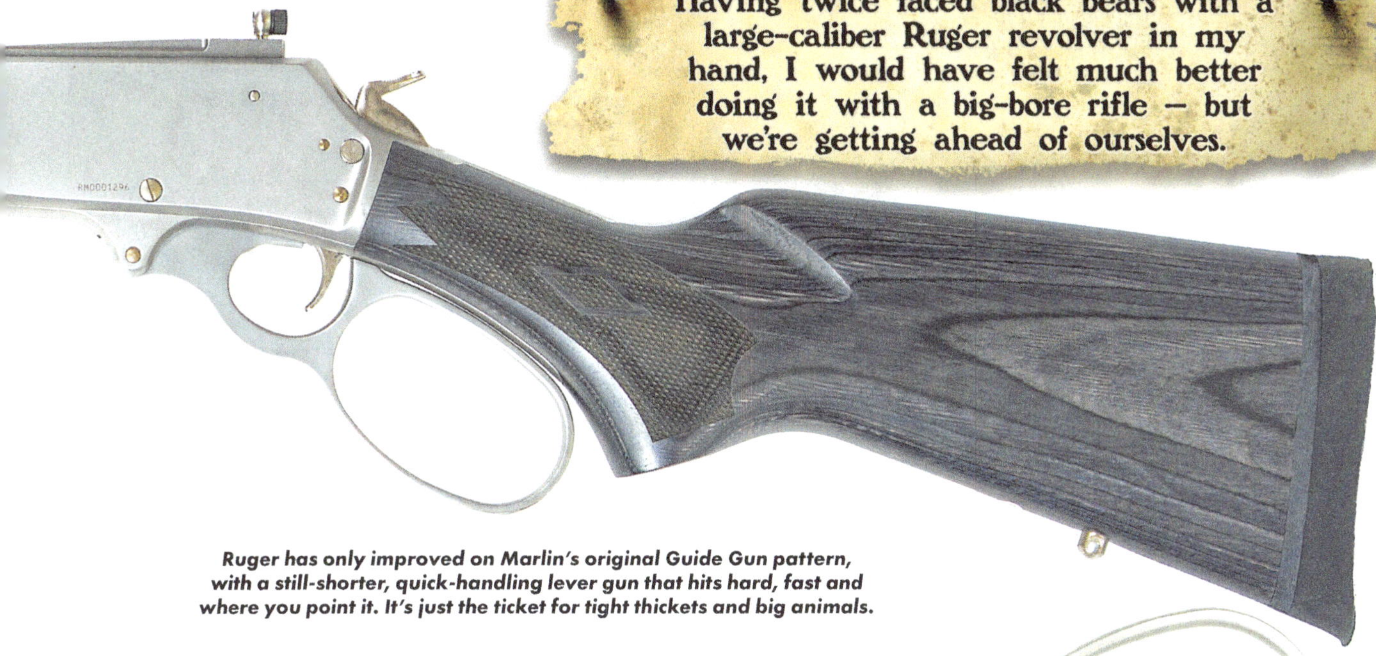

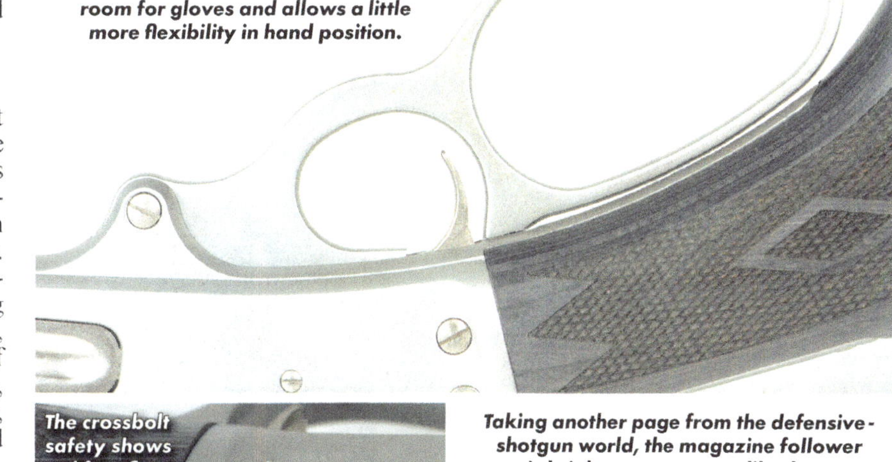

Ruger has only improved on Marlin's original Guide Gun pattern, with a still-shorter, quick-handling lever gun that hits hard, fast and where you point it. It's just the ticket for tight thickets and big animals.

The big loop lever allows plenty of room for gloves and allows a little more flexibility in hand position.

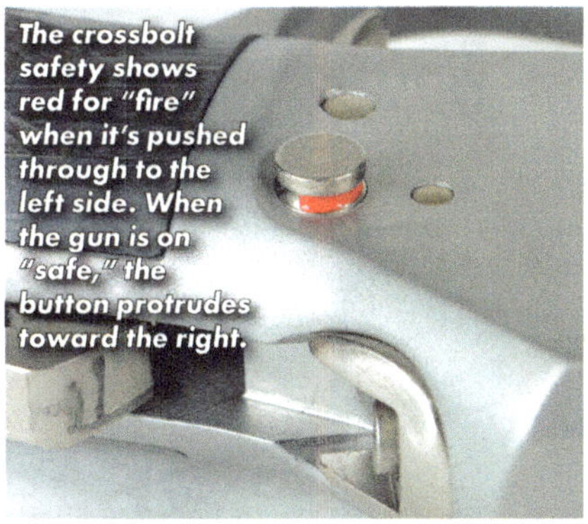

is now made with Ruger's advanced manufacturing capabilities.

Marlin SBL

After a lull in production, the first Ruger-made Marlin introduced was the 1895 SBL. Barely over 3' long with its 19" barrel, the SBL is a vision in polished stainless and grey laminate, with its pistol-grip stock and big loop lever. My lever gun tastes run to the traditional, but this is one good-looking firearm: The classic lines remain, with a Picatinny rail on the top of the receiver (Marlins eject to the side, long appreciated by those using optics), ghost ring sights and a muzzle threaded at $^{11}/_{16}$ x 24. The bolt is nickel-plated, with spiral grooves that give debris a place to go without sacrificing bearing surface. The Marlin horse-and-rider logo is laser engraved on the bottom of the pistol grip, as well as the Marlin bull's-eye logo, which is changed from black-and-white to red-and-white, not unlike the change Ruger made to its own logo several years ago.

I spent some time with the SBL at Gunsite earlier this year and was duly impressed. It was comfortable to shoot, and despite the ghost ring sights — designed to be fast, not precise — it hit. Running the Scrambler rifle course, a multi-station course where you shoot at steel targets out to beyond 100 yards from several different positions, I had no problem hitting the longer targets.

Marlin Trapper

The Trapper differs but little from the SBL: still weather-resistant stainless, but the forged receiver and shorter cold hammer-forged barrel

The crossbolt safety shows red for "fire" when it's pushed through to the left side. When the gun is on "safe," the button protrudes toward the right.

Taking another page from the defensive-shotgun world, the magazine follower is bright orange to readily show whether or not the tube is loaded.

Ruger kept Marlin logos such as the horse-and-rider logo, laser engraved in the bottom of the pistol grip.

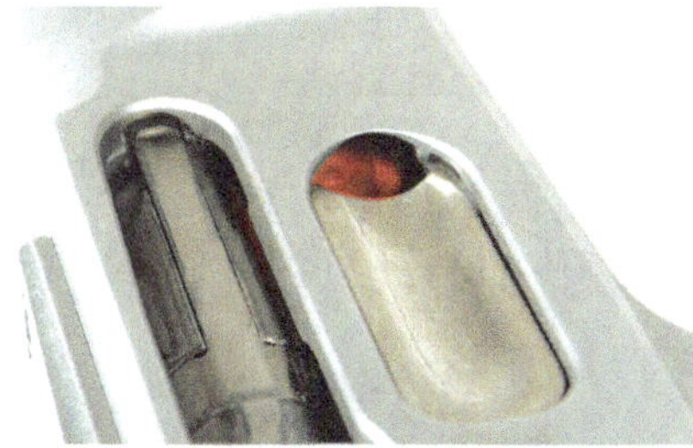

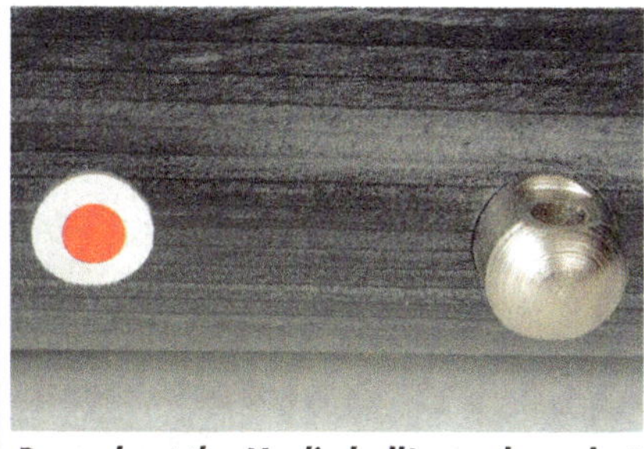

Ruger kept the Marlin bull's-eye logo, but changed it from black-and-white to red-and-white, not unlike the change Ruger made to its own logo several years ago.

Full up, the Trapper holds 5+1 rounds of .45/70, which should be plenty for average bears.

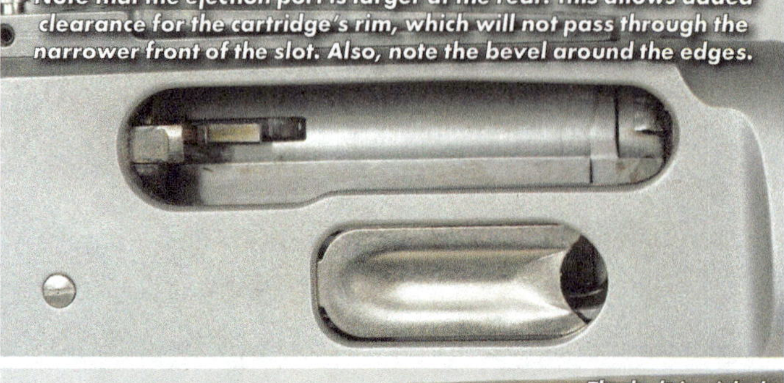

Note that the ejection port is larger at the rear. This allows added clearance for the cartridge's rim, which will not pass through the narrower front of the slot. Also, note the bevel around the edges.

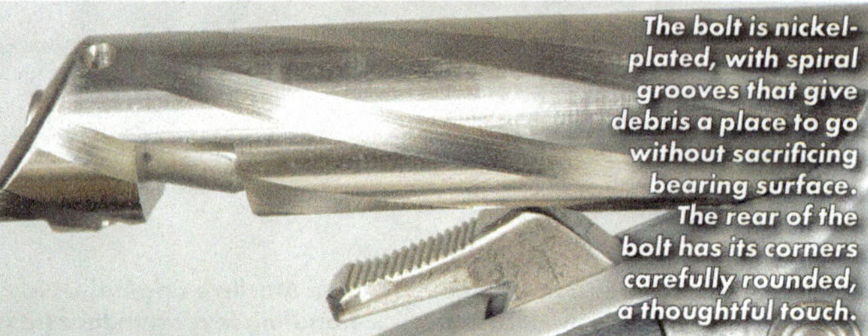

The bolt is nickel-plated, with spiral grooves that give debris a place to go without sacrificing bearing surface. The rear of the bolt has its corners carefully rounded, a thoughtful touch.

The Trapper uses a Skinner rear ghost ring sight.

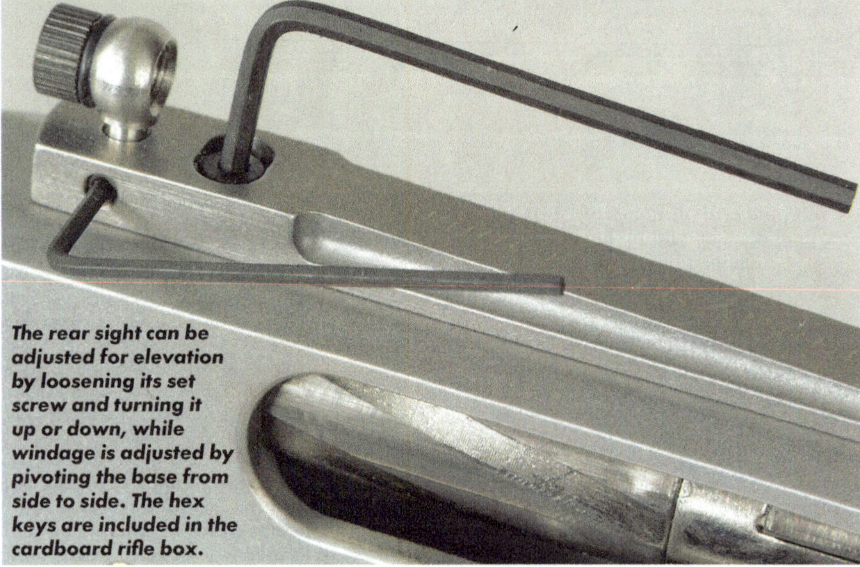

The rear sight can be adjusted for elevation by loosening its set screw and turning it up or down, while windage is adjusted by pivoting the base from side to side. The hex keys are included in the cardboard rifle box.

have a bead-blasted finish instead of polished. And instead of a rail, the rear sight is a Skinner ghost ring mounted on a post, while the front is a bold ramp-type with a white stripe, somewhat similar to the FN MkIII Hi-Power front sight.

The rear sight, which sits at the back of the receiver rather than being dovetailed into the barrel — the slot is still there on the Trapper, just with a filler block in it — is adjustable by loosening a hex-head set screw on the right side of the base and rotating the sight to raise or lower it. Should the large ghost ring rear be too large for you, replacement apertures are available from Skinner in sizes from 0.040" to 0.155" for $11 each ($50 if you want all five sizes to experiment with) or an adjustable insert ranging from 0.022" to 0.156".

Short-Sighted

One of the distinctives of shorter firearms, which probably accounts for some of the popularity of little 1911s, is that a longer sight radius tends to emphasize any slight variance in sight picture, while a shorter radius makes it harder to see those. Think about how much the front end wanders around on a revolver with a 6" barrel versus how rock-solid the sight picture looks on a J-Frame. The variance and wobble are still there with a short barrel, it's just harder to see and adjust for it. This means shorter guns, even when there's no difference in mechanical accuracy, are often harder to shoot well.

No doubt, this comes into play with the Trapper, whose 16" barrel is the minimum legal length without needing a tax stamp. However, the longer sight radius resulting from having the rear sight on the back of

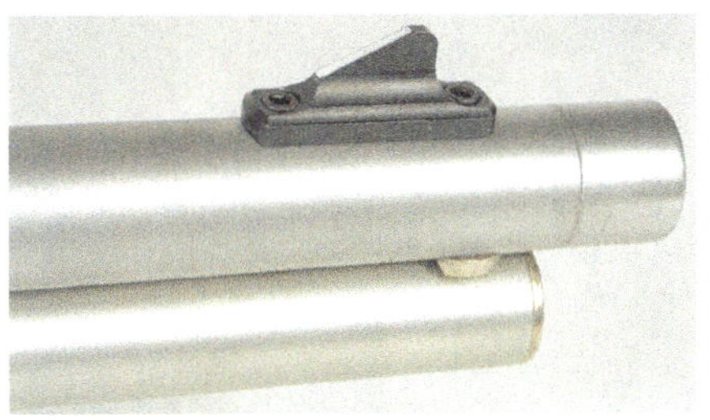

The Trapper's front sight is a bold, rounded front blade with an angled white stripe, not unlike that on an FN MkIII Hi-Power.

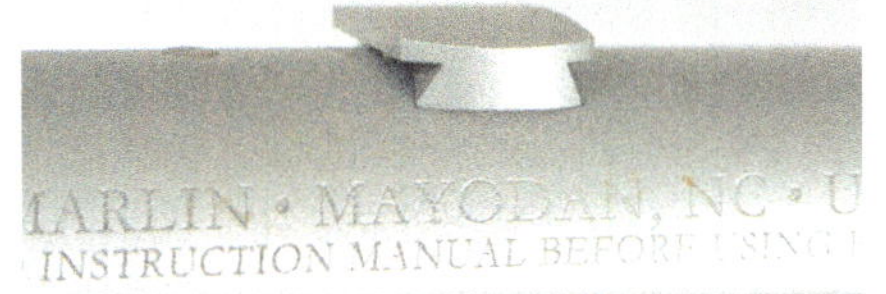

If you want to add a traditional barrel-mounted sight, have at it: The slot is there. But it'll cost you about half the gun's sight radius.

The sort of animal that needs this kind of medicine will be big enough and close enough that hitting is not likely to be the problem. Hitting fast, yes, and it's what ghost ring sights are for: The rim nearly disappears, and you put that big front post in the middle of what ails you.

the receiver helps: It's actually longer than the radius on my express-sighted .375 H&H. And let us keep in mind what the Trapper is for. The sort of animal that needs this kind of medicine is going to be big enough and close enough that hitting is not likely to be the problem. Hitting fast, yes, and it's what ghost ring sights are for. The rim nearly disappears, and you put that big front post in the middle of what ails you. If you need more precision, the 1895 SBL is probably a better choice, or mix and match apertures until you find the mix that best balances your needs for speed and accuracy. If you later decide to add a scope, the Trapper helpfully comes with an offset hammer spur.

Compact ... at a Price

That short barrel is a godsend for brush and thick cover. I've followed trails through laurel thickets where there was barely enough room to get through without turning my shoulders sideways, and always the opportunity of a black bear around the next unseen corner. I would not want to try to swing a full-size, scoped hunting rifle through those clawing branches in a hurry.

As with the sighting, though, there are other drawbacks to a 16" barrel, and some are ballistic. Shooting handloads assembled with 300-grain cast lead bullets over a charge of IMR 4227 through the Trapper side-by-side with my late 1800s era Winchester '86, they lost nearly 250 fps on average compared to the 26" barrel of the Winchester (1,660 versus 1,909). Factory Winchester 300-grain semi-jacketed hollowpoints and handloads assembled with Hodgdon Varget and the same 300-grain cast bullets had velocities from the Trapper of 1,606 and 1,473, respectively.

The thick recoil pad works well and makes the Trapper's recoil easy to manage. It's far better than the steel buttplates on earlier .45/70 rifles.

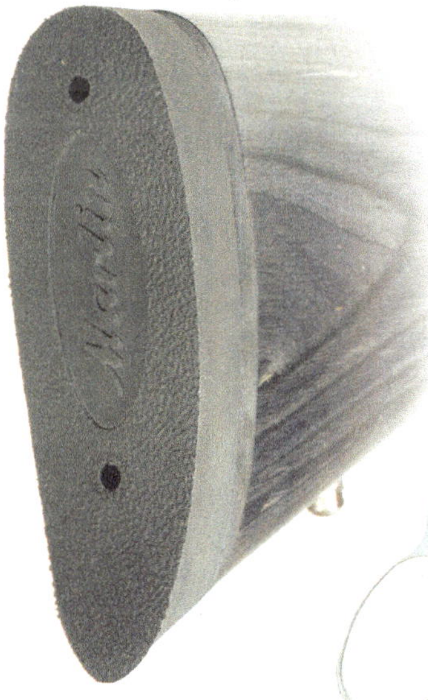

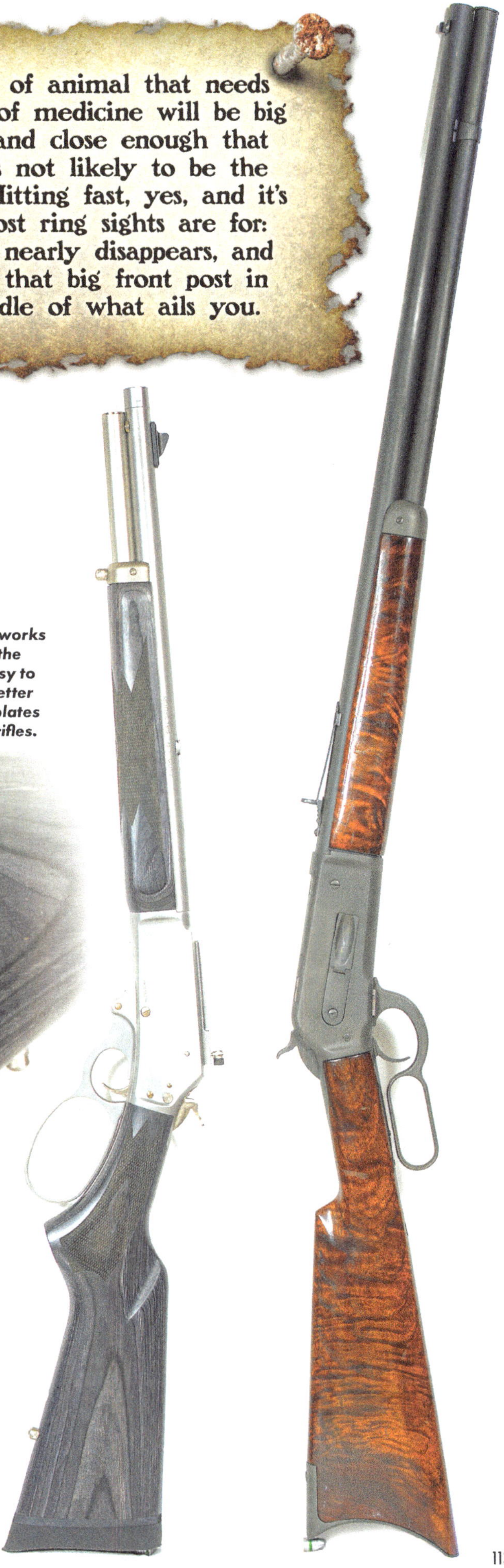

Jeremy running the 1895 SBL at Gunsite. Express sights and all, he had no trouble hitting targets to 100 yards and beyond.

An advantage the lever gun shares with pump shotguns is the ability to "road load" the chamber without first loading the tube. Open the action, drop a round in and pull the lever home. You're good to go.

The muzzle is threaded at ¹¹/₁₆ x 24 for the addition of a muzzlebrake or suppressor.

A brake may be nice, but not necessary, while heavy .45/70 bullets at subsonic speed through a can is next-level awesome.

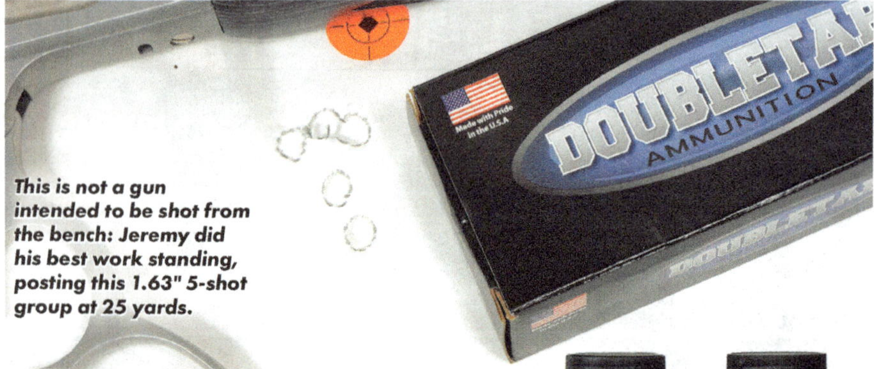
This is not a gun intended to be shot from the bench: Jeremy did his best work standing, posting this 1.63" 5-shot group at 25 yards.

Jeremy assembled .45/70 handloads using RCBS dies, Rock Chucker press and Chargemaster Lite powder measure. Components were virgin Starline brass and grain cast bullets over charges of IMR 4227 and Varget. IMR produced substantially higher velocities.

The Trapper consumed over 200 rounds of full power .45/70, including 40 rounds of (L-R) Winchester 300-grain semi-jacketed hollowpoint, 100 rounds of 300-grain cast bullet handloads and 90 rounds of DoubleTap loads in 300- and 405-grain variants. The 405 is a true thumper.

DoubleTap provided 100 rounds: 40 rounds of its lead-free 300-grain hollowpoint and 60 of its 405-grain hardcast solid. The 300 came out at a manageable 1,509 fps. The 405 makes an even more compelling point, as the added mass and sectional density will give deeper penetration than a 300 and averaged an eye-opening 1,654 fps. While not unmanageable, you won't want to shoot too many at one time. With the mag empty, it kicks hard enough you can actually feel the mag spring vibrate when the shot breaks. Even with the lighter bullet, 6+1 rounds of 300 grainers is pretty fearsome, and while you may find some of the bruiser revolver rounds that deliver similar power, they're much harder to handle at speed than the Trapper.

Range Work

I shot over 220 rounds through the Trapper during the test, most of it at 25 yards. There are guns intended only to shoot tiny little groups, and guns intended to be shot from the bench, and this is neither. While I did shoot it from the bench (punishing because of the lack of recoil control), and from prone (worse because it hits your collarbone), I did my best work standing. At 25 yards, standing unsupported, I was able to post a best 5-shot group of 1.63" and 2.95" when shooting as fast as I could run the lever and acquire a reasonable sight picture. Fifty yards opened it up to 3.78". It hit low as it came out of the box, but three turns up of the rear sight solved this.

One characteristic of the lever gun, shared by the pump shotgun, is the speed of reloading the chamber. When the magazine tube runs dry, you can "road load" the gun by jacking open the bolt, dropping a cartridge in and bringing the lever back home instead of single loading the tube and cycling the action. It won't fill up the gun, but it gets you back into action fast.

Boom

And now for the elephant in the room. Yes, it does kick. However, the thick, soft recoil pad does an excellent job of taming recoil, and it's not at all unmanageable, nor is it liable to injure you unless you do something foolish. When I started shooting hard-kicking rifles, I weighed about 170 lbs. Now, at 5'10" and 215 lbs., a little added bulk helps absorb the recoil, as does better technique. Hang on to the well-checkered forend and lean into the gun, taking care to keep your hand away from the sling swivel if shooting from the bench and take your time pressing the trigger, so you don't jerk it in anticipation of recoil.

The trigger breaks with a very subtle two-stage feel at an ounce under 6 lbs. on my Lyman digital scale. The action smoothed out a little with use, though a couple of times, it took a little extra pressure to make sure I had the lever seated all the way down before firing. I had one mag full where the feeding was a little sticky, something likely ammo related.

I saw two malfunctions, both the result of operator error. The first was in the first 10 rounds, the gun fired when another shooter apparently did not fully seat a cartridge in the mag tube before cycling the lever, and the second was my fault. In an attempt to

What it's for: Jeremy put six rounds into under 3" at 25 yards, shooting as fast as he could run the lever and acquire a sight picture.

keep brass out of the tall grass at the range, I got in the habit of rolling the rifle hard to the right as I jacked the lever, so the brass would eject straight down, apparently doing so hard enough to make the bullet end of the next cartridge pivot toward the ejection port and out of alignment with the chamber. There were no other problems of any kind.

Ruger has only improved on Marlin's original Guide Gun pattern, with a still-shorter, quick-handling lever gun that hits hard, fast and where you point it. I'd take it into a thicket anytime.

For more info: DoubleTapAmmo.com, MarlinFirearms.com, Ruger.com, SkinnerSights.com

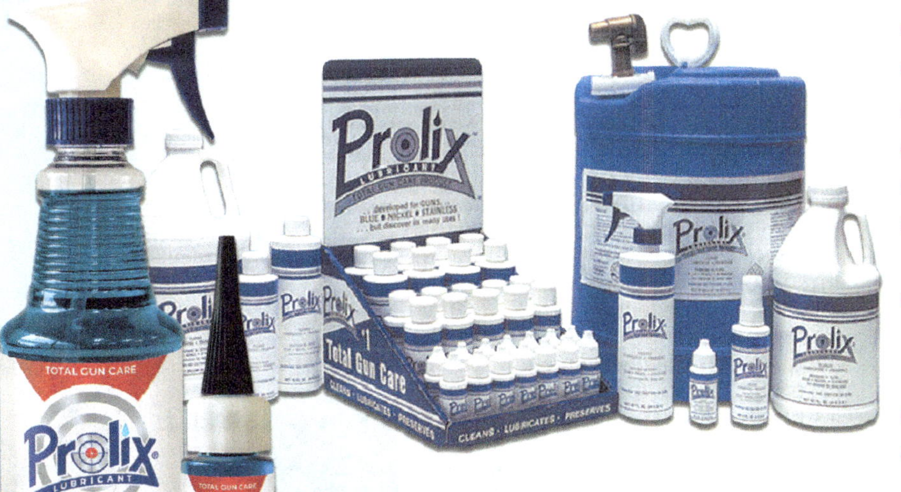

Frank Jardim

THE ORIGINAL ASSAULT RIFLE

Testing the Uberti Replica 1860 Henry Rifle

When it came to practical firepower, the 1860 Henry repeating rifle set the bar high when it hit the market at the start of the American Civil War. The familiar profile of this lever action shows its direct ancestry to the Winchester Model 1866 and 1873. Those models made Winchester Repeating Arms Company a financial success and a household name by dominating what we would today call the personal-defense market in the American West through the turn of the 19th century.

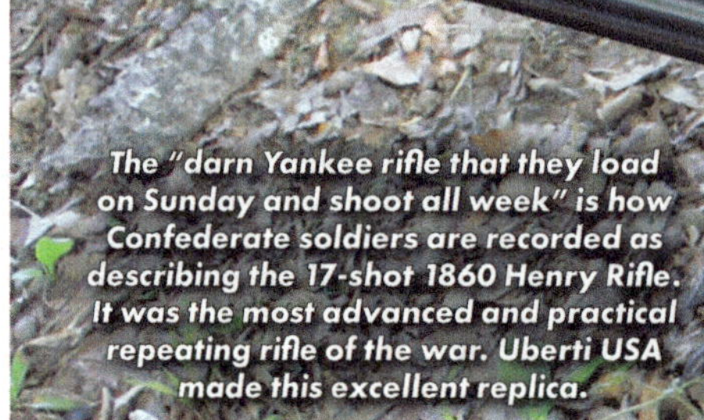

The "darn Yankee rifle that they load on Sunday and shoot all week" is how Confederate soldiers are recorded as describing the 17-shot 1860 Henry Rifle. It was the most advanced and practical repeating rifle of the war. Uberti USA made this excellent replica.

When the Henry appeared in 1860, single-shot muzzleloaders were the norm in America. The Henry and its few repeating peers were looked on by many as just clever novelties. Before the Civil War, entrepreneur Oliver Winchester concluded the firepower of repeating rifles would make single shots obsolete for military and self-defense use. He invested in the new Volcanic Repeating Arms Company in 1855 and became its president in 1856.

Swing and a Miss

The company went bankrupt in 1857. Rather than poor management, the failure lay in the product's shortcomings. The mechanical engineering of the lever action, tubular magazine-fed Volcanic owed much to the contributions of Horace Smith and Daniel Wesson. That much was good. However, the Volcanic was handicapped by its peculiar self-contained caseless cartridge with the powder inside the bullet's hollow base. The cartridge had many drawbacks, the most obvious being its power being limited by the tiny amount of space available for the propellant charge.

Henry's Roots

Though the Volcanic venture was a financial failure, Oliver Winchester saw its ingenious toggle-link lever-action had great merit. In 1857, Winchester created and became the lead investor in the New Haven Arms Company and hired Benjamin Tyler Henry to be his plant superintendent in 1858. Realizing no repeater could succeed without an adequate self-contained metallic cased cartridge, the company first developed a suitably powerful .44-caliber rimfire and then designed a rifle around it. Henry's role was so important Winchester named the new rifle after him and patented it in 1860.

Load on Sunday ... Shoot All Week

At a time when the military forces of the major world powers relied on single-shot, muzzleloading rifled

muskets, the new 1860 Henry had a 15-round magazine and a total capacity of 17 rounds with a round loaded in the chamber and the carrier. A trained soldier could fire a muzzleloader three times in a minute. A ham-handed recruit could reliably fire 17 rounds from the Henry in as many seconds.

Accurate by the day's standards, it was equipped with a folding ladder rear sight graduated to 1,000 yards. Army tests showed it could keep 100% of its shots inside a 25" circle at 500 yards and a 48" circle at 1,000.

Bullet weights were either 200 or 216 grains over 26 to 28 grains of black powder, giving it a muzzle velocity of 1,125 feet per second and muzzle energy of 568 ft. lbs. This falls between today's .44 Special and .44-40 WCF of the same bullet weight; however, based on my tests, I suspect the .44 Henry's specifications were slightly inflated. Even if the Henry was at least as powerful as the 1860 Army Colt pistol, I wonder how much energy the projectile had left at 200 yards, much less either of the outlandish Army test ranges. In any case, what the cartridge lacked in long-range energy, the rifle made up for in sheer firepower. Oliver Winchester had high hopes of marketing the Henry to the Union Army.

Army Bureaucracy

The Henry turned out to be too advanced for the hidebound leadership in the U.S. Army Ordnance Department to realize its merits; only 1,731 were purchased by the federal government for $63,943 (about $50 each). Another 8,732 were bought by individuals and state regiments like the 66th and 7th Illinois and the 97th Indiana.

Though military sales were ultimately disappointing, battlefield reports of the Henry's performance were highly favorable. The Henry could lay down an unprecedented volume of accurate fire, and Confederate soldiers facing it in battle called it "that darn Yankee rifle that they load on Sunday and shoot all week."

Capacity Over Clout

Compared to the charge and projectile used in the standard riflemusket of the era, the .44 Henry was a pipsqueak, and the rifle had no provision for a bayonet or even a front handguard to protect the shooter from burns. Those factors alone probably ensured it would never be selected for general issue to troops,

The toggle action of the Henry had its origin in the Volcanic Arms Company repeater (above). Oliver Winchester was deeply involved in both the Volcanic and New Haven Arms Company before founding the company bearing his name. The patent drawing for the Henry shows its toggle action and magazine system, but the critical breakthrough was its new rimfire .44 Henry metallic cartridge (right).

This view of the bottom of the receiver shows the Italian proof marks along the opening for the carrier.

When the Henry appeared in 1860, single-shot muzzleloaders were the norm in America. The Henry and its few repeating peers were looked on by many as just clever novelties.

Like the original, there is a trapdoor in the buttplate for a cleaning rod.

but its firepower and reliability warranted wider distribution than it got.

Divorce

Henry production ceased in 1866 with a total run of about 14,000 rifles. After the war, Winchester and Henry had a falling out and parted ways. If anything was apparent from Winchester's experience marketing the Henry during the Civil War, it was that the civilian market was more receptive to new technology than the military. Oliver Winchester immediately formed a new company, the Winchester Repeating Arms Company and hired Nelson King as his superintendent with the task of improving the Henry rifle.

The substitution of a lightweight, stand-alone, sheet metal tubular magazine, the addition of a front handguard and a patented side-loading gate known as the "King's Improvement" turned the Henry into the 1866 Winchester "Yellow Boy" and marked the beginning of Oliver Winchester's real commercial success as an arms maker. The Henry was a good rifle, but the Winchester 1866 was a much better rifle that fired the same cartridge. It is primarily due to the popularity of 1866 Winchester that .44 Henry rimfire ammunition remained in production up to World War II.

A Modern "Henry" Rifle

Shooting an original Henry is nearly impossible today unless you are willing to spend a small fortune competing with ammunition collectors for vintage cartridges at least 80 years old and of uncertain reliability. Fortunately, Uberti USA makes a fine replica chambered in either .45 Colt or .44-40 WCF.

The magazine is loaded from the front by pulling back the follower finger toward the muzzle to activate a release latch allowing rotation of the front 5" of the magazine and opening the tube.

Laser engraved on the upper tang in an authentic font is *"MOD. 1860 HENRY"*. Also, *"A. UBERTI-ITALY"* is laser engraved discreetly under the lever. The Henry had no safety other than a half-cock notch on the hammer.

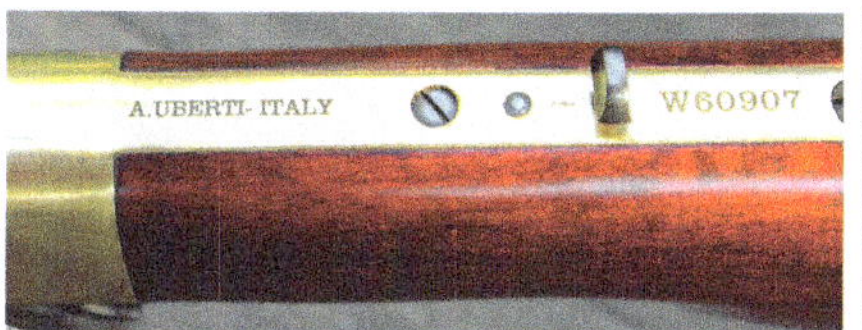

Uberti concealed its maker's marks beneath the lever. The serial number is marked on the lower tang.

Caliber:	.44-40 WCF or .45 Colt
Barrel Length:	24 ¼"
OAL:	43 ⅛"
Weight:	9.5 lbs.
Stock:	Walnut
Sights:	Patridge rear with elevation ladder, stainless front blade
Finish:	Blued, case-hardened (polished brass or color case-hardened steel frame available)
Capacity:	13-round magazine
MSRP:	$1,529

The example I tested was beautifully made with a dark blue finish on the barrel and trigger, case-hardened lever and hammer and a bright polished brass frame and buttplate. The latter had a functioning trap that would have originally contained a four-piece cleaning rod. The straight-grained walnut buttstock was attractively finished and sealed but not overdone. While the finish was thick enough, I couldn't see the texture of the grain; the stock still looked like wood. The Uberti Henry has the pointy crescent buttplate and lever hook of later production rifles that saw service in the Civil War. Because of the greater cartridge length, the replica only holds 13 rounds in the magazine instead of 15. The 24" octagonal barrel is rifled 1:16 twist for .45 Colt and 1:20 twist in .44-40 caliber. Parts fit and finish were excellent.

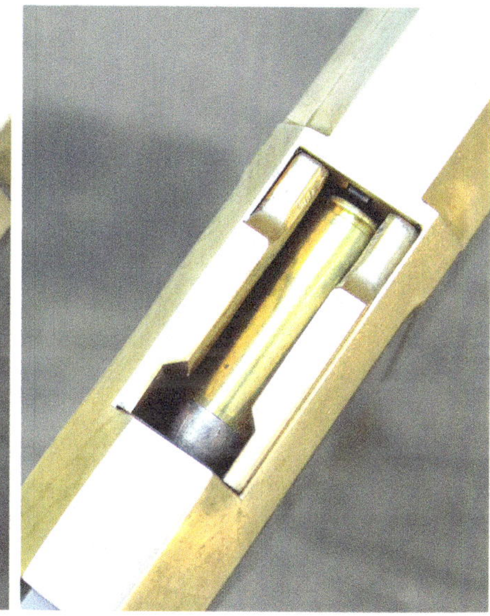

This series of photos shows how the fresh cartridge is pushed into the carrier by the magazine spring, lifted to the mouth of the chamber by lowering the lever and then driven forward and locked in battery by the bolt when the lever is closed.

Magazine Design

Just like the original, the replica Henry's barrel and magazine tube are milled out of a single bar of steel. The Henry was a heavy rifle for its size. The replica weighs in at 9 lbs., 6 oz., about 1.75 lbs. heavier than a comparably barreled Winchester 1873. The Henry's unique tubular magazine runs underneath the barrel in the conventional way, but it loads from the front. This is done by pulling the brass finger of the magazine follower all the way forward against spring pressure until it clears the rear of the 5" rotating sleeve on the front of the barrel. When you push the follower all the way up, it pushes out the sleeve latch on the very tip of the sleeve tube and allows the front of the barrel to rotate to the right. It is a clever, if unnecessarily complicated, design.

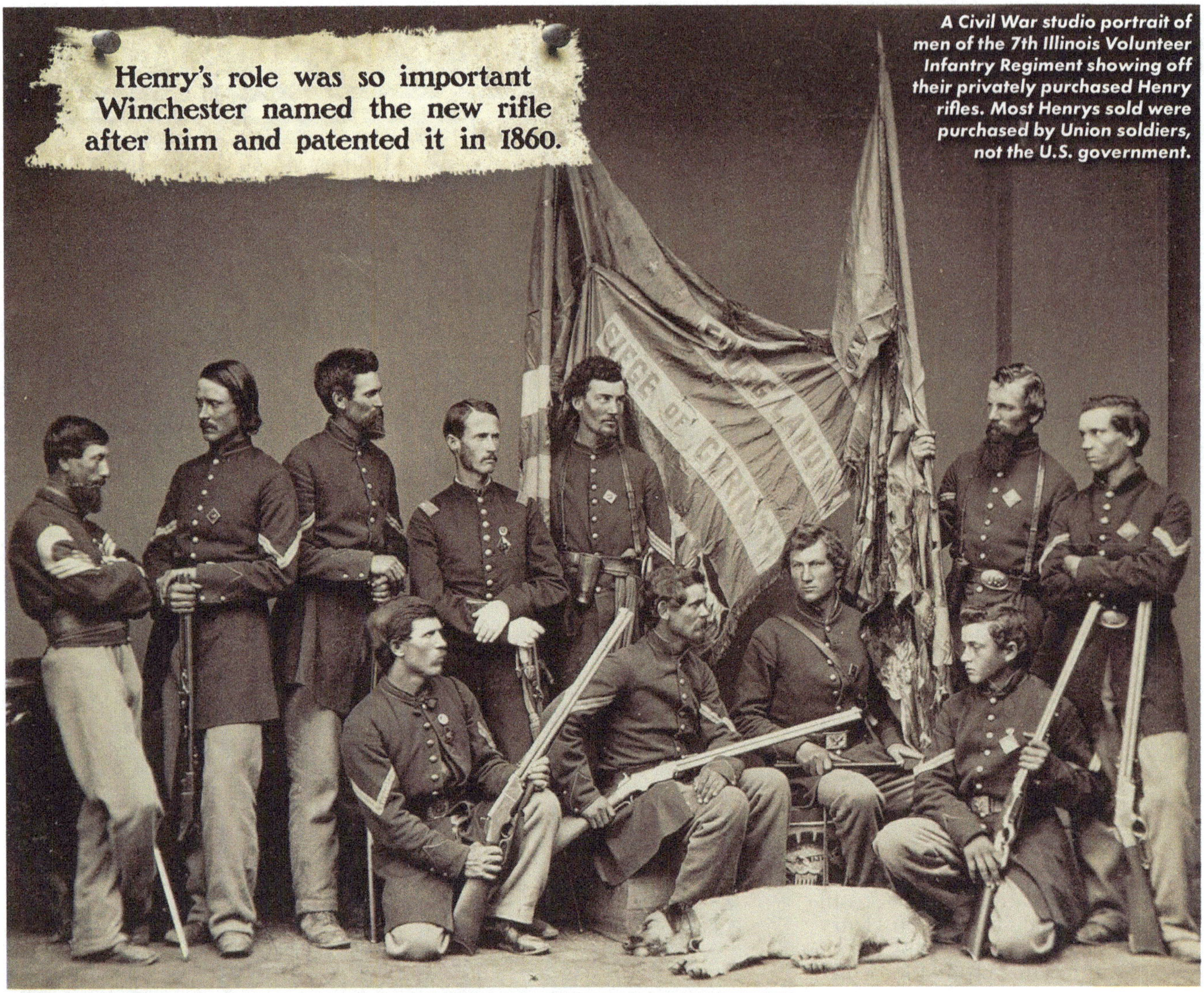

A Civil War studio portrait of men of the 7th Illinois Volunteer Infantry Regiment showing off their privately purchased Henry rifles. Most Henrys sold were purchased by Union soldiers, not the U.S. government.

Note the lack of a loading gate on the side of the receiver. The lever is fully forward in this photo.

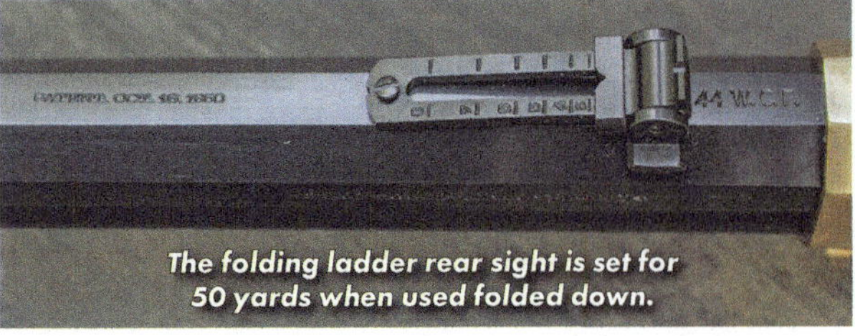

The folding ladder rear sight is set for 50 yards when used folded down.

When raised, the rear sight should theoretically allow for 1,000-yard aimed shots, but the Henry didn't earn its good reputation with long-range marksmanship. It was the best gun of its time for facing down multiple enemies within 100 yards.

The only flaw I found with the rifle was there were a few tooling marks on the front of the sleeve where the latch is fitted, and at first, the little latch didn't always go down into its locking notch after returning the sleeve to firing position. Unlocked, the sleeve can rotate, which might or might not alter barrel harmonics. Close inspection showed the hang-up was due to some tight tolerance machining. After working the latch a bit, I didn't have that problem again.

The bottom of the magazine has an open slot, making it easy to see how many cartridges you have left. Since the brass follower finger moves closer to your hand every time you chamber a round, when it touches you, it acts like a warning indicator signaling you are running low on ammo. A potential downside of this open slot is it might allow dirt or mud to foul the magazine tube, but battlefield reports did not indicate this ever happened.

Care in Feeding

During loading, Uberti recommends you don't drop the cartridges

Union Metallic Cartridge Company long-range .44 Henry Rimfire with a flatpoint bullet.

Original 50-round box of .44 Henry Rimfire.

The front sight is stainless steel. The magazine latch below the muzzle is opened by pulling back the brass finger on the follower protruding through the slot on the bottom of the magazine.

Targets fired with open sights from the bench at 50 and 100 yards with Winchester Super X ammunition.

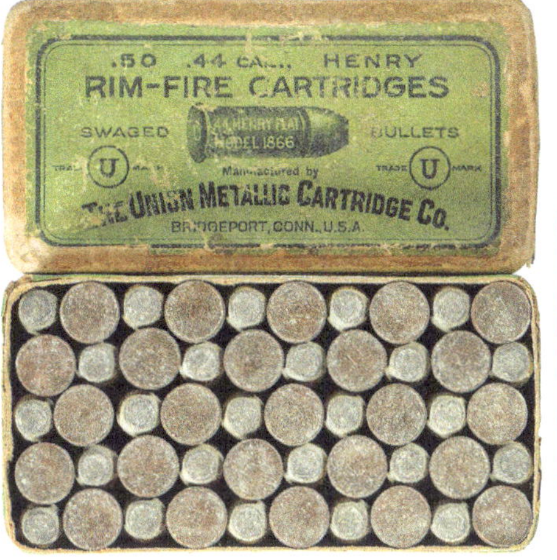

Though the production of the Henry ended in 1866, its .44 Rimfire cartridge remained in production until World War II.

down the magazine tube and never allow the follower to slam down on them. They also won't warranty the rifle if you shoot handloads in it. All this hand wringing is due to the fact the Henry was originally a rimfire. The original rimfire loads for the Henry used an aerodynamic pointed bullet and a flat-point bullet. You could see how even with a flat-point bullet, a high primer in one of your reloads could be detonated if the follower slammed it.

The instructions also point out you should work the lever with all four of your fingers inside to avoid hitting the trigger while cycling the action. I have never seen anyone do this, but Uberti makes a good point. I can see how it might be possible to discharge a round out of battery if you hit the trigger while working cartridges through the action to empty the magazine. Consider it food for thought.

Shooting Notes

On the range, I found the Uberti USA replica Henry had the smoothest action out of the box I have ever encountered on a lever gun. Loading and unloading were flawless with no damage to the fragile .44-40 case mouths on ejection. I chose .44-40 WCF, hoping to get ballistic performance closer to the original caliber. The authentic patridge rear sight and modern stainless steel front sight gave a great sight picture. The trigger was excellent and broke cleanly around 6 lbs. of pull.

The rifle shot to the point of aim at 50 yards with the ladder folded down over the barrel. At 100 yards, it shot about 6" below with the same sight picture. I tried using the lowest sight bar setting on the ladder, but it sent the bullets clean over the target. At 100 yards, you need to use Kentucky windage with the factory sights.

Average velocity of Winchester's Super-X JSP hunting load was only 1,070 fps, but the groups averaged 3.64" at 50 yards and 7.52" at 100 yards. My best groups were 2.5" at 50 yards and 6.63" at 100 yards. This is in line with what you would expect from a 24" barrel in this caliber with open sights. In every case, at 100 yards, I could clearly hear the bullet hit the target after the report from firing, and none of them matched the 1,200 fps claimed for the original black powder .44 Henry loading. I can't help but think this rifle might shoot a lot better with some attentive handloading, but as is, Cowboy Action Shooters shouldn't have any trouble hitting a 16" square rifle target out to 50 yards very quickly.

For more info: Uberti-USA.com

Roger Smith

SNAFU

Situation Normal All F(oul)ed Up

Uberti reproductions of the first run of the Colt 1873, left, and the 1877 run of the S&W No. 3 Schofield, but in .45 Colt.

Anyone with the slightest grasp of mechanics can understand a break-open revolver can never be as strong as one with a top-strap frame.

The term "SNAFU" seems to have entered the U.S. military's informal lexicon immediately after Pearl Harbor. It is thought to have been brought in by seriously needed telegraph operators otherwise too old for military service, who remembered the Old West shorthand for "Situation Normal All F***ed Up."

The acronym was used to describe the chaos of various breakdowns, including transmission lines torn down by the Native Americans and the buffalo who loved to use the poles for scratching posts until they knocked them down. Sharpened spikes were driven through the poles to discourage the buffalo. Instead, the new spikes delighted the deeply wooled thick-skinned animals and caused battles over rubbing rights.

The term probably describes all militaries worldwide and their operations since the beginning of history, so I'm going to limit this discussion to the Old West post-Uncivil War period of U.S. Army small arms and ammunition screwups. Because of space limitations, we'll have to further limit the discussion to the revolvers.

Powder and Ball Forever

Samuel Colt's huge contribution to revolver design was the cylinder locking mechanism he dreamed up in 1830 when he was 16. When he was able to get into manufacturing, he insisted on using an open-top design, and his patents gave him a monopoly on revolver manufacture until 1857. Until his untimely death in 1862, he rejected the new self-contained cartridge technology, insisting people would always prefer to load their cylinders with loose powder and round balls.

Making money by the barrelful on his old-fashioned designs to various militaries certainly did nothing to change his mind — not even nearly losing his shirt in the London factory lasting from 1853 to 1856. Lavish entertaining with plenty of booze and expensive gifts failed to impress the Brits. They did try Colt's revolvers by purchasing about 18,000 in 1854-1855. However, they much preferred double-action top-strap revolvers. If Colt won't make them, we'll just continue to make our own, thank you very much. Which they did, including the 1850 metallic cartridge guns. Except

For mounted cavalry, the S&W No. 3's ability to automatically eject all six rounds when opened, no ejector rod needed, and allow fast reloading of the cylinder made up for the more complicated S&W's finickiness and the inherent relative weakness of all top-break revolvers.

they soon enough went for their own fugly break-action Enfields and Webleys. SNAFU?

Stubborn Doesn't Always Pay

Which brings us to the great 1873 Single Action Army revolver. Remember, percussion Colts and the Thuer cartridge conversion system to evade S&W's patent on bored-through cylinder chambers were still all open-top guns. The sole exception was the short-lived Model 1855 Sidehammer Pocket Revolver.

Rollin White developed the bored-through cylinder concept while working for Colt and patented it. Colt rejected the idea and refused to use it. Colt was known to fire employees for suggesting improvements to his designs and White left in December 1854. He quickly obtained three more patents and was soon welcomed by S&W.

Remington was late to the revolver game like everyone else because of patent restrictions and extensions, but every one of their designs, beginning in 1856, featured a top strap, as did other competitors. Remington willingly paid the $1 per gun royalty, 25 cents to White and 75 cents to S&W to use White's patent for bored-through cylinders.

Samuel Colt was a far better salesman than gun designer. When the Army went looking for a big-bore cap & ball revolver, Colt's 2-oz. lighter Model 1860 supposedly beat out Remington's superior Model 1858. Once again, Sam the Schmoozer received the big juicy government con-

tracts. When the Colt factory burned in 1864, the Northern Army was only too eager to purchase Remingtons.

A New Colt Culture

Sam was gone by the time the Army went looking for a .45 cartridge revolver in earnest, so Colt designers were free to design a lighter weight, inexpensive, shaved-down-wherever-possible (read: profitable) top-strap revolver utilizing the excellent 1851 Navy grip frame. The Army had already purchased quantities of the break-action S&W No. 3 in .44 American and those who counted were suitably impressed with the gun but not the cartridge.

S&W was too busy chasing gold rubles making guns and a better .44 cartridge for the Russians, Turkey and Japan. They couldn't be bothered to make a longer-framed and cylindered version that could accept the Army-specified horse-killer .45 Colt cartridge, which used a 250-grain bullet over 30 grains of powder. Colt's Patent Firearms Manufacturing Company once again got the nod and the contract.

The Case of Soft Cases

Unfortunately, the Ordnance Department insisted on using the same non-reloadable soft copper cases with General Benet's crimped-in inside priming system used for the new 1873 Springfield rifle cartridges that were sticking in their chambers.

The Colt proved to be a rugged (for the era), nice handling but powerful gun that was also slower to reload than the S&W, especially on

horseback. But troopers constantly complained about those soft Frankford Arsenal copper cases sticking in their cylinders. Furthermore, to keep production costs down, its ejector rod was too short to push the empties completely out of the cylinder. The S&W quickly ejected all six empties, if they didn't stick, and could be reloaded much more quickly, making it far superior for cavalry use.

S&W got their comeuppance and nearly went under when the Russians reneged on payment and reverse-engineered the S&W to build in their factories. Army nepotism to the rescue. Major George Schofield was the brother of the distinguished General John McAllister Schofield, who had previously served as U.S. Secretary of War and later would become Commanding General of the United States Army, among other prestigious positions during his long career.

As early as 1871, Major Schofield recognized the superiority of the basic S&W design and made several improvements, which he patented, and S&W adopted. But they adamantly refused to make a slightly longer frame and cylinder for the Colt cartridge.

Instead, S&W offered a shorter cartridge case with 28 grains of powder and a 230-grain .45 bullet that could fit into the S&W's .44 Russian cylinder diameter. It was more pleasant to shoot, but it was no longer a horse killer. Schofield campaigned so long and hard within the bureaucracy, however, that three contracts for a total of 7,000 revolvers were issued in 1875, 1876 and 1877.

Schofield's major improvement to S&W's No. 3 revolver was his 1871 patent to switch the locking latch release from being mounted on the barrel to mounting it on the frame, as shown here, to make it easier for mounted cavalrymen to manipulate.

Frankford Arsenal cartridges: From left to right: 1) The original 1873-74 .45 Colt cartridge produced with a copper case soft enough to allow the firing pin to ignite the priming compound inside, held in place by the base crimp; 2) Soft copper 1875-1882 S&W Schofield cartridge with the same priming system; 3) Reloadable Boxer-primed 1890-1892 tinned brass .45 S&W cartridge; 4) Military .38 Long Colt, dated 1913, and 5) Large-rimmed 1909 .45 Government revolver cartridge.

Ammo Confusion

Now Frankford Arsenal faced having to manufacture two different .45 revolver cartridges. The Colt cylinder was designed for cartridges with 0.503" rims, give or take. However, it could also use the shorter S&W cartridges, with approximately 0.520" rims required to work with the S&W extractor, but not vice versa.

In an all-volunteer army of poorly educated men with poor command of the language, what could possibly go wrong in ordering and shipping?

So much potentially that in anticipation, all .45 ammunition production was quickly switched to S&W only. The mighty .45 Colt round was bureaucratically castrated before it reached its third birthday. The Army had its solution to the short ejector rod problem and production of the original Colt ammunition never resumed at Frankford Armory.

But with Colt ammunition already in the system, the Quartermaster Corps couldn't always keep things straight, and those at fault point fingers and blame others. Major Schofield would have been an easy target. It all had to be his fault. In early 1880, the Schofield revolvers were withdrawn from service and sold off as government surplus. On December 17, 1882, the seriously depressed Major Schofield donned his elegant full-dress uniform and used one of his Schofield-patent revolvers to end his life and dwindling patent royalty payments from S&W.

Ammo Evolution

Winchester showed reliable, reloadable full power brass-cased .45 Colt ammunition in their 1875 catalog. It took until 1882 for the Frankford Armory to finally begin making reloadable .45 S&W ammunition, still in copper cases. Tin-plated brass cartridges to eliminate sticking in the cylinders were produced from about 1890 until the end of .45 S&W production in late 1892.

Speed of Bureaucracy

Then, there's the story about the Colt .45 being withdrawn from Army service in 1892. Some of them were stored instead of being sold off as surplus this time (wonder of wonders!) and replaced by the Colt New Army revolver in wimpy .38 Long Colt. It was such a disaster in the Philippine-American War that began in 1899 that 550 of the old .45s were withdrawn from storage in 1901 and 1902 to be placed back into service. What? Only three years? Instead of being shipped to Manila and immediately re-issued, however, precious time was wasted while they were "refurbished" and reblued, their barrels cut back from 7 ½" to 5 ⅕" and new front sights installed. During this delay, soldiers continued to die at the hands of the native Moro warriors drugged up on stimulants, pain killers and patriotic fervor. SNAFU again, anyone?

And Back to .45 Colt

Colt introduced the superb large-caliber, heavy-duty double-action Model 1899 with a swing-out cylinder, fully capable of using the .45 Colt cartridge. The British quickly adopted it for use in the Boer War, using their own .455 Enfield caliber that was even less potent than the .45 S&W.

The American Army? They chose an upgraded Colt Model 1878 double-action revolver that could use the civilian .45 Colt cartridge. It was introduced as the New Army (Philippine) Model of 1902. It still used the single action 1873/1878-style cylinder and slow poke-it-out reloading. It served until John Browning's automatic .45 ACP pistol was adopted by the Army in 1911 after they finished dinking around with the 1902 design. The Marine Corps wisely adopted its version in 1905. Repeated suicide charges proved to be an unsustainable strategy and the Moro Rebellion finally ended in 1913.

The Army eventually did fiddle around with the 1899 revolver and decreed an improved .45 Colt cartridge was needed. Thus a new .45 Government revolver cartridge was created in 1909 with a 0.538" diameter rim, intended to serve in both single- and double-action revolvers. However, its rim is too large to pass through the loading gate of the great 1873 Single Action Army. Sigh. The bureaucrats' 1909 cartridge was very short-lived.

From what I read, cartoon character Pvt. Snafu of WWII fame lives on to this day in militaries around the world. I wonder how the Russians translate his name.

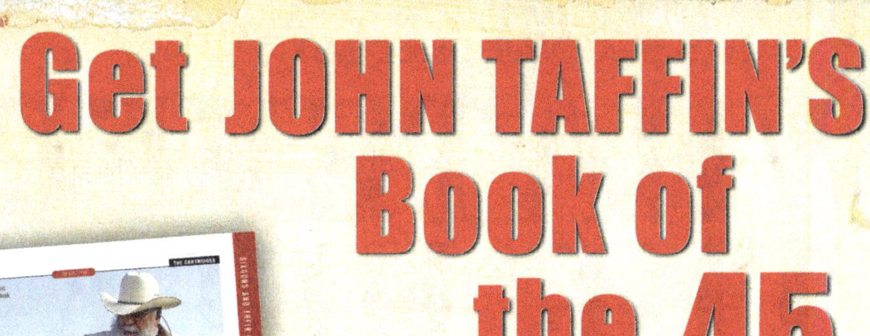

Get JOHN TAFFIN'S Book of the .45 Caliber

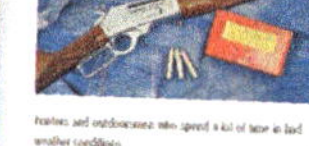

The most comprehensive book on the .45 caliber! This beautifully-colored book is hardbound with over 350 pages.

$58.49
price includes $8.50 shipping (U.S. only)

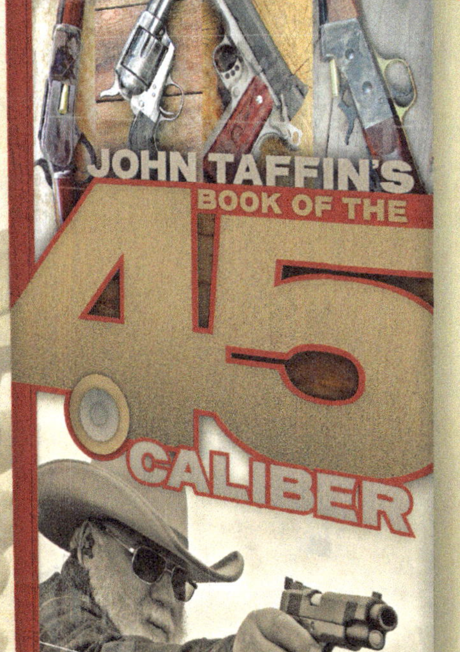

fmgpubs.com/TAFFIN45

Will Dabbs, MD

WHATEVER THE HECK THIS IS ...

Perhaps an Ethan Allen One-of-a-Kind?

I'll let you in on a little secret: There is an element of theater to what I do. One of the reasons we gun writers can seem so omniscient, insightful and wise as regards the minutiae of our quirky little field is that we have time. As you're pulling together a gun article, you can always fall back to your own personal library of gun books or do a little gratuitous Googling to get the facts straight before settling in behind the word processor in an attempt to create a little ballistic literary art. This piece is a bit different.

I have no idea what this gun is. I have found references to some similar pieces but, despite my very best efforts, I can't locate this specific weapon anyplace. I fear there won't be any grand reveal at the end that makes me look all-knowing and awesome. One of you guys likely maintains a massive collection of guns just like this one, but I'm frankly stumped.

Philosophy

Some of the best and brightest minds in the human species have devoted their very lives to the industry of death and destruction. Spinoff technology brought us everything from duct tape to super glue, canned food and the internet. All this stuff began as military tech.

When you get that many smart people working so enthusiastically, you end up with some of the most fascinating ideas. Rollin White's bored-through cylinder changed the world. Walter Hunt's radical Rocket Ball self-contained caseless ammunition, not so much. I find myself mesmerized by all of it.

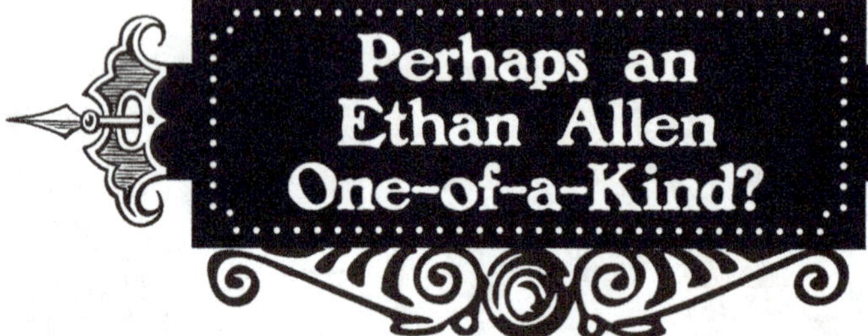

The heavy wire grip really couldn't be much simpler. As for feel in the hand, make your own assumptions ...

This odd little Allen's Patent pistol caught Will's eye because it was just so darn strange.

I am forever on the stalk for unique or historically significant guns. Online auctions are my hunting preserve. I am inexorably drawn to specimens outside the mainstream or technically unusual. This particularly quirky pistol was unlike anything I had ever seen before.

The Quest

The auction in question was liquidating somebody's simply epic vintage firearms collection. You see these things from time to time online. Some guy like me will invest a lifetime amassing a world-class gun collection only to have it liquidated after his passing to fund some forgotten third cousin's cocaine habit. I hope to bequeath something similar to my own family after I'm gone, only without the illicit drug angle.

This offering was a veritable smorgasbord of sweet ballistic goodies. There was an original 19th century Gatling gun, dozens of Civil War and Old West-era long arms and pistols and lots of cool period memorabilia. The damage I can do at these things is driven by the state of the gun fund.

Not everybody knows this, but there are two distinct kinds of U.S. currency in circulation today. These two forms of money look exactly the same, but they really couldn't be more different. Regular money goes toward gas, food, the mortgage and the kids' orthodontics. By contrast, gun money is scraped up from

This Allen's Patent single-shot muzzleloading pistol was likely designed as a low-cost last-ditch defensive tool.

The smoothbore barrel is roughly .25 caliber.

"Allen's Pat. 1857" are the only markings on the gun. Despite being a century and a half old, it appears no one ever fired it.

birthdays, Christmases and sundry other off-the-books revenue streams. When the gun money reaches a certain point, I'm ready to pillage a firearms auction like this one. Alas, on this particular date, the cupboard was fairly bare. It looked like I would have to wait to add a vintage Gatling gun to my collection. However, there were still plenty of eligible low-cost alternatives.

The Gun

This weird little pistol caught my eye simply because … it was such a weird little pistol. The body of the thing was cut from a piece of brass bar stock, while the grip was a crudely formed loop of really heavy steel wire. The gun was a single-shot percussion design featuring an underhammer mechanism. The left side of the frame was engraved with "Allen's Pat. 1857"

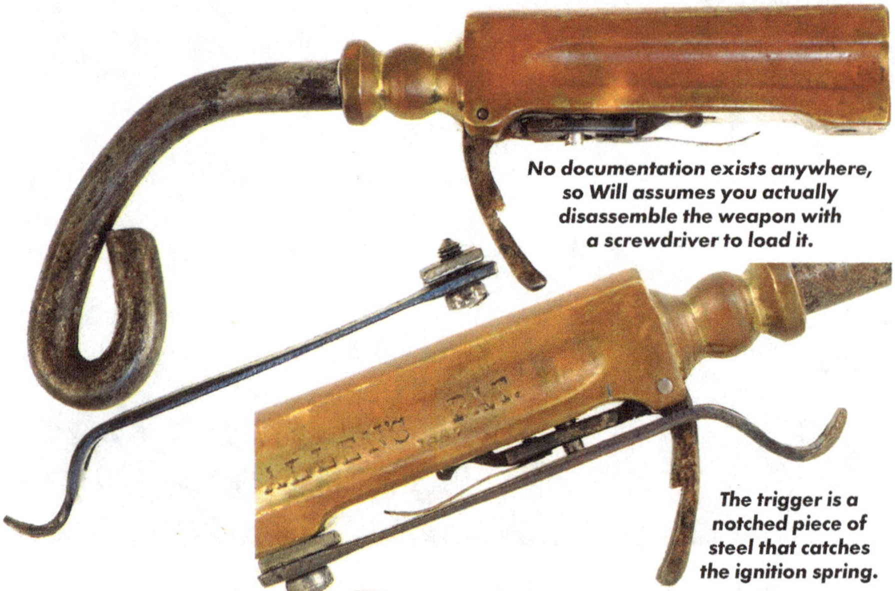

No documentation exists anywhere, so Will assumes you actually disassemble the weapon with a screwdriver to load it.

The trigger is a notched piece of steel that catches the ignition spring.

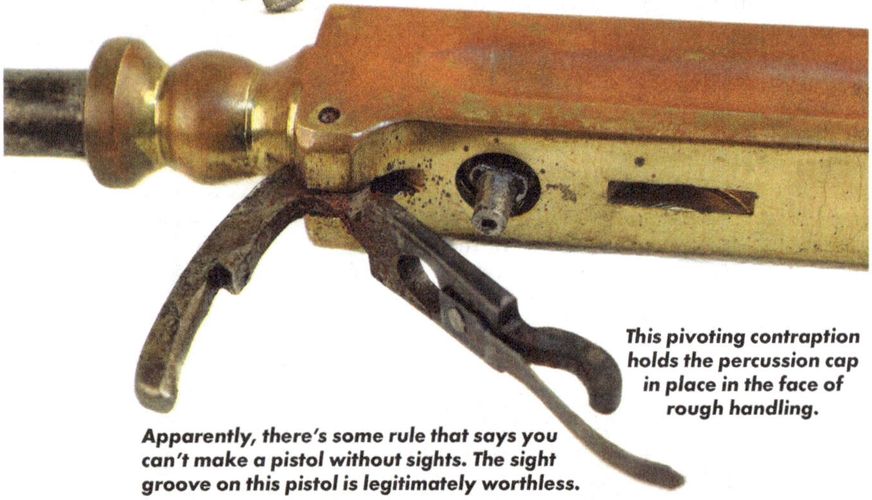

This pivoting contraption holds the percussion cap in place in the face of rough handling.

Apparently, there's some rule that says you can't make a pistol without sights. The sight groove on this pistol is legitimately worthless.

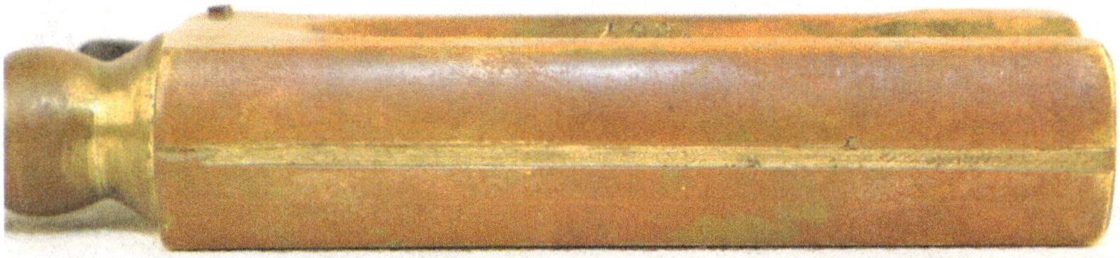

and nothing else. Everything about the weapon was clearly contrived to be inexpensive and compact.

The technical description of the weapon was no help. The associated prose basically said it was an Allen's patent single-shot muzzleloading handgun. However, it was undeniably the ugly duckling among a field liberally populated with beautiful Colts, Spencers and Henrys. That made it an opportunity.

I put a modest bid on the gun and made the homely rascal mine for less than a C-note. As the pistol was obviously dated before 1898, it wasn't considered a firearm in the eyes of the government and shipped straight to my door via the *Brown Truck of Happiness*. Ten days later, I was pawing over it in the living room.

Technical Details

Morphologically speaking, this is a 19th century concealed carry weapon. The gun's modest dimensions and trim architecture make it the sort of thing that could conceivably ride about in the pocket of a smoking jacket. It was also clearly designed for the masses. This gun is bare bones and utilitarian in the extreme. Nothing about the weapon is wasted on frivolity.

The gun appears unfired. It has a roughly .25-cal. unrifled bore and an extremely unusual design. Everything about the weapon conveys modest cost and ease of manufacture. The brass would be easy to work, and the steel bits are simple to the point of crudity. It took me a minute to figure out how to run it.

Manual of Arms

The trigger is an unadorned piece of steel with a notch to catch the hammer spring. This appendage is secured with a steel pin. There is no hammer per se. The firing system is oriented underneath the weapon. The ignition spring is a simple piece of tempered steel retained with a machine screw that strikes the cap directly.

As near as I can tell, you have to disassemble the gun to load it. This entails unscrewing the ignition spring screw and removing the spring. A clever pressed-steel mechanism built into the trigger holds a standard

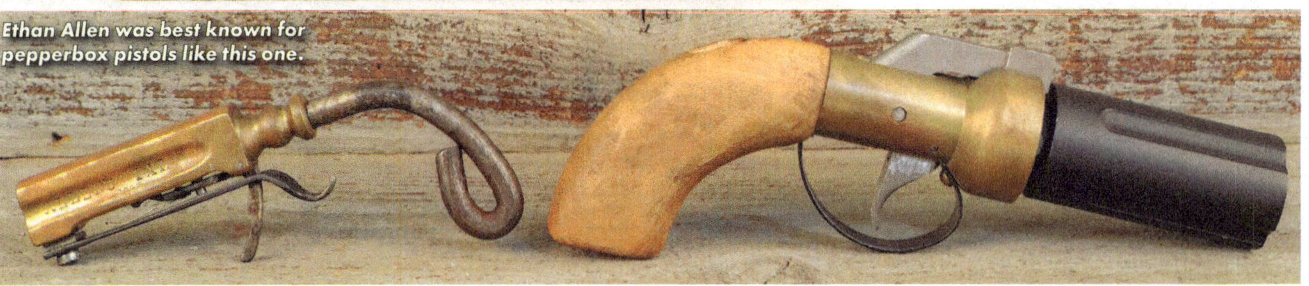

This is the Philadelphia Deringer pistol John Wilkes Booth used to kill President Lincoln. Henry Deringer made his reputation producing small concealable defensive handguns, but unscrupulous gunmakers began plastering his name across their guns to increase sales. Eventually, they added a spare "R," and the new name stuck.

musket cap in place. To access the nipple, you draw the trigger back with the spring removed to lift this retaining arm.

The gun is charged from the muzzle with powder and ball. You would then emplace a cap and reassemble the striker mechanism, presumably with a screwdriver. While certainly clever, this whole contrivance is undeniably cumbersome.

To set the weapon for firing once loaded, you retract the striker spring until it catches in the trigger notch. Point the gun at something you dislike and squeeze. What passes for sights is nothing more than a shallow groove cut in the top of the frame, but you really cannot see it when holding the weapon in firing position.

There is no safety … at all. Apparently, there were not quite so many trial attorneys back in 1857 as is the case today. If you don't want an accidental discharge, then don't cock the gun. If you want to be completely sure, just leave it at home. Given the exposed nature of the firing mechanism, I personally wouldn't be comfortable packing this pistol in a pocket were it loaded. It seems a firm blow to the bottom of the weapon would risk detonation.

Due Diligence

Allen was a common name amongst 19th century firearms. Ethan Allen, purportedly unrelated to the Revolutionary War patriot of the same name, was a Massachusetts arms maker active from 1837 until around 1871. Allen's business went through several evolutionary convulsions over the years, producing a wide variety of rifles and handguns from several manufacturing facilities. They were best known for their pepperbox pistols.

At a time when a typical American could quite conceivably die of disease, hostile attack or starvation, copyright enforcement in the gun world was not the rarefied enterprise it is today. If a certain name became associated with quality firearms, many times, unscrupulous gunmakers would stamp that particular name on the side of their weapons to lend an air of respectability. A great example is the Derringer pistol.

Henry Deringer began producing small single-shot pistols in 1825. While Old Henry produced some 15,000 copies himself, arms makers around the world began plastering his name on the sides of their little pocket guns with wanton abandon. President Lincoln was assassinated with a single shot Philadelphia Deringer. At some point, somebody misspelled his surname with an extraneous "R," and it became the new standard. Today a Derringer is most any compact concealable single- or double-barreled pocket gun, and it's not even the way the guy spelled his name.

So, What is it Exactly?

I honestly don't know. I can only assume it was an early and obscure Ethan Allen offering. This was likely the High Point or Raven Arms handgun of its day, a low-cost, no-frills defensive weapon intended for the masses. With a .25-cal. smoothbore barrel and a reloading cycle measured in hours, I might prefer a decent club in a proper fight.

This odd little Allen's Patent pistol was contrived at a different time. Today, if you get shot in the belly, don't perforate some substantial piece of plumbing and can get to a hospital in a reasonable period of time, you'll likely be fine. It'll be a wild ride, but somebody will put you back together. Back in 1857, this was not the case. Being gut shot in the mid-19th century, even with an anemic little gun like this, meant an agonizing and protracted death bereft of hope. If you survived the initial insult, then infection would more than likely cost you a limb, if not your life.

Guns are the most remarkable tools. The many-splendored methods mankind has contrived to expel a projectile by means of an explosive are simply captivating to those of us who live in this weird little world. In this particularly strange Allen's Patent muzzleloading pistol, we find something just peculiar enough to be cool.

GUNS OLD WEST VOL. 90 AD INDEX

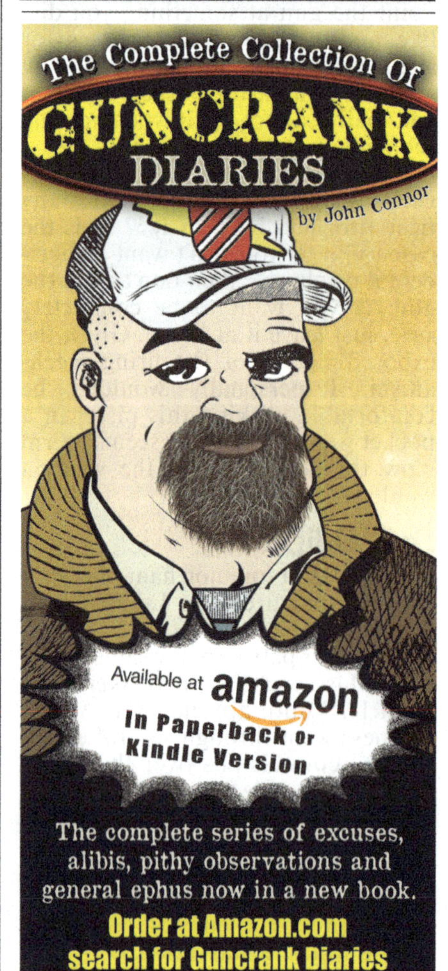

Get our latest SPECIAL EDITIONS for $14.95 each! Order online today!

www.fmgpubs.com

760-975-3880

Skinner® Sights LLC

THE SKINNER HTF GARMENT BAG

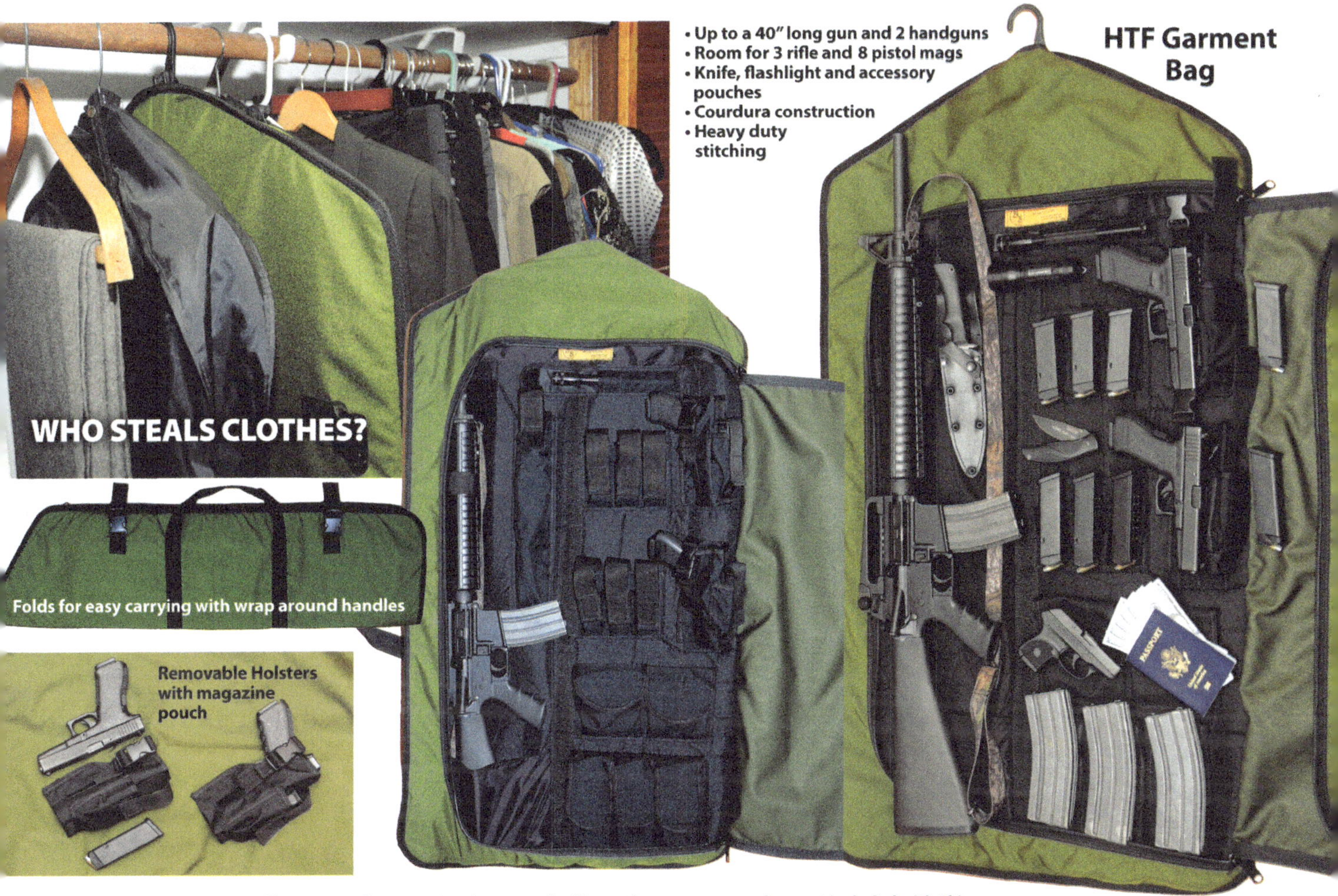

- Up to a 40" long gun and 2 handguns
- Room for 3 rifle and 8 pistol mags
- Knife, flashlight and accessory pouches
- Courdura construction
- Heavy duty stitching

HTF Garment Bag

WHO STEALS CLOTHES?

Folds for easy carrying with wrap around handles

Removable Holsters with magazine pouch

Firearms and accessories shown are for illustrative purposes and are not included with Skinner cases.

THE SKINNER® SIGHTS "HTF" BAG ALLOWS YOUR FIREPOWER TO BE "CONCEALED IN PLAIN SIGHT" YET READY IN CASE OF AN EMERGENCY.

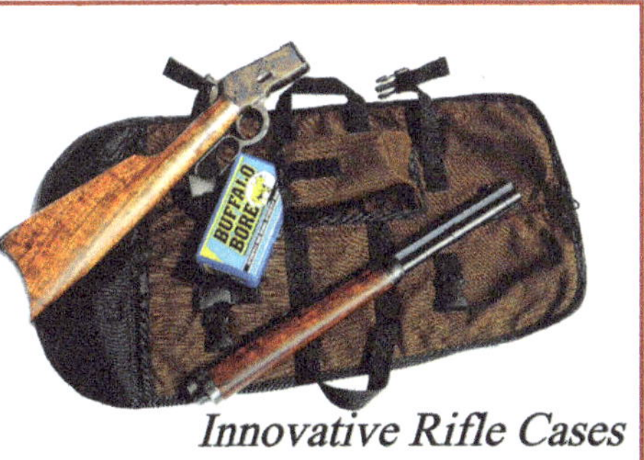

Innovative Rifle Cases

PEEP SIGHTS FOR RIFLES

MACHINED FROM SOLID BARSTOCK

PLEASE SEE OUR WEBSITE FOR MORE INFORMATION

WWW.SKINNERSIGHTS.COM

406-745-4570 • P.O. Box 1810, St. Ignatius, MT 59865

Made in the USA
Monee, IL
07 July 2026

56550201R00072